W9-BUW-886

A QUESTION OF SLAVERY

A QUESTION OF SLAVERY

JAMES DUFFY

HARVARD UNIVERSITY PRESS
CAMBRIDGE, MASSACHUSETTS
1967

PRINTED IN GREAT BRITAIN

Preface

I HAVE tried to clothe the bare bones of a familiar controversy. I have written about the issue of slavery, or its reasonable facsimile, in the Portuguese African colonies in the last half of the nineteenth century and the first two decades of the twentieth century. The traditional misuse of African labour in Angola and Moçambique, the protest this aroused in England, and the reaction in Lisbon form the substance of the book. The discussion on the issue is my theme. I have been more discursive than perhaps I should have been, but I believe that much of the value of the material I have used—legislation, parliamentary debates, consular reports, newspaper accounts, and polemical literature—has been the rhetoric of attack and defence. I have sought to define the controversy in its own terms and I have therefore often followed my material where it went. If most of the language of fifty and a hundred years ago sounds awkward, perhaps absurd, today, this is but another reminder of the momentous changes in modern Africa.

The path I have followed is narrow. In the course of the book I have skirted problems of the greatest importance: the Congo Slave Trade, the Conference of Berlin, the Ultimatum of 1890, Rhodes and the Boer War, the Congo scandals, and the German interest in the Portuguese territories. The question of Portuguese labour policies was marginally relevant to all of these problems, but the complexity of each in its own terms seemed to defy my attempts to make the cogent involvement.

The sources for my study have been the slave trade and consular papers of the Public Records Office, British and Portuguese newspapers and journals, Portuguese legislation and official colonial bulletins, and the publications of English humanitarian societies. My presentation of the Portuguese case is sometimes thin, for lack of more varied and richer sources to which I could not have access, but I am confident that it is essentially correct.

PREFACE

Many of the secret slave depots of the Moçambique coast from Quelimane north to Ibo have disappeared. I have tried to locate them as best I could. There will be some variation in the spelling of place names, but I hope most of them will be recognizable.

I am extremely grateful to the officers and attendants of the Public Records Office for their valuable assistance. Thomas Fox Pitt, Secretary of the Anti-Slavery Society was equally helpful. I thank Professors Charles Boxer, Roland Oliver, and I. Schapera for their guidance on points of history.

Much of the research for the study was made possible by grants from the Social Science Research Council and the National Science Foundation. I am deeply indebted to both, and to the Rockefeller Foundation for the grant which permitted me to complete my research in the summer of 1964. I wish to acknowledge the assistance given by Brandeis University toward the preparation of the manuscript. I also thank Miss Naneen Wendler for typing the original draft of the manuscript and Miriam Sachs for typing and correcting the final draft.

JAMES DUFFY

Contents

CHAPTER I

The Beginnings

By the middle of the nineteenth century Portugal's fortunes in Africa were at a low ebb. For more than a hundred years her position in Angola and Moçambique had been steadily eroded by maladministration, disease, inadequate commerce, inattention and indifference, and by the injuries of a heedless traffic in slaves. The best, sometimes idealistic intentions of colonial counsellors and ministers in Lisbon, and of occasionally vigorous and enlightened governors-general—men like Francisco de Sousa Coutinho (governor-general of Angola in the 1760's)—broke against the ingrained traditions of life in Portuguese Africa. In the north, in Portuguese Guinea and the Cape Verde islands, whose history did not parallel that of the southern African colonies, events had also followed a path of slow decline.

The visible effects in 1850 of the Portuguese presence in Africa were negligible. Measured by what were soon to become the European standards of colonization in the continent, Portugal's effort was wanting. The occupation of territory and control over African peoples scarcely extended beyond the sight of scattered forts and towns. Legitimate commerce was modest. Capital investment in the colonies was insignificant. Communication was uncertain. Educational and health services did not exist. The missionary programme had collapsed into oblivion. In such condition Portuguese Africa entered the most critical half-century of her history.

Over the years different patterns of policy and behaviour had formed in the three areas of Portuguese Africa. Guinea had importance only as an intermittent source for slaves, while Santiago in the Cape Verdes served as occasional entrepôt for slaves and as a trading and administrative centre for the archipelago and Guinea. Angola was from an early date the most prolific supplier of slaves for the new world. Dominated by arrogant and selfish men, Angola took on a personality unique in African history. Moçambique, more leisurely, more decadent perhaps, was a colony of mixed and uncertain identity. Administered until 1752 as part of Portugal's eastern empire, Moçambique was important for her island port and the *prazos*, or great estates, of Zambézia.

What the territories, notably Angola and Moçambique, held in common was a recession from an early promise and, in each, the subsequent inability to alter a fundamental way of life. With the failure or petering out of trade, agriculture, evangelization, and of the campaigns of conquest, Portuguese activities were progressively set. In Angola the evolutionary process was rapid: by 1650 all other considerations had gone, to be replaced by an earnest dedication to the slave-trade. In Moçambique Portuguese interest had flagged; not until over a century later did the traffic in slaves begin to reach Angolan proportions.

Portugal's progress down the West Africa coast had produced but one steady article of commerce—the Negro slave. If the serious traffic in slaves came late to Moçambique it was because the great distance to the Americas and Portugal's policies in the Indian Ocean delayed the inevitable reliance on the sale of slaves. Probably only the discovery of great deposits of gold or silver, with their demands for native labour, or the annihilation of the Portuguese community by African armies could have substantially changed the history of Portuguese Africa. In neither Angola nor Moçambique were there conditions for the emergence of a colony like Brazil. In fact, one reason why Angola became what it did was because there already was a Brazil. What happened in those years before 1850 created enormous obstacles to change in the years after 1850.

The habits of slaving created habits of thinking as hard to change as the conditions which formed them. No matter what the specious moral justifications for slavery and the slave-trade said, no matter what modern Portuguese writers have had to say about the historic tolerance in black and white relationships, 'another result of Portugal's concentration on the slave trade was the rooted conviction that the Negro could legitimately be enslaved and hence was indisputably an inferior being to the white man'.[1] The fact that the Portuguese male did take as wife or mistress an African or mulatto woman had very little to do with mitigating either slavery or the slave-trade, and, as Charles Boxer says, it had nothing to do with changing racial prejudice. By 1850, then, Africans in Portuguese colonies were generally regarded as inferior beings, 'niggers', whose function was to labour.

If the attitudes of the Portuguese residents in Africa were fixed by the middle of the nineteenth century, English attitudes towards the same Portuguese, if not fixed, were perceptibly hardening. English interest in the Portuguese territories was another aspect of an ancient relationship—the 'oldest alliance'. From the fifteenth century England had held a paternal concern for the affairs of Portugal. The Treaty of 1661 was a symbolic expression of that concern: for a number of concessions England agreed to give protection to Portugal and her colonies. Subsequent treaties and understandings strengthened England's paternalistic sentiments. A real acknowledgement of the position of each power within the alliance was seen during the Peninsular War with England's occupation and control of Portugal.

England's official—and humanitarian—reaction to Portugal's dilatoriness in suppressing the slave-trade from her African possessions in the first half of the nineteenth century was typical of the relationship. England ordered and bullied Portugal in the manner of an impatient parent. Portugal was seen to be resisting in the manner of a stubborn child. Now a curious quality began to intrude into the English attitude, something not discernible in earlier centuries. This was an intolerant morality and a kind of neo-racial prejudice. Lord Palmerston, outraged by another of Portugal's seeming evasions in the curtailment of the slave-trade, said to Lord Russell: 'The plain truth is that the Portuguese are of all European nations the lowest in the moral scale. . . .'[2] Palmerston's remark was more

[1] Charles R. Boxer, *Race Relations in the Portuguese Colonial Empire, 1415–1825* (Oxford, 1963), p. 40. This set of three essays by the most distinguished of historians of the Portuguese world demolishes the myth of Portuguese racial tolerance.

[2] Quoted in Christopher Lloyd, *The Navy and the Slave Trade* (London, 1949), p. 148.

than a reflection of British impatience at not being able to infuse the Portuguese spirit with larger doses of anti-slaving morality; it was also revealing of the neo-racial prejudice with which British humanitarians were wont to regard the Portuguese. English philanthropists looked upon the Portuguese as degenerate slavers to be scourged from the sea—and maybe even from their African possessions.

Anglo-Saxon impatience at the dilatory tactics of the three Latin nations—Brazil, Portugal, and Spain—was in part the natural impatience of the reformed turned reformer. From 1807 to 1850 England had laboured to check the African slave-trade, and then to abolish it. The Governments of Brazil, Portugal, and Spain were slow, in British eyes, to enforce on their subjects the obligations of their anti-slaving treaties, and even though economic changes had diminished the Atlantic slave-trade, it was not until British cruisers began to patrol African waters that the final extinction of the traffic became a possibility. By 1850 the traffic to Brazil was virtually finished. Treaties of 1839 and 1842 with Portugal, enforced by the British Navy, had good effect in Angola, where Livingstone was pleased to observe in 1854 an upsurge of legitimate commerce. From Moçambique ports there was still a sizeable local and international trade in slaves which would be difficult to eliminate.

For another twelve years American and Spanish slavers slipped away from the Congo shores or from the inlets of Moçambique with their miserable cargo bound for Cuba. These shipments were the last tremors of the moribund transatlantic trade. But in Portuguese Africa the habits of centuries were not to be broken easily, and the slave-trade continued, on a much reduced scale, in devious ways and under different names. Slavery became free labour, contract labour, forced labour, and the slave became a worker, but a traditional relationship was unchanged. The problems of slavery, in one guise or another, were to bedevil Portuguese territories in Africa for another century; they were to engage Portugal for the next sixty years in a running quarrel with the English Government and with a group of still vigilant English humanitarians.

CHAPTER II

Angola to 1870

BY the 1850's the time had come for reforms in Angola and Moçambique. Part of the reform would be directed to an attempt to finish off the slave-trade and to abolish slavery. The reforms, however, were envisioned in Lisbon, which was distant from Africa, and by a relatively small group of humanitarian colonialists (chief among them being the Marquês de Sá de Bandeira, prime minister from 1836 to 1840, and overseas minister through most of the 1850's into the 1860's), who could not command the authority to have them carried out. For twenty-five years, 1853–78, the reformist aspirations of Portuguese Governments would be contained in legislation and decrees. Most of these failed in their purpose, and where they succeeded they led to a perverted continuation of traditional practices. There was the law and there was the reality. And there was the British Government, disbelieving and impatient, urging, prodding, rebuking.

When David Livingstone came to Luanda in late May 1854, he found a town of some 12,000 inhabitants, 'most of whom were people of colour'. Fifteen years earlier Luanda had still been a thriving port for the slave-trade, which paid the greater part of the colony's revenue. Now the trade had diminished almost to extinction, and lawful commerce in coffee, cotton, and beeswax produced a greater revenue than slaves. Livingstone's heart was gladdened, but he was uncertain about the future:

The intentions of home Portuguese Government, however good, cannot be fully carried out under the present system. The pay of the officers is so very small, that they are nearly all obliged to engage in trade; and owing to the lucrative nature of the slave-trade, the temptation to engage in it is so powerful, that the philanthropic statesmen of Lisbon need hardly expect to have their humane and enlightened views carried out.[1]

On the journey eastward from Luanda, Livingstone had opportunity to observe domestic slavery as well as small caravans of slaves being taken by *pombeiros* (African traders) to the country of Matia Yamvo to be traded for ivory. These activities the missionary viewed with some tolerance, if not approbation.[2]

Although he was but another in a lengthening list of English visitors to criticize Portuguese practices in Africa (Captain William Owen, who made a coastal survey of Moçambique in the 1820's, was perhaps the first), Livingstone was destined to be the most important. He spoke with greater moral authority and greater personal knowledge than any of his predecessors and most of his successors. And he spoke to a larger audience. Livingstone came to be a fearful antagonist of Portugal in Africa; what he had to say about slavery and the slave-trade in the Portuguese territories of southern Africa provided a text for English humanitarians for the next sixty years. The text read: The African policies of Portuguese Governments were usually honourable and enlightened; the conduct of many officials in Portuguese Africa was corrupt; Lisbon's policies were ignored; Portuguese residents and their African or half-caste protégés were inveterate slavers; and conditions in Portuguese Africa, the result of the attachment to slavery and the rejection of progress, were atrocious.

While the control over the slave-trade from Portuguese African possessions was effectively determined by various international

[1] David Livingstone, *Missionary Travels and Researches in South Africa* (2 vols; London, 1857), ii. 396.

[2] Perhaps Livingstone's harshest commentary is on the attitude towards the slave. 'The way in which slaves are spoken of in Angola and eastern Africa must sound strangely even to the owners when they first come from Europe. In Angola the common appellation is "O diabo", or "brute". . . . In eastern Africa, on the contrary, they apply the term "bicho" (or "animal") and you hear the phrase, "call the *animal* to do this or that". In fact, slave owners come to regard their slaves as not human, and will curse them as the "race of a dog." ' (*Missionary Travels*, ii. 447.)

Livingstone was kindlier in *Missionary Travels* towards the Portuguese in Africa than he was privately in his journal. See *Livingstone's African Journal, 1853–1856*, edited by I. Schapera (2 vols.; Berkeley, 1963).

treaties Portugal had signed, notably the treaty of 1842 with Great Britain, within the colonies themselves Portuguese Governments made efforts to curb the traffic. The Decree of 10 December 1836 was the first shot in a barrage of decrees which ended with the final abolition of slavery in 1878. The 1836 decree prohibited the traffic of slaves in Portuguese dominions. Two important exceptions made by the law were: first, slaves could be imported into Portuguese territories by land, and second, colonists could import up to ten slaves with them when they went from one Portuguese territory to another. This decree—and almost every other anti-slavery law promulgated for the next thirty years—was the inspiration of the Marquês de Sá da Bandeira, who was at once Portugal's greatest humanitarian and foremost colonialist. The nub of his African policy was contained in a report he submitted as prime minister to the Portuguese Parliament in 1836, wherein he argued that there would be no hope for the African colonies so long as the slave-trade continued and agriculture did not flourish.[3]

In his own day, and later in the century, Sá da Bandeira was regarded as either foolish or mad by more practical Portuguese colonialists, particularly those living in Africa. Even though Sá had his own way in the overseas ministry during his long tenure there, the Portuguese Government, beset by domestic difficulties and uncertainties, was usually indifferent to his colonial programmes. Overseas the reaction was often more pointed. Earlier, in response to the Decree of 1836, Governor-General Noronha wrote the Marquês that he had cut off the only branch of commerce in Angola, had caused a deficit in the budget, and had made anyone who tried to impose the decree mortally hated by the residents of the colony. The resistance in Moçambique to the law was even stronger.[4] But Sá da Bandeira persevered, arguing that the abolition of the slave-trade and of slavery was an indispensable condition for the

[3] See J. M. da Silva Cunha, *O trabalho indígena* (2nd ed.; Lisbon, 1955), pp. 126–7. Sá da Bandeira envisaged not only the abolition of the slave-trade and slavery, but also the formation of an African administrative corps, African judges and magistrates. It was in this period that free Africans in Portuguese territories were enfranchised as Portuguese citizens.

[4] Bernardo de Sá Nogueira de Figueiredo. (Marquês de Sá da Bandeira), *O trabalho rural Africano e a administração colonial* (Lisbon, 1873), p. 17.

prosperity of Africa. In the 1850's he issued a series of decrees against both practices.

The first of these was the Decree of 14 December 1854. The decree was an omnibus anti-slavery Bill. All slaves were obliged to be registered within a thirty-day period. All slaves not registered were to become *libertos*, or freed men. Slaves belonging to the state were to be made *libertos*, with the obligation of serving the state for a seven-year period. Slaves and *libertos* were to come under the tutelage and protection of a special board created for them—the *Junta Protectora dos Escravos e Libertos*, the so-called Board of Protection. Any *liberto* who had achieved the eminence of being a university graduate, a priest, an officer in the army or navy, a professor, a rural landowner, or a book-keeper was to be considered exempt from tutelage. Other provisions of the decree provided processes by which slaves could purchase their liberty.

Without a doubt the 1854 Decree was filled with good intentions. It did not provide for the abolition of slavery in Portuguese Africa, but it was an important step in that direction. Unfortunately the creation of the status of *liberto*, which was supposed to provide a healthy transition for both master and slave, planted the germ of the idea that a slave could continue to be a slave in the absence of slavery. The *Junta Protectora*, which was to assume various other names as the century progressed, was supposed to be the supervisory agency in colonial capitals; in practice the Board was a failure from the beginning.

The 14 December 1854 Decree had been anticipated in the Decree of 25 October 1853, conceding to Angolan planter João Maria de Sousa a Almeida a tract of land on the island of Principe for agricultural purposes. The concessionaire was permitted to export to Principe some 100 slaves that he owned in Angola, on the condition of giving them their certificate of freedom. The regulations annexed to the decree provided that the slaves should be baptized before being freed. The *libertos* were to labour seven years without pay for their former master. At the end of seven years without trouble the *liberto* would be freed of any further obligations. For his part, the employer was subject to several obligations with regard to food, lodging, clothing, religious instruction, and medical assistance.

To oversee the conditions of the arrangement a Board for the Protection of Libertos was set up in São Tomé Island, with a branch in Principe.[5] In this insignificant grant decree were the beginnings of a contract labour system. Here also was the beginning of the system of exporting slaves from Angola to São Tomé, which was to erupt fifty years later into a notorious scandal and controversy.

In June 1856 slavery was abolished in the disputed district of Ambriz[6]—as well as in the territories of Cabinda and Molembo—which Portuguese forces had begun to occupy the year before. Ambriz and the lands north to the Congo were areas to which England had denied Portuguese sovereignty, and the abolition of slavery there was an attempt to head off English humanitarian protests against Portugal's take-over. In the same year, on 28 July, still another Bill sponsored by Sá da Bandeira became law. Children born of slave mothers were born free, the mother's master having the right to their services, however, until the children reached the age of twenty. Also in 1856 Sá da Bandeira had to abandon a Bill which would have authorized the expulsion of well-known slave-traders from Portuguese African possessions.

Two years later, on 29 August 1858, the decree was published abolishing slavery *twenty years hence* in all the lands of the Portuguese monarchy. The first phase of Sá da Bandeira's efforts were completed. His accomplishments over the twenty years since 1836 may seem absurdly small, but there was no widespread support in Portugal for his programmes. The overseas minister accomplished his legislative record by force of his prestige and will. Sentiment in the colonies was in favour of slavery, and colonists there had vocal supporters in the Portuguese press and Parliament. The idealism of Sá da Bandeira was limited by this opposition and by his own practical (or impractical) concerns for the economic development of Portuguese Africa, but seldom in the history of the Portuguese

[5] See Silva Cunha, *O trabalho indígena*, pp. 132–3.

[6] A port on the coast north of Luanda, once a slave-trade centre. Sovereignty over this area of the coast and north to the mouth of the Congo was claimed by Portugal and denied by England. See Roger Anstey, *Britain and the Congo in the Nineteenth Century* (Oxford, 1962) for a full discussion of the complicated issue.

overseas empire had the spirit of philanthropy shone so clearly—even if most of its achievement was the shadow of legislation, not the substance of fulfilment.

English members of the Mixed Commission Courts in Luanda kept the British Foreign Office informed of Portugal's success and failure in coping with the problems of slavery and the slave-trade. The courts, set up under the Treaty of 1842 for the suppression of the slave-trade, were made up of an English and Portuguese commissioner and both an arbitrator and secretary for each nation, though they rarely met in full body. Their formal function was limited, but in the 1850's and 1860's the English commissioners were sometimes successful in getting Angolan officials to take anti-slavery actions. The reports of the Luanda Commission to the Foreign Office are the most reliable sources of information on slaving practices in Angola. In 1856 Sir George Jackson was commissioner and Edmund Gabriel, arbitrator. Both men had had long service in Luanda, and Gabriel was to succeed Jackson.

Reviewing for 1855 the state of slavery and the slave-trade in Angola, Jackson and Gabriel[7] wrote to the Foreign Office that the traffic 'has been in a state nearly of abeyance, giving here and there, indeed, indications of life and a readiness to spring up afresh as vigorously as before whenever opportunity may offer . . . but showing no proof of that open and daring activity which once characterized it'. The British representatives were fearful that the recent Portuguese occupation of Ambriz to the north would not bring any diminution in the slave-trade from that port, for experience had shown that when Portuguese jurisdiction and 'fiscal restrictions' took over, no significant decline might be expected in the slave-trade. Jackson and Gabriel were firm advocates of the notion that free trade provided the surest death for the slave-trade.

Of the slave registration decreed by the Act of 14 December 1854 they reported that the governor could not find two individuals in the province who were able to agree on its provisions.

[7] A similar mixed commission court was situated in Cape Town. The Moçambique coast was in its jurisdiction, but the distance was so great and the information so diluted that it was not a successful enterprise.

The promiscuous use of the terms *livres, libertos,* and *ingénuos* made it difficult to affix any precise meaning to the Africans affected by the legislation. One thing did seem certain, that the 26,000 slaves registered in Angola would not be freed. For Jackson the principal recommendation of the decree was 'the formal recognition thus solemnly put forth by the Crown of Portugal of the many and serious inconveniences resulting from the present state of the Negro population in her transmarine possessions, and the facilities it may afford for that further and more perfect legislation in favor of that unhappy race'.[8]

Although Jackson and Gabriel feared a serious revival of the overseas slave-trade from the Angolan coast, their fears were never realized. Over the next ten years an occasional slaver did slip away and an occasional slaver was apprehended either at Ambriz or Benguela (on 18 February 1856, for example, the Portuguese brig *Serro do Pilar* captured the *Isla de Cuba* with a cargo of slaves, 210 tons burden, off Benguela Velha). The resurgence of the slave-trade occurred to the north, at the mouth of the Congo River, an area which offered most of the amenities which helped the clandestine traffic to flourish.

Portugal, though she had not renounced her historic claim to the Congo estuary, had no control or influence over events. Nor did British members of the Mixed Commission have political influence in the area, although their reports to the Foreign Office were filled with information about the slave-trade. Only British naval squadrons asserted any practical authority, and so long as slave traders had the protection afforded by flying the American flag, their power was limited. In no way could the Portuguese Government be held accountable for the outrages committed during this last violent flurry of the West African traffic, but the participation of Portuguese subjects in almost every phase of the illicit operation—as contractors, supercargoes, crew members, and, finally, as slave merchants in the Congo—was an exasperating element in the relations between England and Portugal and reinforced a particular association in an English humanitarian attitude. The corrupting Congo traffic brought shame to all who took part in

[8] F.O. 84/985, Luanda Commissioners to Foreign Office, 22 Jan. 1856. F.O. references are to Foreign Office series in the Public Records Office.

it—from American financiers to slave-trading African chiefs, but perhaps the largest share of the guilt was imputed, in most cases incorrectly, to the Portuguese.

The horrors of this latter-day traffic were equal to those of a century earlier. Francisco de Assis Tavares, commander of the *Villa Flor* of the Portuguese West African naval squadron, describes a raid on the factory of José da Silva Correa at Punta da Lenha on the Congo River where slaves were waiting to be embarked.

> I landed on the third inst. [3 June 1857] at six o'clock in the morning and, on proceeding to search the place, I came to a Barracoon. . . . In this place I discovered hidden under mats, 47 slaves of different sexes and ages, amongst whom were 4 with neck irons, and one in a dying state, besides another dead in a state of incipient putrefaction. The insupportable effluvia proceeding from the dead slave and from several tanks with deposits of filth obliged us immediately to leave the Barracoon. It was horrifying to look upon this scene of inhumanity. I caused all the Negroes to be brought out and those who were prisoners to be set at liberty: on interrogating some of them they said that they were waiting for a ship, in which to be embarked. They were very badly treated and received but little food.[9]

On hearing of the case the governor-general, José Coelho do Amaral, stated that Correa would be tried and his factories burned down, but nothing came of these threats.

In Angola the seeds of a historic controversy had been planted by the Decree Grant of 25 October 1853 to planter Sousa a Almeida. In his conversation with Governor-General Amaral on 26 July 1856, Sir George Jackson took up the question of the shipment of Africans from Angola to the islands of São Tomé and Principe. He raised two points: one, that slaves were being shipped out of Angola in the guise of household servants, this in violation of Article 5 of the Treaty of 1842, and two, that the forty-seven Negroes shipped on 16 June to the island as *libertos* were really to serve as slaves on island estates. On the second point Jackson picked out the inherent contradiction in

[9] F.O. 84/1013, Tavares to Pedro Valente da Costa Loreiro e Pinho, 18 June 1857.

the regulations for the Decree of 25 October 1853 fixing the procedures by which slaves were sent to the islands.[10]

Amaral's response to the first point was that slaves were slaves and servants were servants; the ten Africans were listed in their passports as servants. To the second point he admitted the necessity of the *liberto* to work for seven years, but the governor argued:

> Slaving does not consist alone in being bound to labour. If that were the case, who could boast of being free? The condition of a slave is a much broader one; it consists in the almost absolute privation of all that by natural right pertains to the dignity of man. The *libertos* in question are given to the care of curators and of a Protection Board who have carefully to attend to those comforts which they may justly claim; to their suitable instruction, in a word, to every kind of legitimate interest belonging to them. . . . Because they do not at once receive their complete freedom can it be said that they continue slaves?

In no way did Amaral admit that compulsory labour for an appointed time (seven years in this case) constituted a state of slavery. He cited the use of contract labour in European countries. And he denied that plantation owner Almeida had purchased slaves to send to Principe, it being well known that Almeida had more than enough slaves in Benguela to fill the quota.[11]

The classic lines of dispute were being drawn, the Portuguese position being that compulsory labour, even exported compulsory labour, was in no legal sense slavery, and the English position being that compulsory labour, especially exported compulsory labour, was nothing less than slavery. In his answer to the Governor Amaral, Jackson went to the root of the *liberto* problem. The freed Negro, he argued, 'really has no voice in

[10] F.O. 84/985, Jackson to Amaral, 26 July 1856. The Foreign Office sent instructions to Henry Howard, British Minister in Lisbon, to complain of these procedures. F.O. 84/989, F.O. to Henry Howard, 16 Feb. 1856, 8 Apr. 1856, and 26 Dec. 1856. Howard followed the instructions in his discussion, and correspondence with the Viscount of Althoguia, Portuguese Foreign Minister, but the Lisbon Government from the beginning did not view the compulsory labour of *libertos* as any form of slavery. F.O. 84/990, Howard to Althoguia, 25 Feb. 1856.

[11] F.O. 84/985, Amaral to Jackson, n.d.

the matter'. And the Africans sent to the islands were not domesticated slaves, but almost invariably either children or 'Negroes in a state little removed from savage life'. He regarded the contract as deceptive and 'entered into without the full consent of all parties'.[12]

In Angola African interests were usually neglected by the Luanda Board of Protection for Slaves and Freed Men. On most issues between slaves or *libertos* and Portuguese residents, the Board decided in favour of the latter. One member of the Board complained that funds collected from slave registration fees were misused. Protesting the use of these funds to subsidize a Portuguese-sponsored mining expedition, the philanthropic mayor of Luanda said that, since the Board was created to defend the slave and protect the *liberto*, the money should be used for their education. He urged the purchase of a fertile tract of land where *libertos* might be brought together and given agricultural instruction. Sunday schools should be established for instruction in the Christian religion and morality so that by degrees the *libertos* might become useful citizens. The early proposal of techniques for cultural assimilation was not without its practical side; from the farm would come a steady flow of agricultural labourers, always in short supply in Angola. The proposal failed to find majority support on the Board.[13]

In Lisbon the issue of slavery arose several times in the Portuguese Parliament, notably on 14 and 15 February 1856, in a debate on alterations to the Decree of 14 December 1854 which had created the status of *libertos*. Two liberalizing amendments were proposed by Deputy Afonso de Castro, the first being the extension of freedom to slaves belonging to colonial municipalities and to charitable organizations (*misericórdias*), and the second, the abolition of Article 29 which obliged the *libertos* to serve the state for seven years. Castro, in support of his amendments, observed that slavery was condemned by philanthropy, that it was no longer an economic necessity in the

[12] F.O. 84/985, Jackson to Amaral, 23 Sept. 1856.

[13] F.O. 84/985, Jackson to F.O., 30 Sept. 1856. In another instance the mayor (president of the municipal council) mortgaged part of his properties to lend money to a slave to purchase his freedom after the slave's petition to the Board had been turned aside.

colonies, and that the state of liberated Negroes was a condition for the most part worse than slavery. The majority of the chamber was in agreement that slavery should be abolished overseas, but it was believed that it would not do to be precipitate in depriving colonial communities and agricultural interests of their property rights. As a further caution the majority noted that the interests of slaves, who would scarcely know what to do with freedom suddenly pressed upon them, had to be considered. The first amendment carried, the second failed.[14]

At the same time the Portuguese Overseas Council was attempting, as a result of continuing queries from the British minister in Lisbon, to find a solution to the *liberto* problem that would simultaneously guarantee a flow of labour to the developing plantations of São Tomé and Principe and meet British objections to the traffic. On 4 September, the Council issued a report recommending that *libertos* from Angola to São Tomé be permitted to embark only at Luanda,[15] that they be furnished with certificates of registration, that the embarkation be under the supervision of the Angolan authorities, that the liberated Negroes should be conveyed directly to São Tomé where they should be placed under the supervision of the local Board of Protection, and that a limit of ten *libertos* be shipped at one time on one vessel. Several additional recommendations, irrelevant for Angola and São Tomé but quite pertinent for Portuguese East Africa, suggested that no *liberto* be carried in foreign vessels and that no liberated Negroes be engaged outside Portuguese African territory.[16]

The Portuguese Government was sensitive to British criticism of its African policies, particularly those touching labour questions; this sensitivity was to remain well into the twentieth century, withstanding even the difficult decade of the 1890's. By 1856 the customary Portuguese reaction to English inquiries was set, to continue basically unchanged. That was to promise to look into the complaint, then to try to curb the excesses or

[14] F.O. 84/990, Howard to F.O., 16 Feb. 1856.

[15] The supply of labour came from up and down the coast. Gabriel wrote that the want of labourers created a traffic in slaves—carried in small African craft—from the mainland opposite the islands. F.O. 84/1013, Gabriel to F.O., 5 Sept. 1857.

[16] F.O. 84/991, Howard to F.O., 27 Aug. 1856 (enclosure).

abuses of a particular practice through additional legislation or bureaucratic control. This tactic was seldom successful, and the abuse itself, essentially unquestioned by the colonial planners, went on for generations, to become more deeply ingrained in the Portuguese African way of life.

But so long as Sá da Bandeira was a member of the Government, Portugal's policy was not always a counteraction, goaded into being by English inquiries. There was frequently a creative aggressive quality to Sá da Bandeira's humanitarianism, which may be seen in the Decree of 3 November 1856.

It is strictly in accordance with justice to abolish as soon as possible the abusive practice which has existed from remote times in a portion of the territories of the province of Angola, consisting in obliging free Negroes, Portuguese subjects, to do the laborious work entitled 'Porter's Service' (*Serviço de carregadores*), considering that the right, which, according to the constitutional character of the monarchy, belongs to all Portuguese subjects, without distinction of race, colour, or religious creed, or disposing of their own labour and industry as it best suits them . . . and inasmuch as this abuse being promoted and maintained by avarice . . . has annulled the right of the above-mentioned Negroes to depose freely of their own labour; considering that the argument put forward for preventing the abolition of this vexatious practice, viz. that if the Negroes were not forced to perform the said service . . . all trade with the interior of the province would cease, as well as that with the independent tribes of the interior, is a pretext to be classed with those made use of by the advocates of slavery against the adversaries of such iniquity; insomuch as in all the Portuguese territories of Angola where the said forced labour is not exacted, free Negroes are to be found who voluntarily hire themselves for the purpose of conveying the merchants' goods . . . finally, considering that such violence ought no longer to be tolerated, it having for more than a century been stigmatized by various zealous and intelligent authorities of that province, who considered it as the cause of serious impediment to the advancement of the province . . . I think it right to decree the following:

Article 1) The forced labour called 'serviço de carregadores' is hereby abolished and prohibited in all the territories of the province of Angola without any exception.

Article 2) All forced labour of whatsoever denomination is also abolished.

Not included in the two provisions were military service and local road building.[17] The decree had little practical effect, but more than a hundred years were to pass before African labour in Angola was again declared so free.

Sá da Bandeira's banning of compulsory labour, particularly carrier's service, was resentfully opposed in Angola, and representatives were sent to Lisbon for revocation of the ban. The principal argument put forth by Angolan merchants and officials was that commercial interests in the province were suffering because free Negroes, naturally indolent, refused to sign on to carry produce from the interior to the coast. But the fault lay with subordinate authorities in the interior who had previously gained a considerable part of their income recruiting Africans in their districts to act as *carregadores*. Now they strove to frustrate the new legislation by placing obstacles in the way of merchants trying to hire voluntary labour.[18] Without the support of his subalterns in the back-country the governor-general could do little and in effect he did little. After an article appeared in a Lisbon paper, *A nação*, 5 April 1858, detailing abuses still perpetrated under the old system, Sá da Bandeira instructed Amaral to make a complete investigation and to punish the administrative officers who permitted the abuses.[19]

The extensive correspondence between Amaral and Sá da Bandeira led to a long decree issued on 22 September 1858.

[17] *Diário do governo*, 9 Nov. 1856. The Minister for Marine and Overseas was not totally impractical. In another decree, to accompany the *portária* abolishing forced labour, an increase in taxes was declared in those districts of Angola where the decree had effect, this 'in consequence of the great benefits conferred upon the Negroes by the abolition of forced labour'.

[18] F.O. 84/1043, Gabriel to F.O., 31 July 1858. In a Decree of 19 Jan. 1858 the overseas minister stated that the term *carregadores* ought not to be used, since the service had been abolished. He also ordered that under the new system of free labour, chiefs were to be remunerated for the use of their people. *Diário do governo*, 5 June 1858.

[19] *Diário do governo*, 5 June 1858. A year later Sá da Bandeira was again inveighing against subordinate authorities in the bush who had neglected their duties and abused the confidences placed in them. They had continued to demand money for supplying *carregadores*. In some areas they had monopolized the whole traffic, 'this to reserve to themselves illicit gain', Again, in the Decree of 5 Feb. 1859, Sá told the governor general to remove such officials from office or to transfer them or to retire them from office. From time to time a minor official was removed from office. *Diário do governo*, 14 Feb. 1859.

Absurd in some sections, generous in others, the decree was a mixture of the practical and the ideal, another attempt to reconcile the impossible elements in Angola's labour problems. The decree took note that the governor-general had attributed the difficulties of enforcing the November 1856 measure 'to the inveterate reluctance on the part of the blacks to labour' and that this had led to the atrophy of trade with the interior. Left to their natural indolence, the Africans would be unable to pay the new tax—which had already led to a certain amount of emigration to those parts of the interior where taxes could not be collected. Sá da Bandeira countered by saying that only in the districts of Golungo Alto, Ambaca, and Pungo Andongo were free Africans reluctant to work. It was *here* that their labour had been extorted, and it was these districts which Africans left. In other districts, Benguela, Cassengo, and Duque de Bragança, where forced labour was prohibited, there had always been a good supply of porters and workers.

Sá da Bandeira then reiterated the real purpose of the 1856 decree: to encourage African agriculture and industry. He urged that the chiefs and headmen be gently persuaded to bring in a stipulated number of pounds of cotton (in proportion to the number of inhabitants in their village or district) to the principal city of the area each year where it would be purchased by the Government at a fixed price. Should the head of a household fail to bring in the stipulated amount of cotton, or a substitute article, he should be bound to work for the colonial government on the roads or an agricultural project until he had earned an amount three times the value of his required contribution. At that time his services could also be hired out to private employers. Parish priests and missionaries must regard it as their task to indoctrinate the African population with the necessity of application to labour and of dressing in the European style. Chiefs especially should be clothed in the European manner. And at the end of the *portária*, the overseas minister stressed that it was necessary to root out the idea that the white population of the Portuguese African colonies have a right to the labour of natives without giving them due remuneration.[20]

[20] *Diário do governo*, 4 Oct. 1858.

At a relatively early date the notion that work and European dress made the difference between an African and a Portuguese was fixed in the official mind, from which it was not to be easily dislodged. Sá da Bandeira had previously expressed himself in a letter to the President of the Board of Guardians in Angola who had asked for the minister's interpretation of several points in the Decree of 14 December 1854, among them the statement that all unbaptized slaves should be baptized and the suggestion that all slaves and free Negroes of Luanda should be dressed in European clothing and be addressed in the Portuguese language so as gradually 'to civilize them'. He wrote that the Board and more specifically its President were bound to use every effort in their power to induce the owners of slaves to cause them to enter the pale of the Catholic Church to convince them to abandon their uncivilized habits and superstitious practices. Towards these ends much would be done by the diffusion of public instruction and by the establishment of primary schools in many settlements and districts, which would facilitate the introduction of the Portuguese language. His Majesty commanded further that the Negroes under the guardianship of the Board should dress in the European style.[21]

The combination of plans for the assimilation of Africans and for the use of their labour in the development of the Portuguese territories, the bed-rock of all Portuguese African policy, liberal or conservative, led Sá da Bandeira to reject an accumulation of British requests asking the Portuguese Government to rescind a licence granting José da Costa Pedreira, merchant and landowner of São Tomé, permission to convey 100 slaves there from Angola. Sá da Bandeira said that the development of agriculture in the islands not only increased their prosperity and aided Portuguese commerce but also worked for the civilization of the province. Since slaves, by Portuguese law and by international treaty, could not be shipped and since the conveying of Africans from the continent had the effect of delivering them from slavery, the Portuguese Government did not hesitate to grant the concession to Pedreira. Certainly, Sá went on, the Portuguese Government could not with good conscience deprive Angolan slaves from entering upon the enjoyment of

[21] Decree of 18 Jan. 1858. In *Diário do governo*, 29 Jan. 1858.

civil rights common to all Portuguese subjects. The concession, therefore, was no enfringement of treaty, and could not be considered slave traffic. 'It would be a great advantage', he concluded, 'that similar enterprises should be multiplied . . . because many slaves would thereby pass to the condition of liberated Negroes.'[22]

Edmund Gabriel wrote to the Foreign Office for the year 1856 on the decline of the slave-trade in Angola and the rise in legitimate commerce, notwithstanding 'that the restrictive policy of the Portuguese government is enough to paralyze everything like active and energetic commerical enterprise'. Anti-slavery legislation had made little change in the colony's customs. Gabriel inquired from time to time about the execution of the Decree of 14 December 1854, but he had not 'become aware of any beneficient or satisfactory results from it'. Nor had the Board of Protection for slaves and *libertos* adopted any measure for promoting either the physical or moral well-being of those whose interests were entrusted to its care. In another dispatch Gabriel commented on Portuguese anti-slavery legislation. 'It is one thing to enact laws, it is another to execute them, and experience has unhappily shown with what facility all laws against the slave trade are evaded in this country.' He recommended that the Mixed Commission oversee the shipping of liberated Negroes to São Tomé and Principe.[23]

Agricultural hopes for the future seemed to rest on slave-labour. In order to respond to an inquiry sent out from Manchester on the cotton supply in Angola, present and potential, the British consulate in Luanda had the Austrian botanist Friedrich Welwitsch prepare a report on the cotton-growing possibilities of the Angolan interior. A Luanda business firm did a sort of economic analysis. The transition of the native-grown crop into a plantation crop, they agreed, would almost certainly involve slave-labour. 'The existence of slavery in the province and especially the employment of slaves by all the agriculturists in the interior render it doubtful whether any

[22] F.O. 84/1043, Sá da Bandeira to the Duke of Loulé (Portuguese Foreign Minister), 8 Mar. 1858.

[23] F.O. 84/1013, Gabriel to F.O., 11 Feb. 1857 and 2 Mar. 1857.

large plantations would be made without having recourse to slave-labour.'[24] The same fears were held for mine workings in the interior should they prove profitable.[25]

Another disturbing factor to Gabriel was the appearance of French ships at the Congo to carry off African workers to France's island possessions in the West Indies. In 1857 an agent of Régis Frères, a trading house of Marseilles, began purchasing slaves who were afterwards embarked, 1,000 of them, from the Régis factory at Loango and sent as emigrants to Guadeloupe. Gabriel wrote: 'The Africans being carried off . . . whatever they may be called and whatever may be the guarantees given them for their future rights and liberty are . . . bought like any other article of merchandise from those who, in violation of the laws of God and man, continue to traffic in human flesh—the slave dealers on this coast.' The anticipation of a quasi-legal purchase of slaves aroused great interest and revived the hopes of slave-dealers all along the coast.

The governor-general of Angola was fearful that these proceedings would encourage the slave-trade in that section of the coast the Portuguese claimed as their own. 'No free labourers' could be obtained by the French agent unless they were slaves and bought from slave-traders, and the governor vowed to prosecute any Portuguese subject participating in the business. The commander of the French naval force along the coast declined to intervene, dwelling at length on the freedom given the Africans after their purchase. For several years French ships called regularly at the Congo for workers for West Indian and Indian Ocean estates. For a short while the traffic reached the proportions of thousands of slaves a year.[26]

[24] F.O. 84/1043, Gabriel to F.O., 3 Apr. 1858.

[25] F.O. 84/1043, Gabriel to F.O., 30 July 1858.

[26] F.O. 84/1013, Gabriel to F.O., 1 Oct. 1857. The French had strong objections to a memorandum sent out by the Overseas Ministry to the governer-general of Angola instructing him to prosecute Portuguese subjects doing business with the French traders. French Foreign Minister Count Walewski told Lisbon that France had every right, under the Convention of Madrid, 30 Jan. 1786, to export Negroes from the Congo and would use force to do so, if this became necessary. Portugal, because of her equivocal position at the mouth of the Congo, tried to involve England in the discussions with France. F.O. 84/1048, Howard to F.O., 8 May 1858.

To Gabriel the importance of the French arrival was really the encouragement it gave Africans to sell their fellow men.

> It is a pursuit by which they easily obtain their necessities and all that is essential to their subsistence, and so long as it is open to them, they will never exert themselves in cultivating the natural products of their country.... The civilization of Africa is a measure which affords but little hope of ultimate success, so long as the prejudices of the natives are fostered and their wants supplied by the French, Spanish, and Portuguese agents employed in purchasing slaves.[27]

Gabriel believed that if the full facts were made known to the Emperor Napoleon, France would put a stop to the Congo trade. Régis had constructed barracoons at Embomma and Banana Creek, from which 4,000 workers were being shipped. Agents for the firm were now buying most of the slaves coming down the river. The French with their better goods were outbidding Cuban agents. Whether the workers were slaves or free labourers, Gabriel could not say, but 'to Africa, my Lord, the effects are the same. Their collection brought war and bloodshed to the interior of the country.'[28]

Merchants and ships chandlers in Luanda were involved with the burgeoning Congo traffic. Some Luanda traders had factories on the Congo coast which were supplied by coastal launches. At times these vessels did not have proper papers and were destroyed by cruisers of the British squadron, whose officers claimed they could not differentiate between these and other launches used to carry slaves and provisions to the slave ships. It was not impossible that some Portuguese launches were engaged in both legitimate and illegal commerce. The issue became a bitter one between Gabriel and Governor Amaral; it was one of the reasons for the breakdown of what had once been a cordial relationship. After eighteen years in West Africa (four in the Navy and fourteen in the Mixed Commission), Gabriel was exhausted and overworked, and his patience in diplomatic amenities sometimes wore thin, especially when he had good

[27] F.O. 84/1043, Gabriel to F.O., 25 Feb. 1858.

[28] F.O. 84/1075, Gabriel to F.O., 15 Apr. 1859. A year later Gabriel saw no improvement in the situation. The French were still busily buying slaves for their colonial plantations. F.O. 84/1104, Gabriel to F.O., 25 Feb. 1860.

information that Cabinda launches had helped ship 518 slaves from the coast to the waiting *Tavernier*.[29] Nor had Amaral's temper improved during his four years of residence in Luanda. The troubling problem of Portugal's claims to the coast north of Ambriz also increasingly exacerbated relations between the two men.

Edmund Gabriel was a remarkable man. Indefatigably zealous in his efforts to curb and extinguish the sale and abuse of Africans, he was a formidable force in keeping the problems of slavery and forced labour alive in the Foreign Office. Until 1859 he had been able to assert an influence in Angola, when he chose, only a little less powerful than that of the governor-general. Gabriel had now come into a troubled period, and his problems with the colonial government were made more difficult by the appointment of Sir Henry Vere Huntley as Arbitrator to the Mixed Commission and British consular official. Formerly a naval officer in the West African squadron, Huntley was a callow and foolish man. In a pretentious report on a Portuguese project to build a railroad from Luanda to Cassengo, Huntley gave his views on what this would mean to slavery in the interior. He did not foresee any serious change. African chiefs who formerly sold their people would now enslave them to bring in produce to ship on the railway. Nor did he recommend any change in the practice of using forced labour for carrying services. It might be that a new moral order would emerge in the interior and the demon of slavery be struck down, 'but if the tropical African cannot feel the falling fetter, will not demand his right of freedom, and remains insensible to the example of justice set before him—he must wallow, as he has from time immemorial, in his wretchedness and debasement'.[30]

[29] F.O. 84/1075, Gabriel to F.O., 11 Nov. 1859 and 25 Nov. 1859.

[30] F.O. 84/1082, Huntley to F.O., 1 Mar. 1859. Huntley was the author of *Seven Years Service on the Slave Coast* (2 vols.; London, 1850) and a novel *Peregrine Scramble*. In *Seven Years Service* (ii. 1–17) Huntley described the slaughter of the king's slaves in Dahomey, saying that legitimate commerce had no influence whatsoever in ameliorating savage life in West Africa. He regarded the whole work of 'civilizing and christianizing West Africa as a melancholy failure'. He was equally harsh towards England's 'self-styled Philanthropists'.

English attitudes towards Portuguese policies in Africa have formed almost without exception (the most notable being Sir Harry Johnston) two distinct categories. There has been the one opinion, sternly moral, philanthropic, and inflexible, which has held that the African population in Portuguese territories has been mercilessly exploited. The other, tolerant and flexible, held that Africans were savage children and Portugal, or any other white authority, was perfectly justified in dealing harshly with them. Gabriel represented the first opinion, Huntley the second, and for two years, 1860 and 1861, the controversy between the two men was as unrelenting as any taking place then or later between English and Portuguese.

Gabriel's report of 25 February 1860 was in large part a studied response to Huntley's observations on the Negro race. He began by giving high praise to Portuguese anti-slavery legislation, but denied that new laws would do the work. First it would be necessary 'to correct public opinion in this country on the subject of slavery, for I will venture to say that with the exception perhaps of a few officers of the Government, there does not exist one individual in this province who wishes that the slave population should rise a single step in the scale of civilization above its present degraded levels'. Then in direct rebuke to Huntley:

One of the arguments most prominently advanced in support of the system of enslaving the Africans is that their intellectual facilities are of an inferior order, that they are in fact an inferior race of beings, and that inasmuch as their own indolence and apathy show that they are indifferent to the blessings they would derive from their freedom, it is useless to teach them the habits of civilized life and impolitic to grant them their liberty. Parties who hold these views no doubt, far from aiding to promote the moral and intellectual culture of the Africans, consider it more expedient that they should be allowed to remain in the present state of ignorance and barbarity.

I believe . . . that the African character is susceptible of improvement and civilization in a degree little inferior to that of any race of men similarly circumstanced, but it is obviously only when slaving and the slave trade should have been totally eradicated from amongst them that any marked progress can be looked for, or that this country can be expected to make its natural advance in civilization.

> Teach the natives of Africa the benefits and blessings of freedom, and they will soon not only aspire to it, but make an effort to obtain it . . . but leave them in the deplorable state of darkness in which they are now and they will be forever held in subjection and degradation to supply the means of profit and labour to their European task masters.[31]

Not a man to avoid controversy, Huntley took issue directly with Gabriel in *his* report to the Foreign Office, written while Gabriel was on leave. A long section of his report, 'Consideration of Processes on which the Extinction of African Slavery is Based', attacked Gabriel head on. Huntley questioned both the proposition that no man had a right to enslave another and that Africans were 'susceptible to improvement in a degree little inferior' to other races of men. He could not be bound by such propositions. In his years of travel up and down the coast he had seen no proof. Where Gabriel's ideas on Negro freedom had been in practice for half a century, nothing had happened. 'Millions of Africans comprising the population of Western Africa have not produced one instance of a patriotic leader—instructions in aid of learning, arts and sciences are totally unknown. Invention, that divine and natural gift, which unbidden suddenly flashes some wonderous application upon minds of other races, has never animated the features of the Negro.' Africa, Huntley continued, had shown itself hostile to industry, either its own or European. And if slavery, he asked in conclusion, dulled perceptions and broke down the energy of the mind, how was it that chiefs who were never slaves, were not 'one jot nearer civilization than the slaves they sold'?[32]

Earlier in the year Gabriel had refused to sit with Huntley on the Mixed Commission because of the latter's pronouncements. On his arrival in Luanda in late 1859 Huntley had taken residence in a house owned by the notorious former slave-dealer Francisco António Flores and had subsequently dined with him. Huntley had made other associations which offended the severely moral Gabriel. In his turn, Huntley regarded Gabriel as a martinet who could 'see no fidelity of service in others, unless they yield homage to the estimates he has thought proper

[31] F.O. 84/1104, Gabriel to F.O., 25 Feb. 1860.
[32] F.O. 84/1105, Huntley to F.O., 18 Nov. 1860.

to frame with reference to the Negro, his emancipation and ultimate education'.[33] Huntley sought to undercut Gabriel's position in Luanda and London, and when Gabriel became seriously, if advertently, involved in the case of the Congo prince Dom Nicolau, Huntley in effect worked with newly arrived Governor-General Carlos Augusto Franco to embarrass, if not destroy, Commissioner Gabriel.[34] On his return from leave in 1861 Gabriel's luggage, through a series of complications, was unloaded on the beach instead of at the customs warf. It was thereupon impounded, and Gabriel was harrassed for a number of months. Huntley took the side of the Portuguese authorities and wrote several dispatches accusing Gabriel of breaking Portuguese law. This was too much for the men in the Slave Trade Department of the Foreign Office, who now saw a possible conspiracy—worked out by Flores!—to compromise Gabriel out of his position. Huntley was transferred in 1862.

On the question of the labour traffic to São Tomé and Principe, Gabriel and Huntley were usually in agreement. It was becoming an important business, and their report of October 1861 was the first lengthy study of practices which were to change very little thereafter. Slaves were being sent to São Tomé under

[33] F.O. 84/1105, Huntley to F.O., 5 July 1860. On the margin of Huntley's dispatch, an aide in the Slave Trade Department, where people were sympathetic to Gabriel, has written: 'This is a perfect reflection of Sir H. Huntley's own feelings.'

[34] The case is that of Dom Nicolau d'Aqua Rosada e Sardinia and it takes up most of the correspondence for the year 1860. The affair is too complicated to sum up briefly. The nub of the matter is that Nicolau, a *quondam* Portuguese *assimilado*, was murdered at Quissembo by a group of African dissidents. The governor-general sought to take advantage of the murder to put down rebellious Africans in the north and to push Portuguese sovereignty up the coast from Ambriz to Quissembo. His little army was roundly defeated in late Feb. 1860. Men from an American ship and a British ship anchored at Quissembo refused to let Amaral enter the town to rest his troops. Amaral rankled under the failure of the expedition and took the occasion to charge Gabriel with the responsibility for Nicolau's murder on the ground that Gabriel had helped Nicolau to get out of Luanda to escape the wrath of Portuguese authorities over some articles Nicolau had written for a Lisbon newspaper. The charge was only partially, and accidentally, true. Amaral then refused to correspond with Gabriel and talked only with Huntley, a situation Huntley greatly relished. The behaviour of Huntley and Amaral brought no particular credit to either. Amaral was relieved of his duties in June 1860, to be replaced by Carlos Augusto Franco.

various denominations: domestic slaves, servants, *libertos*, or simply 'ten Negroes'. Each was provided with a passport and his name appeared on the passenger list published in the *Boletim oficial* of the province. This procedure, the two men supposed, was a deceit to evade the Treaty of 1842. From February to October of 1861, 415 Africans were carried to the islands with no attempt at concealment, not to mention the clandestine traffic. Slaves sold for twenty dollars in Angola fetched one hundred on São Tomé. The extensive coffee plantations established on the island within the last few years had created a demand for labour, which dealers in both the Congo and Angola had begun to fill. The voyage from Luanda to São Tomé on a new line of steamers plying between Luanda and Lisbon was a matter of six days. Dealers or middlemen made three of four voyages a year accompanied by the ten domestic slaves permitted by the treaty to be shipped from colony to colony. When this did not suffice, *libertos* were shipped as passengers. Commissioner and consul feared that the traffic would increase and draw into it all the unprincipled characters who had formerly been active in the slave-trade to the New World.[35]

The next two years saw the São Tomé traffic develop into a controversy of great importance in Luanda, Lisbon, and London. Gabriel was relentless, in the last painful year of his life, in his urgings to the Foreign Office and in his communications with the governor. Foreign Secretary Russell and Slave Officer Wylde fumed in London, and in Lisbon the Portuguese Government pertinaciously and courteously refused to admit that it was either a question of traffic in slaves or that it was a treaty matter.

By January 1862 Gabriel's predictions of an increase were being borne out. In the last three months of the previous year, 467 Africans had been embarked for the islands in one guise or another: 22 as domestic slaves, 48 as *libertos*, and 397 as *pretos livres* (free Africans). Accompanied by Commander

[35] F.O. 84/1105, Gabriel and Huntley to F.O., 10 Oct. 1861. The Foreign Office, using this and other reports, requested the British minister in Lisbon, Arthur Magenis, to take up the matter directly with Portuguese authorities and to tell them to take measures. F.O. 84/1142, F.O. to Magenis, 31 Dec. 1861.

Edmundstone of the *Arrogant*—whose presence was calculated to give strength to threats of intervention by the British naval squadron—Gabriel had a long and heated interview with Governor-General Sebastião Calheiros de Menezes. The new governor maintained that a passport was sufficient evidence that the embarking Negro was no slave. Gabriel argued that passports neither conferred liberty nor gave evidence that the holder was free, and that to the planters of São Tomé the passports were meaningless. He suggested that if England exercised her power under the 1842 Treaty, she would find that 'these Negroes were carried off by force and doomed to compulsory separation from their own country: that they belonged in fact to parties who, under the specious pretence of requiring labour for the cultivation of their estates, bought the Negroes brought to them by the dealers in slaves, and whatever the form of emancipation . . . gone through, shipped them to São Tomé as objects of commerce, in open violation of treaty engagements.' On no point was the governor-general disposed to yield, and Gabriel realized that the matter would not be set right in Luanda without stringent instructions from Lisbon.[36] Two months later Gabriel wrote that 'small coasting craft, schooners, palhabotes, and large launches, none of whose names appear in the *Gazette* [*Boletim oficial*], are constantly sailing off to São Tomé with human cargo'.[37]

In one of his many letters to Calheiros, Gabriel wrote that the system encouraged a criminal traffic which England and Portugal had once decided to suppress. Certainly the Treaty of 1842 did not apply to bona fide voluntary emigrants to São Tomé, but could anyone acquainted with Angola really believe that 2,000 Negroes could be found in one year who would of their wish and consent go off to the islands. Gabriel warned that the national feeling in England on the momentous question was as strong now as it ever had been. There were men in his

[36] F.O. 84/1166, Gabriel to F.O., 8 Jan. 1862.

[37] F.O. 84/1166, Gabriel to F.O., 8 Mar. 1862. On receipt of this communication, W. H. Wylde wrote a memorandum saying that the matter had reached such proportions it was time to take decisive action. Earl Russell sent off instructions to Magenis to seek an audience with the king in order to tell him of 'the bad impression created in England . . .'. See F.O. 84/1166, Memorandum of 5 May 1862.

country determined 'to affect the final extirpation of a traffic which had not only carried desolation to Africa, and checked the course of civilization, but doomed so many victims to misery and torment'.[38]

The Secretary-General of the Province of Angola, responding for Calheiros, who refused to answer Gabriel, informed the Commissioner that the emigrants were Portuguese subjects moving legally from one Portuguese province to another Portuguese province. Any infringement by the British Navy with their passage would offend the freedom and dignity of Portugal. Nor could His Excellency believe that England would want 'the world to witness such excesses and abuses practised on this coast by the English naval forces towards Portugal because she is a small nation—and compare them with the condescension and forbearance shown for so many years towards France because she is a great nation—she having exported from the Zaire [Congo River] tens of thousands of Negroes without England raising the slightest difficulty'.[39]

No matter how strong or frequent his protests to the colonial authorities in Luanda, Gabriel found that he got no results. Local officials would not yield, and Gabriel set about more earnestly than ever to present a case for the Foreign Office to use with the Portuguese Government in Lisbon. In a long letter, dated 19 April, he reviewed his correspondence. 'It is absurd to say that these Negroes are Portuguese citizens merely from the fact of their being brought into this city from the interior as slaves, sold here, and passports given to authorize their shipment to St. Thomas.' He went on to assert that many of the Africans came from parts of the interior where Portugal had not even nominal jurisdiction, were bought from tribes 'as independent as Portugal itself'. How can they be Portuguese citizens, he asked again and again. And 'if they are Portuguese citizens we presume they are not criminals, and whence, therefore, their arbitrary and forcible action from this country?'[40]

[38] F.O. 84/1166, Gabriel to Calheiros, 24 Mar. 1862. Several weeks afterwards, Calheiros, arguing that treaty matters were the business of the consular corps, not of commissioners, refused to receive Gabriel's letters.

[39] F.O. 84/1166, Secretary-General Barboza Leão to Gabriel, 7 Apr. 1862. By the end of March this correspondence had trickled to nothing.

[40] F.O. 84/1166, Gabriel to F.O., 19 Apr. 1862.

The reports began to have more effect in London. A minute by Russell on Gabriel's letter of 10 July 1862 reads 'Why should not our cruisers be ordered to deal with these shiploads of Negroes as slave ships and send them for ajudication?'[41] The serious discussions removed to Lisbon. Gabriel, now a very sick man, had two satisfying moments in the last months of his life. In July the commander of the French naval forces on the coast called to inform him that 'the system of exporting Negroes to the French West Indian colonies was formally put an end to by him on the 30 ultimo, in accordance with the orders of his sovereign'.[42] And on 17 September a new governor-general, José Baptista de Andrade, arrived in Luanda to replace Major Calheiros de Menezes. Gabriel hoped that he would be 'more co-operative than his predecessor' who had recently been awarded the Legion of Honour by the Emperor of France, for, Gabriel implied, his determined support of the *émigré* system in the Congo.[43]

Gabriel died of dysentery at sea on 14 December 1862. 'All who are engaged in the noble and humane cause'. Arbitrator Hewett wrote from Luanda, 'must lament the loss of his vigilance and assiduity.' The greater part of the population of Luanda followed his coffin from the place where it was landed to the grave where it was deposited. The orders due the highest judicial authority were paid to the remains.[44]

As Gabriel's last reports were received in London, the instructions of the Foreign Office to Arthur Magenis, Minister in Lisbon, became more pointed, for there was a notion in the Slave Trade Department that Magenis had not been carrying

[41] F.O. 84/1167, Gabriel to F.O., 10 July 1862.

[42] F.O. 84/1167, Gabriel to F.O., 12 July 1862.

[43] F.O. 84/1167, Gabriel to F.O., 27 Sept. 1862. Calheiros also received a sword of honour from the grateful inhabitants of São Tomé as an acknowledgement of the services he had rendered that colony. *Jornal do comércio,* 22 May 1864.

[44] F.O. 84/1167, Edward Hyde Hewett to F.O., 20 Dec. 1862. Wylde's minute of 4 Feb. 1863 reads: 'The public have lost a valuable servant, and whatever had been effected towards suppressing the slave trade from the Portuguese possessions on the West Coast of Africa is mainly due to the unflinching zeal and energy with which Mr. Gabriel and his predecessor Sir George Jackson denounced and pursued all who were engaged in the traffic.'

out earlier instructions with visible enthusiasm. 'You will state', he was told on 18 April, that you are instructed not to disguise the fact that if effectual measures are not taken by the Portuguese authorities to check this traffic, stringent instructions will be given to our cruisers to do so.'[45] A month later Magenis was ordered to ask for an audience with the King of Portugal to bring to his attention the substance of the reports from Gabriel which had been forwarded to Lisbon. The king was to be presented with a British threat to seize vessels suspected of the trade.[46]

Magenis had previously discussed the São Tomé problems with the Duke of Loulé, Portuguese Foreign Minister, who had in turn asked the Minister for Marine and Overseas, José da Silva Mendes Leal, for a report. Mendes Leal had gone to Governor-General Calheiros for information. Thus he was able to inform Loulé that the passages were 'in strict conformity with the laws': ships carried only ten Negroes, either slaves or freedmen; no passports were given free Negroes unless the application was accompanied by a document from the administrator of the Negroes' district declaring them to be free individuals. 'It would be an abuse of authority and a transgression against the fundamental law of the state to refuse passports to Portuguese citizens . . . and to hinder them from going where it may suit their purposes.' The Secretary-General of Angola had gone to São Tomé and he was pleased to inform his government that every precaution was taken there. According to the governor of that island: 'Free negroes were only employed in such work as they voluntarily sought after, and only worked as long as it suited them.' Those Negroes who were rude and inexperienced were watched over by the administration, although such was the scarcity of labour on the island, all workers, free or slave, were treated well.[47]

[45] F.O. 84/1177, F.O. to Magenis, 18 Apr. 1862.

[46] F.O. 84/1177, F.O. to Magenis, 16 May 1862. Magenis was at the same time being pressed to get Portuguese action on conditions in East Africa where Consul Livingstone was describing scenes of slavery and moral bankruptcy. In one letter accompanying a Livingstone report, Russell wrote: 'The governors and agents who permit these foul acts will be removed and replaced by honest and honorable men.' F.O. 84/1177, F.O. to Chargé Harries, 20 July 1862.

[47] F.O. 84/1177, Mendes Leal to Loulé, 24 Feb. 1862.

After Magenis had his interview in May 1862 with the king, 'who was obviously embarrassed', Loulé called in the British minister to tell him that steps would be taken and that Governor-General Calheiros was a man to inspire confidence.[48] On 29 August, Loulé said that effectual measures had now been taken. The problem had been, the Portuguese Government discovered, that the system had been, 'if not encouraged, at any rate tolerated by the provincial authorities, owing chiefly to erroneous notions entertained by the late colonial secretary, who had believed that the prosperity of São Tomé might thereby be promoted without any violation of the letter or spirit of the Treaty of 1842'. But this attitude, Loulé admitted, had turned out to be an embarrassment and a potential danger which could no longer be permitted. Both the governor-general and the secretary-general had been suspended, 'their direction of the affairs of the colony having met with the disapproval of the home government'. British Chargé Herries observed: 'It is possible that one of the reasons for their recall may have been the obstinacy with which they persisted in abetting the slave trade transactions.'[49]

But by November 1863 Portugal's position had hardened. Loulé told Magenis plainly that under the Law of 14 December 1854 his government could not hinder the shipment of *libertos* to the islands and that no aspect of the practice violated the Treaty of 1842 which had reference only to 'slaves properly so called'. He inquired on what grounds the British Government sought to prohibit workers from the islands. The Portuguese Government had the right to permit any number of free Negroes or freedmen (*libertos*) to go there. 'Where, when, and in what manner was it settled, that not even that which the

[48] F.O. 84/1177, Magenis to F.O., 23 May 1862.

[49] F.O. 84/1177, Herries to F.O., 1 Sept. 1862. Calheiros defended his actions and their legitimacy to the last. He continued to maintain that both free men and slaves who entered the city of Luanda were free when they left it with a passport. It was not enough for Gabriel to shout fraud; he must prove it. And then the reason for it all: 'Nature has adapted a race of men for these regions, and if they cannot be peopled by free Negroes, when blacks alone can resist the climate and apply to labour, what can be done to people them and cultivate them when they are in want of cultivators? Are they to be condemned to be perpetually abandoned?' Calheiros to Mendes Leal, 16 July 1862, enclosure in F.O. 84/1200, Magenis to F.O., 5 June 1863.

Treaty authorizes to be done with Negro slaves [the permitted shipment of domestic slaves] cannot be allowed with respect to free Negroes?' With that question unanswered, Loulé said his government would not take another single step in the matter.[50]

In Angola, Edward Hewett innocently assumed that with the change in governors the practice would be extinguished and so he informed the Foreign Office in February 1863.[51] But Watson Vredenburg, Gabriel's successor, had another story. It was told in Luanda that *libertos* shipped to São Tomé were there sold and enslaved again. In spite of the governor's personal honesty and his attempts to establish precautions, he had not really succeeded.[52] In a later conversation with Vredenburg, Andrade confessed that he was misled and deceived by the persistent efforts of 'those people who send these blacks to São Tomé'. When Andrade denied the issuance of passports to Africans of whose freedom he was not convinced, other Africans with an undoubted right to passports, applied for them. The documents were then transferred.[53] Coffee production had doubled in São Tomé in the last five years, and the demand for labour continued to increase.

To the south the last small flurry of the Atlantic slave-trade occurred in 1863 and 1864. With more active American participation in the naval squadrons patrolling in the vicinity of the Congo, slavers began to come to the more tranquil waters off Benguela. In the two years apparently from four to six ships took on loads of from 200 to 400 slaves south of Benguela and slipped away. There were few British patrols along that coast, and Portuguese forces were inadequate, although on 26 February 1864 the Portuguese schooner *Napier* captured the Spanish brig *Virgen del Refugio* which was then condemned.[54] The governor of Benguela district was seriously implicated in the resurgence of the trade. He resigned in April 1864, and an investigation was made of his conduct.

[50] F.O. 84/1200, Loulé to Magenis, 24 Nov. 1863.
[51] F.O. 84/1194, Hewett to F.O., 28 Feb. 1863.
[52] F.O. 84/1194, Watson Vredenburg to F.O., 31 July 1863.
[53] F.O. 84/1194, Vredenburg to F.O., 1 Sept. 1863.
[54] The officers of the ship were turned free on a ridiculously low bail and immediately absconded.

Vredenburg had established with Governor Andrade a friendship similar to that which had existed between Gabriel and Amaral. Andrade was under attack in Lisbon because of this friendship. The former secretary-general of the province, Barboza Leão, had taken to accusing him of being under the influence of British authorities in Luanda and of having sacrificed the island of São Tomé to the British by preventing the migration of labour. In confidence Andrade told Vredenburg that Calheiros and Barboza Leão had given passports to slaves and let them be shipped as so-called free men. The Angola Government had in those days been virtually in the hands of the secretary-general, who had received a heavy fee on the passports he had issued. The ease of shipping slaves off to São Tomé had led slave owners throughout the province to dispose of some of their slaves for a large profit.[55]

Andrade attempted to check the traffic by making a close examination of the free Africans who applied for passports. By now the flow of labour was a constant stream which could not be dammed. Obstructed here, the stream sought another course. Now it was the trade in *libertos* which began to assume large proportions. There was no question of credentials or passports, expatriation was compulsory. The source remained the same, slaves from the interior or slaves belonging to Portuguese masters; only the name had to be changed. Andrade confessed to Vredenburg with mortification that he did not see how he could control the traffic. Any number of boats had been engaged for the sole purpose of carrying *libertos* to the islands. Since no *libertos* could go unaccompanied by a 'colonist', a whole new industry came into being; colonists shuttled back and forth between Luanda and São Tomé accompanied by ten freed Africans. 'There is no difference between a *liberto* and a slave', Vredenburg wrote. 'Both do the same job and submit to the same authority, both are taken against their will.' He asserted, probably wrongly, that the planters of São Tomé could get enough free labour if they were willing to pay good wages for it.[56]

[55] F.O. 84/1214, Vredenburg to F.O., 30 July 1864.

[56] F.O. 84/1214, Vredenburg to F.O., 14 Aug. 1865 and of 7 Oct. 1865. On the margin of the second dispatch is a long minute by Wylde, dated 4 Dec.,

The Foreign Office instructed the minister in Lisbon to tell the Portuguese Government that *libertos* were slaves, that they were sold as slaves, and the fact that they were obliged to work for only a ten-year period didn't make them any the less slaves. The minister should tell the Portuguese Government that they were playing with language when they said that the Treaty of 1842 did not consider the matter of *libertos*.[57] The instructions were carried out carefully in a series of communications. Neither the Portuguese Foreign Ministry nor the Ministry for Marine and Overseas paid much attention. The economic success of São Tomé and Principe, one of the few successes in the colonies in the nineteenth century, was more important than the importuning British dispatches. The Portuguese Government launched a minor counter-attack by demanding the recall of Vredenburg for alleged improprieties.[58]

In another direction, however, the colonial administration in Angola was more concerned for the welfare of the colony's African inhabitants. In a circular letter of 4 December 1865, the acting governor-general, José Mendes Affonso, President of the Council, instructed governors of districts, administrators, and chiefs of posts to pay attention to the many *portárias* forbidding the hard and forced labour of *serviço de carregadores*. Some officials had frustrated the instructions. He acknowledged that the system was deeply rooted in the habits of the country and philosophically defended on the ground that 'the indolent and obstinate blacks refused to work unless forced'. He also knew that the system promoted many abuses. In an eloquent passage, whose rhetorical spirit can be found in almost every

saying that the British Government had again to take a strong stand or the practice was not likely to get stopped. The earlier farce of sending slaves as so-called free emigrants had been stopped by British threats. He argued that the new practice of sending slaves with alleged colonists also be halted.

[57] F.O. 84/1258, F.O. to Edward Lytton, 25 June 1866.

[58] The Foreign Office steadfastly refused to consider the matter. The Portuguese allegations were so contrived that there was no difficulty in refuting them with the statements of Portuguese authorities in Angola. Vredenburg regarded the episode as a 'dirty trick'. 'The truth is that the Portuguese, who are by nature a shifty race, consider that the treaty was extracted from them, that it is against their interests and prevents their determination to render it valueless.' F.O. 84/1271, Vredenburg to Wylde, 8 July 1866.

piece of Portuguese African legislation from 1854 to 1964, Mendes Affonso reminded the officials of the interior:

> It is a sacred duty of the administrative authority to treat the governed as a good father of the family, consulting their interests, aiding and protecting them to the utmost extent of their beneficient and paternal authority, among these duties being that of the noblest mission, of stimulating by every lawful means commerce and agriculture in the interior of this province, convincing, persuading, and stimulating by gentle and bland manners the uneducated and indolent blacks to the work of cultivating their own or another's land, for that end mediating and facilitating private agreements, animating and inviting them to this work, but at the same time taking care that they are duly paid, and that the arrangements are fulfilled by both parties, acting as by their office bound as diligent and benevolent mediators between the wretched and the powerful, the rich and the poor, the educated and the uneducated, thus guiding and conducting these natives to the love of labour which does so much honour to and so ennobles the man who devotes himself to it and subsists by it.[59]

Eloquent and dangerous words. So long as this was the nature of humanitarian sentiment in Lisbon and Luanda, some form of impressed labour would never be far away.

An African Commission had been formed in Lisbon (including Sá da Bandeira as Chairman, Count Lavradio, another former Overseas Minister, Carlos Bento da Silva, former Governor-General Silva Mendes, and several deputies) to study the matter of the Portuguese African possessions. The first inquiry to be made was to see how soon slavery could be abolished. The commission was also to consider in what manner labour was to be organized after the abolition of slavery, how to reconcile the needs of the owners with the liberty of the Africans. And to consider 'what kind of control ought to be exercised by the government in this case, and what special measures are called for by the transformation of slaves into

[59] It was Mendes Affonso who welcomed the new governor-general, Francisco António Gonçalves Cardoso on 12 Mar. 1866 with these words: 'What I can happily and with the greatest satisfaction assure Your Excellency is that the vile and wicked traffic, that most ruinous cancer of this province, is extinct on the coast. . . .' *Boletim do governo de Angola*, 17 Mar. 1866.

labourers'.[60] Even in Lisbon, attitudes were taking a familiar cast.

Any substantial measures to control the slave-trade of Angola and to ease the transition from a régime of slavery to one of free labour had to have the support and participation of lesser officials in the province. This would be difficult to obtain in the easy-going moral climate of Angola where colonial officers had been intimately involved, officially for most of the time, with the slave-trade for 250 years. Not only had Calheiros, Barboza Leão, and Governor Gamitto of Benguela profited from the transport of African workers from one area to another, but there were many more men of lower rank whose livelihood had come to depend on facilitating the supply of labour to those who needed it. Paid a pittance—which often arrived six months to a year late—many colonial officials had become a vital link in the slave-trade of the interior. 'How is it possible', asked the *Jornal do comércio*, 'to expect that people should nowadays serve for the paltry salaries of the last century when everyone carried on the slave trade?'[61] Andrade had described some of the officials under him as 'persons whose character filled him with disgust and abhorrence'. But to English public servants, immorality in government service, particularly when it abetted the slave-trade, could not be explained—or excused (the Foreign Office had a generally low opinion of Portuguese governmental employees, and, probably for that reason, consistently tried to bully them in one way or another). It was too easy an answer to blame part of the traffic in human beings on 'corrupt and venal officials', men the Foreign Office took great pains to tell the Portuguese Government to drum out of the service.[62]

On 2 April 1867 the Board for the Protection of *Libertos* met at 1 p.m. in the Government palace in Luanda and

[60] *Diário do governo*, 3 Dec. 1866. The commission was also to consider questions of tariff and administration.

[61] *Jornal do comércio*, 16 Sept. 1865.

[62] Chargé Edward Lytton was particularly high-minded (and high-handed) on the subject. F.O. 84/1258, Lytton to F.O., 14 Aug. 1866; Lytton to Foreign Secretary Cazal Ribeiro, 14 Aug. 1866. In the latter communication Lytton did admit that it *was* difficult for petty functionaries 'to maintain a standard of public virtue so high as to be beyond the reach of temptation'.

decided to suspend activities and to free the six *libertos* left to the charge of the Board. From the beginning the Board had been a failure, its meetings a formality, and its superintendence of the handful of *libertos* in its charge a sham. The Overseas Ministry in Lisbon could have learned from the Board's failure that to entrust the protection of African subjects to a local committee was not a practical way to deal with colonial problems. Lisbon did not learn, and for fifty years one elaborate commission or board after another was set up in Portuguese Africa to mitigate the harsh realities of oppression. They all failed.

The *libertos* the Board had not taken under its care were the ones sent off to the islands to be watched over there by a similar board. Some of these men were now being dispatched from the Luanda jail, and Hewett suggested that the time had come for another full examination of the practice. One would like to know, he said, for how long the emigrant was a *liberto* before he was embarked, how long he had belonged to the *colono* before going off with him, how long he remained on the islands. The Portuguese Government knew nothing of the facts of the system and should inform itself.[63]

All slaves in Portuguese Africa, by the Decree of 25 February 1869, still another transitional measure to abolish slavery gradually, were to cease to be slaves and pass into the condition of *libertos*. Vredenburg was unimpressed. 'The decree in question changes the name of "slave" to "liberto", but it does no more.' The Decree of 1854 had been totally disregarded. The many thousands who ought now to be their own masters were to be counted in the dozens, and most of them were in Luanda where a meticulously honourable police chief, Lt. Nascimento Sampaio, had given them redress. The rest had been forced to labour for all of their lives. 'In what way does this differ from slavery?' The *Juiz de Direito* of Benguela had told him that in that city, the second in the province, not one *liberto* had been set free. Slaves who had been registered ten years ago had been so often sold, resold, and transferred that it was impossible to keep track of them. Nobody cared, nothing was done, and the *liberto* was hopelessly confused. After serving one master for eight years, a *liberto* was frequently

[63] F.O. 84/1299, Hewett to F.O., 29 July 1868.

transferred to another master, registered again, and condemned to another ten years of service. Amaral had returned as governor-general. Vredenburg had a long and discouraging conversation with him. The governor dwelt on the difficulties of carrying out Lisbon's regulations in Angola, and Vredenburg was obliged to agree. The absence of system, the want of communication, the lack of roads, and the utter disorganization and immorality made the task a hard one. Ten years of labour was in fact forced and unremunerated labour for life.[64]

The reply of Foreign Minister Mendes Leal to sour comments like these was at once noble and righteous. 'Today it is happily for humanity an established principle that no civilized nation can accept slavery as an institution.' But a serious economic crisis would ensue if slaves were all suddenly emancipated, and it would be equally difficult for slaves, 'destitute of education and possessing, in general, very little intelligence', who would then turn to idleness and vice. Portugal had therefore 'an obligation to humanity, a duty to civilization and even to religion' to have a well-prepared transition. No one should consider being forced to labour for ten years excessive. Slaves could buy their freedom through their own industry and merits, and the price was bound to get lower as the years passed toward 1878. The efforts of the Portuguese Government would never cease to obtain complete liberation for all slaves.[65]

As a consequence of the suppression of the transatlantic slave-trade the British Government in 1869 entered into negotiations with the United States and Portugal to do away with the mixed commissions at the Cape of Good Hope, Luanda, and New York. England proposed to keep a vice-consul in Luanda to guard against a revival of the traffic. On 4 July 1870 the Mixed Commission was broken up and 27 July, Watson Vredenburg boarded the Portuguese steam packet *Coanza* to return home. The Atlantic trade had been extinguished, but other labour problems, more complicated and almost as vexing and controversial, had come into being. They would not disappear for many years.

[64] F.O. 84/1315, Vredenburg to F.O., 12 June 1869.

[65] F.O. 84/1322, Sir Charles Murray to F.O., 27 Jan. 1870. A copy of Mendes Leal's letter, dateless, is forwarded with the dispatch.

CHAPTER III

Moçambique to 1870

THE slave-trade came relatively late to Moçambique, but it was to remain an acknowledged reality longer than it did in Angola. The Moçambique trade was a diffuse reality, more the result of stimulus and organization outside the territory than of any coherent efforts within Moçambique to perpetuate the trade. The problem was that conditions within the colony were sufficient to assure a supply of African labour to anyone who wanted to come and get it. Lisbon was more set against the export of workers from Moçambique than from Angola, but the Government was powerless to prevent it. Moçambique became a supplier of workers. There was little official will to resist; out of inertia and the active connivance of some officials there were created continuing conditions and attitudes which made it possible subsequently for treaties and conventions to be written, in which it was *formally recognized* that Moçambique was a reservoir of African labour.

In Moçambique, David Livingstone was the agent of English humanitarian sentiment. Livingstone characterized life in Moçambique in such terms that the territory never really lost the image of slavery and moral bankruptcy. Livingstone regarded most Portuguese in Africa as denizens of some lower moral society. An addiction to corruption and slavery set them apart. It became the duty of England to rebuke them for their inveterate ways and to expose their Philistine spirit to the new order of progress and commerce.

Arriving in Tete on his journey from West Africa, Livingstone found decay and anarchy in Zambézia.

The more intelligent Portuguese . . . frankly ascribe the present ruinous condition of eastern Africa chiefly to the Slave Trade having withdrawn the European population from agriculture and every other source of wealth. Our country has, therefore, been nobly labouring to confer a double benefit—preventing the unhappy victims of slavery from being torn from their country and friends, and compelling the slave trader to turn his attention from a traffic which rarely enriches, to more permanent sources of wealth.

And then:

Having formerly been led awry by the specious pro-slavery reasoning against our cruisers, I am now proud that I belong to a country whose Government possessed the high moral courage to go on in its efforts to benefit the slave, in spite of all the plausible sophistry brought to bear against it. . . . That the Portuguese Government has not done more to prevent its own people from the illicit traffic is not so surprising here as it is in England; it has been very much hampered in action because the small pay received by the officers who are the chief authorities in her colonies almost impels them to engage in trade for a living. They do not feel inclined to put the law in force against brother merchants, with whom they may be in pecuniary relationship.[1]

Moçambique was in a state of near collapse in 1855. Zambézia was in the hand of *prazeros*, or estate owners, whose associations were only remotely Portuguese. Only at Tete 300 miles up the Zambesi was there a real semblance of Portugal's presence in the interior. Moçambique island was a fairly active trading centre, and the lesser ports at Ibo, Quelimane, and Inhambane had a Portuguese or Goan commercial post or two, some administrative officers, and a scanty garrison of African soldiers and Portuguese convicts. Portuguese authority seldom extended beyond these centres. Moçambique had never been agriculturally important, and commerce was now in a questionable state. Most African leaders were hostile, and the governor-general had few forces at his disposal to confront them. In Lisbon the Ministry for Marine and Overseas did not have the same concern for the development of Moçambique which it had for Angola, which seemed to promise great riches and easy development. Slaving, which had flourished extraordinarily in the first forty years of the century, had gone into a relative decline in the 1840's; but it was now in resurgence with new

[1] F.O. 84/985, Livingstone to Clarendon, 19 Mar. 1856.

demands from Cuba and from the French sugar islands. English cruisers sailing the coast were not very successful in checking the traffic.

In the absence of any serious efforts at prevention, the slave-trade thrived and occasionally boomed. Cargoes for Cuba were loaded near Ibo and sometimes in the vicinity of Quelimane and Inhambane. A coastal traffic in dhows carried Negroes to Zanzibar, Madagascar, and Comoro. And there was the *engagé* (or *émigré*) system for procuring workers for the French sugar plantations of the French Mascarene Islands. Each type of activity presented its own problems, but in the 1850's the collection and sale of slaves in Moçambique for the island of Réunion presented problems of conscience. In practice the system did not vary a great deal from the traffic in *libertos* from Angola to São Tomé, which the British Government opposed and Portugal encouraged. In Moçambique the traffic to the French islands came to be banned by Lisbon authorities who looked to England for encouragement, but on this issue England's position was sometimes less forceful than in Angola.

For more than a decade French planters in Réunion, and to a lesser extent on the islands of Mayotte and Nossi Bé, had been getting labour under the 'Free Labour Emigration System', mostly from Kilwa where French agents bought slaves from Arab traders, set them free and then engaged them for work on the plantations. In the view of Livingstone and the officers of the Mixed Commission the system was a considerable stimulation to the slave-trade of the interior. Some of these slaves came from the coast of Moçambique by way of dhows and it was not unknown for a French ship to recruit directly in Moçambique. In 1854 formal permission was obtained from Moçambique authorities to extend the system there. When England protested, France said so long as Indian labour was denied the islands, nothing else could be done.

A decree of 27 February 1855 had prohibited the departure of Moçambique Africans under the denomination of colonists to the island of Réunion.[2] The decree originated in a request

[2] George Frere and Frederic Surtees of the Mixed Commission at Cape Town reported that for 1855 and 1856 the exportation of Negroes from Moçambique under the names of colonists and free labourers had been carried on to a

of the previous year from several French planters in Réunion for permission to extend the recruitment to Inhambane. The request, coming through Paris, had the approval of the French Government. The Colonial Council in Lisbon studied the petition and recommended on 3 February 1855 that it be turned down, because no free Africans would contract their services and a slave-trade would spring up to supply the new demand. The Council also foresaw that such a concession might be a violation of the Treaty of 1842.

In a long dispatch the governor-general replied that stopping the system was detrimental to Moçambique's interest. On 30 July 1856, Overseas Minister Sá da Bandeira issued another *portária*, reaffirming his order of 1855 and strengthening it. He said that his government was absolutely determined to do away with the traffic in slaves in all the Portuguese possessions. The practice of letting Africans, brought from the interior by local traders, be sold to 'Arab and other speculators, who sold them to the commissaries of Réunion', was giving direct encouragement to the slave-trade in the interior. Sá da Bandeira instructed the governor to submit particular information on every individual exported from the province.[3]

Not only was this second decree ignored in Moçambique, but it drew the ire of the French Government, which was not disposed to suffer inconveniences caused by lesser powers. In April 1857 the French insisted, through their minister in Lisbon, that permission to recruit labourers for Réunion be given. They pointed out that the Negroes became free on their expatriation and that their lives were ameliorated in Réunion; they would

very great extent—by permission of the governor-general and of the governors at Ibo and Quelimane. 'It is with some concern', they wrote, 'that we have observed that the Portuguese authorities seem powerless to carry out the measures ordered by the government at Lisbon for the suppression of the slave trade.' F.O. 84/1014, Frere and Surtees to F.O., 14 Apr. 1857.

[3] *Diário do governo*. 2 Aug. 1856. In Lisbon a long defence of the governor's action was published in a newspaper by his secretary, the ubiquitous Barboza Leão, who stated that His Excellency was animated by the purest motives. Since slavery had been abolished in Réunion, he thought five years of labour there could only tend to civilize the savage inhabitants of Moçambique—which hardly spoke well for the civilizing influence of Portugal. F.O. 84/990, Howard to F.O., 8 Aug. 1856.

return to their own country 'improved in civilisation and religion'.[4]

Sá da Bandeira replied bluntly to the French. Having been the author of the greater part of Portuguese legislation on slavery in the past twenty years, he was not disposed to repeal any part of it. Not only did the *émigré* system encourage Arab traders to stir up wars to get slaves, but the loss of workers was an impediment to Moçambique's own agriculture. He suggested that France go back to India for coolie labour which had been used in the Mascarenes until it was discovered that Moçambique labour was cheaper (Mauritius, a British colony, could get workers from India, but the Indian Government would not permit them to work on foreign soil. In 1861 the ban was revoked). He invoked the treaties between Portugal and England that prohibited Portugal from permitting this sort of traffic in Negroes. To support his statements he quoted from letters he had received from Moçambique showing that French ships were 'publicly taking in shipments of Negroes under the modest title of engaged labourers, having, however, iron collars round their necks' (letter of 25 December 1856) and that 'the exportation of engaged labourers (slaves) to Réunion continues on a large scale: six shipments have been effected at Ibo, six at Moçambique, and six vessels have started for Quelimane to ship the same cargoes' (letter of 6 January 1857).[5] Sá da Bandeira even refused French requests for permission to recruit *free* Africans, commenting that there weren't many free Africans left in Moçambique, anyway, most of them already having been sold as slaves.[6]

A full report on the traffic from Moçambique was sent to the British Foreign Office in December 1857 by the newly appointed consul to Moçambique, Lyons MacLeod (MacLeod had been appointed consul in order to provide a closer report of slaving conditions along the coast). French ships of 200 to 1,000 tons burden were allowed to carry one Negro per ton from Moçam-

[4] F.O. 84/1018, Howard to F.O., 6 May 1857.

[5] F.O. 84/1018, Sá da Bandeira to the Marquis de Lisle, 5 May 1857. *La Presse* of Paris, 27 June 1857, quoting *Le Moniteur* of Réunion, gave the account of the murder of the captain and crew of one small French vessel by so-called free Negroes being carried to the islands.

[6] F.O. 84/1018, Howard to F.O., 27 May 1957.

bique to Réunion. Before leaving Réunion the ships were inspected by the authorities and a French government officer put on board who was to witness the legalities and certify to the voluntary nature of the engagement. Most of the ships went to Ibo where the planter's agent paid a price of thirty to forty dollars a head for the workers; some of the money was rumoured to pass into the pockets of Governor-General Vasco Guedes de Carvalho e Menezes. Slaves were marched down from the Nyasa district, sometimes on a journey of several months, and kept in stockades two or three days distance from the coast until they were called for. On Réunion they were vaccinated, put in fourteen days quarantine, and then hired out to sugar planters for a five-year period. The workers had no choice of masters and received from six to eight shillings a month wages in addition to their keep, clothing, and medical care. In each district there was a Protector of Emigrants whose business it was to see that the workers were not ill treated. Punishment was reserved to the authorities, and corporal punishment was not permitted. After five years the labourer had to be returned, at the expense of the original importer, to the mainland, but usually the Africans stayed on as free workers receiving higher wages.[7]

Consul William Sunley made a similar report from Johanna (Anjouan), whence traffic to Réunion had also been brisk. French ships had carried off about 1,000 slaves in 1857. Forty to forty-five dollars was paid for the manumission of each slave taken from Johanna. When Sunley complained to the sultan, he was assured the traffic would stop, but so long as slaves could be picked up on the Moçambique coast for twelve to fifteen dollars, the temptation in Johanna was strong to continue the trade. 'The price of engagements, were, I am informed, 140–150 dollars last year and should they rise still higher those engaged in procuring labourers will be able to offer a higher price for slaves. Under these circumstances it will be extremely difficult to keep the people from engaging in the traffic of

[7] F.O. 84/1019, Lyons MacLeod to F.O., 7 Dec. 1857. This traffic was vigorously harassed by the British Navy. Commander Oldfield in the *Lyra* captured twelve dhows from Feb. to Aug. 1858. Most of them were fitted and provisioned for slaves, but had no cargoes when captured. F.O. 84/1078, Cape Commissioners to F.O., 2 May 1859.

slaves, unless men of war are sent and traders made to feel they cannot avoid capture.' Traders in the last year had paid about 30,000 dollars on the coast for slaves and had put seven new dhows into service. Even if the sultan closed the traffic at Johanna, Sunley feared it would remove to Comoro where no check was placed on the migration.[8]

Although most of the workers came from Ibo and the vicinity of Moçambique island, French agents sought new sources at Quelimane and Inhambane. Supplementing this supply line were the Swahili dhows sailing to the north-west coast of Madagascar; this trade was described by the Cape commissioners:

> The slaves are first taken to depots in St. Augustine's Bay and Bojanna Bay on the west coast of Madagascar from all parts of the east coast of Africa, but principally from Quiloa and Ibo during the northeast monsoon and from St. António and Quizungo during the southwest monsoon. This trade is chiefly carried on in dhows conveying from 30 to 140 slaves each; and we are informed there can be no pretence styling this portion of the operation at least a voluntary emigration. . . . The mortality among African immigrants to Réunion during the voyage and on board while lying at the anchorage of St. Denis is very great from smallpox and dysentery . . . One vessel . . . landed only 72 Negroes out of 300 received on board.[9]

The commissioners estimated that 3,000 *engagés* had been taken from Moçambique in 1858, as against some 4,000 in 1857.

When in October 1857, João Tavares d'Almeida took over the governorship of Moçambique, he immediately had published in the *Boletim oficial* the next of the two decrees prohibiting the export of workers in the name of free emigration. Speaking for himself, Almeida took the occasion 'to make known in a most positive manner that it is his determination immediately to supersede any authority who shall be less than zealous in exact performance of his duty in curbing this prohibitive traffic, or that of the slave traffic, and to send to trial all those

[8] F.O. 84/1056, Sunley to F.O., 31 Mar. 1858 and 5 July 1858.

[9] F.O. 84/1078, Cape Commissioners to F.O., 23 Jan. 1859. The most informative source for the East Coast trade in this period is R. Coupland, *The Exploitation of East Africa, 1857–1890* (London, 1939).

who might protect either of the two traffics or connive at them'.[10]

Tavares d'Almeida's determination precipitated a crisis between Portugal and France. A French barque, the *Charles et George* from Réunion, arrived at Quitangonha (a score of miles north of the island of Moçambique) and anchored for several days. On 21 November 1857, twenty Portuguese troops marched up the coast to prevent the embarking of slaves, whereupon the barque sailed off. When on 27 November the troops again went up the coast to Conducia, this time they found the *Charles et George* with 110 Negroes on board. The ship was seized, and was taken the few miles down the coast to Moçambique. A commission carried out an inquiry, and the case was then turned over to the judicial courts where the ship was condemned and the French captain sentenced to two years in irons at hard labour.

In the report of the commission of inquiry (15 December 1857) the captain stated that he had been bound for Mayotte, but because of an officer's illness had been obliged to put in at Quitangonha. He had found no Portuguese officials there, only some inhabitants who offered labourers for sale, which he bought. The commission found 110 Negroes on the ship: 19 women and 31 men had been shipped at Comoro and 47 men and 13 women in the Bay of Quitangonha. The greater part of the slaves were old men and children. The captain presented no passports and no documents to prove the engagements.

The testimony of some of the slaves before the commission revealed the uncertainties of life in East Africa. José, the slave of Domingos José Ferreira of Moçambique, stated this his

[10] *Boletim do governo geral da província de Moçambique*, 10 Oct. 1857. In a circular issued on 20 Nov. 1857 Almeida told the local governors how to proceed: 'After a scrupulous examination of all the ship's papers, in which are included the title deed of ownership, the character of the French nationality, the master roll of the crew, the manifest and the instructions of the delegate given by the administration of the Island of Réunion, and having made known to the captain the orders of His Majesty's Government prohibiting the shipment or engagement of colonists, you will require from him a declaration according to the annexed form, and to the delegate you will officially communicate the positive prohibition which you are bound to enforce against the carrying out of the intended arrangements, and require a written acknowledgement of the said communication.' *Boletim*, 19 Dec. 1857.

master had sold him to a 'Moor' (the term used by the Portuguese for all Muslims from Morocco to Mindanao) who took him to Comoro and there sold him to the French. António, the slave of Patrício of Quelimane, said that he had been kidnapped by a Moor from Angoche and there sold against his will to a dhow of Swahili traders and taken to Comoro where he was sold to the French. Emílio Muquema, a slave of Francisco de Menezes of Moçambique, said that he was kidnapped on the mainland by the Makuas and sold at Quitangonha to the Moor Ali, who sold him to the French captain. Victorino and Carlos, the slaves of Jacinto de Jesus e Silva of Moçambique, said that they had gone to the mainland to cut firewood, had been kidnapped by Makuas, and sold in Quitangonha to persons unknown to them. Iria, the slave of Abuldurama, captain-general in Quitangonha, stated that her master had caused her to be sold. Rebema Binte Muça and Ali Umar said they were kidnapped at Kilwa by Moors and then shipped to Comoro where they were sold. Every Negro on board said he was there against his will, that he had been forced or sold.[11]

France's reaction to the episode was sharp. They demanded the release of the captain. The Foreign Minister, the Duke of Loulé, and Sá da Bandeira were secretly embarrassed, since the previous governor-general of Moçambique had permitted the traffic and profited from it. Early discussions between the two countries led nowhere. In August 1858 a prize crew brought the *Charles et George* into Lisbon under the Portuguese flag. Captain Rouxel arrived to appeal his sentence. From the beginning the French maintained that the seizure was illegal, since the Arab chief of Matibane had produced his licence from ex-Governor Menezes permitting the engagement of labourers. They also argued that Portugal had no jurisdiction over the area. Papers which Captain Rouxel had not produced in Moçambique now appeared in Lisbon; the Portuguese regarded these as forgeries. The French Government demanded restitution of the vessel, the freeing of the captain, and compensation of not less than 20,000 pounds sterling for the workers lost.

[11] The commission's report was sent to the Foreign Office by Howard. F.O. 84/1048, Howard to F.O., 7 Sept. 1858.

If the Portuguese Government was privately dismayed by the difficulties the zealous Tavares d'Almeida had created, it publicly stood firm in September 1858 and said that France was badly informed of the facts of the case. When France sent two men of war up the Tagus on 4 October, Portugal offered to refer the matter to mediation. A week earlier Loulé had asked England to use her good offices to bring about an amicable settlement. But on 23 October Portugal was obliged to yield to France's peremptory demands, agreeing to release the captain and the vessel and to pay indemnity.[12]

In the street and in Portuguese newspapers England was abused in the days after the humiliation. 'The violence is perpetrated', wrote the *Jornal do comércio*. 'Portugal had passed under the Candine Forks, but not alone. At her side is a powerful nation—England. This power was the originator of the abolition of the slave traffic, and it would not uphold its own principle, nor sustain the right of its ally, who had sacrificed so much towards a faithful observance of the treaty concluded between them for a purpose so moral and civilizing.'[13] In London the Portuguese minister Count Lavrádio had a violent interview with Lord Malmesbury in which he accused the foreign secretary of betraying Portugal. The debate in the Portuguese Chamber of Deputies was more constrained, the opposition contenting itself to ask why Portugal had not begun its negotiations with France earlier and why the assistance of England had not been demanded. Sá da Bandeira and Loulé replied that as there was no danger of war, there was no need to involve England. That nation was not bound to support Portugal in all of her disputes. António Avila, the finance minister,

[12] One of the aftermaths of the affair was the challenge to the French minister given by the former governor-general, Vasco Guedes de Carvalho e Menezes who had taken exception to the minister's remark that he had make a scandalous fortune on the slave-trade. Lisle told Menezes that if he persisted in his insults, he would blow his brains out. F.O. 84/1081, Howard to F.O., 8 Jan. 1859.

[13] *Jornal do comércio*, 24 Oct. 1858. The article went on: 'It remains for England and Portugal to declare that the French Government have the right to traffic in slaves. Let the present fact be legalized. Then at least something will be saved from the wreck of treaties. The cause is lost, but honour is safe. . . . Shame and dishonour belong to those who misuse their power, trample upon treaties, and despise justice.'

added that by appealing to England, Portugal would have given the appearance of resorting to force in the absence of right.[14]

There had been no real cause for English intervention on Portugal's behalf, but it was true that England shared in Portugal's humiliation. During the dispute England had taken the role of conciliator (in Paris the British minister had tried to persuade France to submit the question to mediation), and Portugal was deprived, in a sense, of her ally's moral support. Portugal's legal position was not good in the somewhat complicated case, but her moral position was impeccable—if one forgot that Portugal approved a full-scale *émigré* system of her own on the west African coast. But England, which had prodded Portugal periodically to stop such abuses and indirectly bore some responsibility for what happened, came out of the affair with her anti-slaving position *vis-à-vis* Portugal considerably weakened.

There was an unease in Malmesbury's dispatch to Minister Howard containing suggestions for the Portuguese Government on how it should behave from then on.

With regard to the future, Her Majesty's Government are of the opinion that in order to prevent further complications which may be caused by the adherence of the French Government to their scheme of Negro emancipation, it will be desirable for the Portuguese Government to ascertain . . . exactly under what forms and circumstances a French suspected ship may be visited to verify its nationality and also whether it is to be understood that the presence of a French delegate protects the ship and justifies its proceedings, whatever they may be in respect of carrying Negroes, in the eyes of the French Government . . .

Her Majesty's Government sincerely trust that neither the unfortunate dispute . . . nor the apprehension of increasing difficulties for the future will shake the constancy of the Portuguese Government in abiding by those treaties which in common with Great Britain and Spain it has established for the suspension of the slave traffic. Doubtless the views adopted by France . . . must weaken our hands for that great and just object; but it is our duty, while submitting to a system which renders a moral principal subservient to a strict legality, to persist, as far as we are permitted by inter-

[14] F.O. 84/1049, Howard to F.O., 29 Dec, 1858.

national law, to diminish, if we cannot eradicate, a great public evil.[15]

In Moçambique Consul Lyons MacLeod had been singularly free of his government's inhibiting cautions. On any issue touching the slave-trade, or the moral degeneracy of the Portuguese in East Africa, MacLeod was a man of spontaneous and forceful opinion. Suspicious, resentful, quarrelsome, and perhaps a little mad, MacLeod was an ardent and diligent abolitionist whose nine-month stay in Moçambique was marked by constant furor.[16] His failure to win the confidence of the Portuguese colonial administration was a serious hindrance in the Anglo-Portuguese campaign to suppress the slave-trade along the Moçambique coast. In one of his first communications, in October 1857, he broke with the governor's opinion that it was the population of Moçambique who made the slave-trade possible. Should the Foreign Office grant him a 'Commission of Inquiry' (perhaps the Mixed Slaving Commission from Cape Town) he would prove 'that the authorities alone were implicated in the slave trade'. For the coming monsoon season he predicted a hundred slavers in the Moçambique channel and estimated the number of slaves exported in the last three months as 14,000.[17]

From the beginning MacLeod was contemptuous of Portuguese officials on all levels; from the beginning he openly quarrelled with them in so far as they would be drawn into controversy. On 29 August 1857 he suggested to Governor-General Vasco Guedes that he dismiss the governor at Ibo in order to regain MacLeod's confidence.[18] On 10 September he informed the governor-general that the slaver *Minnetonka*,

[15] F.O. 84/1047, F.O. to Howard, 6 Nov. 1858.

[16] See MacLeod's *Travels in Eastern Africa, with the Narrative of a Residence in Moçambique* (2 vols.; London, 1860).

[17] F.O. 84/1019, MacLeod to F.O., 3 Oct. 1857. The consul closed his letter, 'Trusting that my unaided exertions to suppress this horrid traffic in our fellow beings will meet with your Lordship's entire approval.'

[18] F.O. 84/1019, MacLeod to Vasco Guedes de Carvalho e Menezes, 29 Aug. 1857. Mr. Hammond at the Foreign Office, warned MacLeod that his 'style of addressing the governor of Moçambique is too dictatorial. . . . Your representations will be equally forcible if made in courteous language. . . . If the Portuguese authorities resent your want of civility and become your personal enemies, your power of usefulness will be impaired.' F.O. 84/1050, Hammond to Macleod, 7 Jan. 1858.

flying American colours, had shipped 1,200 slaves at Ibo—although MacLeod had warned him ten days earlier of the ship's presence. The captain of the *Minnetonka* had 70,000 dollars on board and was able to outbid the captains of seven French merchant ships who had come for free labourers, or slaves, as MacLeod called them, who were purchased at Ibo for forty dollars a head to be sold at Réunion for from 80 to 100 dollars a head.[19]

For a few weeks in October relations between the irascible MacLeod and the newly arrived Tavares d'Almeida were cordial. Following the *Charles et George* episode, Tavares d'Almeida, in MacLeod's view, gradually came under the influence of a group of men the consul identified as 'the slave party'. Obliged to live on the mainland for want of accommodation for his wife and himself on the island, Macleod felt isolated, at bay, constantly tormented, and persecuted by 'the slave party'. His house was stoned. African villagers, of whom MacLeod and his wife had deep fears, walked in and out of his house at will. His wife had to chop wood and carry water. The governor-general refused to give him police protection or to put a launch at his disposal for trips to the island. Portuguese authorities did not observe the diplomatic amenities of calling at his home and inviting him to theirs. Such was the recitation of MacLeod's complaints. His letters to the governor became increasingly abusive, those of the governor, replete with injured dignity.[20]

During a shortage of food in February, March, and April 1858, MacLeod supposed that a conspiracy had been formed to starve him from his post. In a parting shot to Tavares d'Almeida, he wrote:

> When her Majesty's Sloop *Persian* arrived here on Saturday, 10 April 1858, I had neither bread nor flour in my house with my wife and female servant, both sick. While the guns of HMS *Persian* were saluting the Portuguese flag, Her Majesty's Consul was starving in his house; simply because he did his duty in suppressing the slave trade, and the Governor General of the Province of Moçambique allowed the exequatur of the King his Master to be dishonoured.

[19] F.O. 84/1019, MacLeod to Menezes, 10 Sept. 1857.
[20] The whole of F.O. 84/1050 is a file of MacLeod's absurd correspondence.

The noble spirit of endurance manifested by my wife and her maid during all this persecution is worthy of the nation whose women they represent here. They have suffered in a holy cause, that of the slaves.

God has guarded those whom Your Excellency would not guard.[21]

Long after his departure MacLeod was regarded as a meddler and a trouble-maker, and the British consuls who came to serve in Moçambique in the 1870's and 1880's were still regarded with suspicion.

MacLeod had been right in one regard: the slave traffic was now a serious problem. A Pandora's Box had been opened four years before by the *émigré* system. It did not matter that in January 1859 Prince Napoleon, Secretary of State for French Colonies, prohibited the raising of free labourers on the east coast of Africa, in Madagascar, and in the Comores. A dhow traffic of formidable proportions had developed in the Moçambique channel, which the Portuguese naval forces were totally inadequate to control.[22] And there were slave ships arriving from Cuba.

A secret departmental report of November 1860 by Brigadier W. M. Coghlan, in charge of the Muscat–Zanzibar Commission, gave the British Government a dismal picture of Portuguese East Africa. He quoted Captain C. P. Rigby, the British Resident at Zanzibar, who said the trade 'was carried on in the most shameless manner, all the Portuguese authorities aiding and abetting it and dividing their nefarious gains'. By all accounts the cruelties of the traffic were equal to those in West Africa; the Portuguese were destroying the last faint traces of civilization in their possessions. Large tracts of land

[21] F.O. 84/1050, Macleod to Tavares d'Almeida, 16 Apr. 1858.

[22] On 31 Dec. 1858 the Minister for Marine and Overseas sent a letter to Portuguese naval stations in East and West Africa to the effect that the *Charles et George* affair would probably provoke increased activity by slavers. Portuguese naval officers were to redouble their efforts—though they were not to arrest ships carrying either the French or American flag. Territorial officers were instructed to extract added vigilance from their subordinates. The instructions were more pretentious than the forces to carry them out.

The Foreign Secretary, Lord Russell, wrote Count Lavrádio that England did not doubt Portugal's intention to do away with the slave-trade, but she did doubt Portugal's ability to do it without the aid of British cruisers. F.O. 84/1082, Russell to Lavrádio, 22 Oct. 1859.

were being depopulated and 'the semi-barbarous tribes were being driven to a state of desperation which threatens at no distant period to be the scourge and ruin of their degenerate and inhuman masters'. Ibo had again become the centre for the Spanish trade. Coghlan suggested that the cruiser force be strengthened with new bases established at Johanna and Delagoa Bay. All captives should be taken to Natal for Christian instruction; there was a constant want of labourers there.[23]

David Livingstone, now back in Africa on the Zambesi expedition—and as English consul at Quelimane—wrote about life in the interior of Moçambique. He described the efforts of the *prazeros* on the Zambesi to sell their people down the river.[24] It was boasted that English men-of-war dared not interfere with these slaves, and it was believed in Zambézia that in Lisbon 'no one knows or cares about what is done in this country except the Viscount de Sá da Bandeira. It is vexatious to witness the infatuation with which the Portuguese again commence the trade. . . . It may truly be said that they export their labour for a trifle and neglect fortunes lying at their feet.' What was needed, according to the missionary, was lawful English commerce. 'The French Emigration Scheme threatening to render all our past efforts fruitless, the conviction is forced in the mind that a small colony of our own nation in the healthy highlands beyond the Portuguese influence and pretensions would eventually be of immense value both to Africa and to England. . . . And the English, far from being intruders, would increase the high moral influence which the French scheme is damaging.'[25]

In 1862, while describing the expansion of the island slave traffic by the people of Tete, Livingstone averred that the Portuguese in Zambézia, with the connivance of officials, were enslaving Africans faster than Lisbon could emancipate them.[26] In a later letter:

> And yet it seems essential to a practical change of the system

[23] F.O. 84/1120, W. M. Coghlan to H. L. Anderson, Bombay, 1 Nov. 1860.
[24] For a description and bibliography of the *prazo* system, see James Duffy, *Portuguese Africa* (Cambridge, Mass., 1959), pp. 82–89.
[25] F.O. 84/1082, Livingstone to F.O., 4 Mar. 1859.
[26] F.O. 84/1177, Livingstone to F.O., 22 June 1862.

that has allowed the region between Cape Delgado and Delagoa Bay to be virtually a 'private slave preserve' that our countrymen should have free access. The way in which the passions of the natives are turned to account is quite beyond the government at Lisbon. The Ajawa for instance were furnished with arms and ammunition by means of Tette slaves, to be paid for in Manganja captives. The forays that followed drove the Manganja away from their well cultivated fields. Famine followed and now the fugitives as well as the victors are almost compelled to sell their people to the Tette agents to keep themselves from starving.[27]

The trade up the left bank of the Shire by the Tete people was of recent origin, Livingstone went on, but east of the Shire, *prazeros* and renegades like Mariano and Bonga had ravaged the country for seven years stuffing their stockades with slaves to be shipped from Quelimane. The country was in a constant state of alarm. Only the English commanded respect in the region. At the whipping post in Tete African slaves cried out, 'Oh for the English! When will the English come?'[28] As the failure of the Zambesi expedition to accomplish anything of consequence became clear, Livingstone shunted the blame more and more onto Portugal's shoulders. He complained that no good could come of his work when his steps were dogged by slave-traders and all of his efforts were neutralized with the sanction of the Portuguese Government. The corrosive hostility which Livingstone bore the Portuguese by 1864—which is so apparent in the *Narrative of an Expedition to the Zambesi*—strengthened an anti-Portuguese prejudice in English humanitarian opinion.

Now the official British remonstrance became sharper. Reports from the Admiralty and from the commissioners at Cape Town gave details of an increasing traffic—and the connivance of Portuguese officials. Four shipments of slaves from Ibo to Cuba were reported in the last eight months of 1859 and at least one cargo a month from Quelimane to the French islands. Laying these charges before the Portuguese Foreign Secretary, Sir Arthur Magenis admitted it was difficult to obtain evidence of the complicity of Portuguese officials, but that it

[27] F.O. 84/1177, Livingstone to F.O., 29 Dec. 1862.
[28] F.O. 84/1200, Livingstone to F.O., 28 Jan. 1863.

was also difficult not to attach some credit to the report that the governor at Ibo received ten dollars a head for each Negro shipped from his district.[29] By the end of 1860 the Foreign Office was ready to instruct Magenis 'to deliver a strong remonstrance to the Portuguese Government on this subject, and you will express the regret of Her Majesty's Government that a traffic which strikes at the root of all legitimate trade, and which impoverishes and ruins the country from whence the slaves are exported, should still be carried on from the Portuguese territories and connived at by Portuguese authorities'.[30]

The suspicion grew in the British official mind that not only were district governors culpable of complicity but that Tavares d'Almeida himself was also guilty. Commander Oldfield of the *Lyra* reported that it was said in Moçambique that the governor-general had on several occasions received large sums of money for closing his eyes to the dereliction of duty on the part of his subordinates.[31] The commissioners at Cape Town gave other details of the Moçambique trade in 1866.

The principal traffic from the Portuguese possessions to the northward of 13° South Latitude is in slaves who are shipped at a cost of about 30 dollars a head. At Ibo, Point Pangane, Matemo, Lambuo, Quisanga, and Quirimba from 5000 to 6000 slaves were seen ready for embarkation.

The Governor at Ibo, Major Siccard, who while commandant at Tette was considered to be opposed to the slave trade, is said certainly to countenance the traffic since his promotion to the government at Ibo.

At the settlement at Pemba Bay . . . the Cape Commission is informed that there is no traffic carried on except in slaves who are kidnapped from the tribes in the neighbourhood and sent to Ibo in the dhows employed in provisioning Pemba Bay.

This traffic is so profitable to the Portuguese officials at the Port of Ibo, and the succession of governors so speedily acquire a com-

[29] F.O. 84/1113, Magenis to the Duke of Teixeira, 23 Mar. 1860. The usual response of the Portuguese Government to such communications was that new instructions had gone out to the governor-general in Moçambique.

[30] F.O. 84/1113, F.O. to Magenis, 8 Dec. 1860.

[31] F.O. 84/1142, F.O. to Magenis, 16 Apr. 1861, From Zanzibar Captain Rigby excoriated Portuguese officials at Ibo. They had developed such a competence for bribing that no representations would succeed. F.O. 84/1146, C. P. Rigby to F.O., 5 Oct. 1861.

petence from those bribes they receive for permitting it, that they appear to care for no representations made respecting it. An instance is known in which the Governor of Ibo paid a bribe of 500 crowns to an Arab at Zanzibar to induce him to withhold information of the supercargoes of slavers being then in town.[32]

Tavares d'Almeida resented the accusations and denied them flatly. It was true that there were centres of slave-trade along the Moçambique coast. Where there was no Portuguese authority such trade was impossible to curtail. Naval units at his disposal were completely inadequate for the task. But he rejected out of hand the British charges of connivance brought against his subordinates. Smuggling of slaves would be carried on so long as there were people to buy them. He, for example, did not accuse the British Navy of connivance because it failed to halt the traffic by sea.[33] Later in the year, Tavares d'Almeida made an impassioned statement of his own honesty ('My conscience is tranquil'). Perhaps the British Navy had reason to doubt some local Portuguese officials, he said, but since British officers knew so much about what went on in the channel, since they violated Portuguese territorial waters, and since they violated treaties by wantonly stopping legitimate shipping, why hadn't *they* put an end to the traffic? 'The points occupied by troops (and not very good ones) from Cape Delgado up to this island . . . are the town of Ibo and Cape Muamembo in Pemba Bay.' From Moçambique southward to Quelimane the only point occupied by a regular garrison was Angoche, and this only about a year ago. From Inhamissingo or Luabo to Sofala, the only point occupied was Sofala. From Sofala to Inhambane, the points occupied were Chibane and Bazaruto. And from

[32] F.O. 84/1177, Magenis to António José d'Avila, 14 Jan. 1862. All the details came from the Cape commissioners' report in 1861.

[33] Letter of 15 Feb. 1862 from Tavares d'Almeida to the Overseas Ministry. In F.O. 84/1177, Herries to F.O., 18 Sept. 1862. In his minute on this dispatch, Wylde did not believe much reliance could be placed on the governor's word, but Lord Russell took a more detailed if somewhat uncomprehending view: 'I think the accusations of Dr. Livingstone and the replies of the Governor of Moçambique are both very obscure. The carrying slaves across the sea can be prevented by cruisers to a certain extent, but if Dr. Livingstone is to engage to prevent slave hunts in the interior we may be involved in many little wars. The naval officers give a good report of the Governor General of Moçambique.'

Inhambane to Lourenço Marques there were no intermediate points that were occupied. Tavares d'Almeida concluded by asking the minister for overseas to find a successor, so he could resign and cease to be the object of embittering accusations.[34] This kind of accusation and response would go on throughout the 1860's. Deep and long lasting resentments were being formed.

Although a pattern of activity was now set, the Cape commissioners reported in 1862 that the trade all along the Moçambique coast was declining. Slaves were cheap and plentiful at Ibo, from which they concluded that business was bad (the last short flurry of the Cuban traffic which began in 1859 had virtually died out, though as late as 1864, two shipments were made from Inhambane). South of Ibo the dhow traffic was greatly reduced. From Angoche captives were still sent to supply the French islands.[35] A year later, thanks to the efforts of Tavares d'Almeida, the dhow traffic to Madagascar and Comoro had fallen off still further, though some thousands of Africans were still taken.[36]

But in 1864, in so far as these things could be measured, recent information indicated that the dhow traffic had again increased. A Portuguese cruiser arrested two dhows carrying a total of 291 Negroes; another eleven were known to be working the coast. The Cape commissioners drew the familiar moral.

> Whether shipped in the Moçambique or further northward . . . it must be borne in mind that unhappy slaves are almost all supplied by the country lying in the Portuguese territory, and the continuance of the traffic may fairly be attributed in a great degree

[34] Tavares d'Almeida to Overseas Ministry, 14 Oct. 1862. In F.O. 84/1200, Loulé to Magenis, 30 May 1863. In the same dispatch is another letter (8 Nov. 1862) from Tavares d'Almeida to the ministry. He did not deny that there may have been, or perhaps still was, some connivance by Portuguese officials, but the British had only made assertions, not offered proof. The trade at Tete was in the hands of Arabs whose religion permitted them to buy slaves. African tribes in some areas of the territory theoretically yielded obedience, but they could not be controlled by Portuguese authorities. 'The honor of the Portuguese authorities, the demands for civilization, the good name of her Portuguese nation, and the future prospect of the province' were all involved in the campaign against the slave-trade.

[35] F.O. 84/1169, Cape Commissioners to F.O., 18 Sept. 1862.

[36] F.O. 84/1197, Cape Commissioners to F.O., 1 Oct. 1863.

to the restrictions with which the Portuguese authorities have fettered commerce along the 600 miles of coast over which she claims sovereignty. In the opinion of Captain Gardner, after an experience of three years upon the station, Portugal has by these restrictions stopped legal trade on the whole coast, and left her own subjects and the native chiefs nothing but the slave trade to depend upon.[37]

William Sunley calculated that about 3,000 slaves from Moçambique had landed in Madagascar during the southern monsoon. Most of the slaves were embarked at António River, at Mohamba, and at Port Conducia, and were landed at Majunga and Movambsanga on the north-west coast of Madagascar.[38]

The trade fluctuated throughout the decade, but it did not die. The flow of slaves to Madagascar increased after 1860; slaves were sent from there to Nossi Bé and Mayotte, and there they were often contracted for by planters from Réunion.[39] Tavares d'Almeida had spoken truthfully when he said the Moçambique Government was powerless to prevent the dhow traffic. In fact it would go on for more than twenty years. By 1870 it had given Moçambique a fame as being a repository of workers. That reputation would last 100 years.

[37] F.O. 84/1238, Cape Commissioners to F.O., 1 May 1865.

[38] F.O. 84/1249, William Sunley to F.O., 5 Jan. 1865. In the middle of the year Sunley's consulship, unpaid, was withdrawn because he used slave labour on his sugar estates. He had been unable to get free labour, and given the choice of yielding his consulship or his estates, Sunley chose the latter. By general agreement, he had done much in the past five years to help reduce slavery.

[39] F.O. 84/1147, F.O. to Sunley, 5 Nov. 1861; Sunley to F.O., 2 May 1861. Also F.O. 84/1265, W. Pakenham (British Consul at Madagascar) to F.O., 17 Jan. 1866.

CHAPTER IV

Transition, 1870–1900

IN the last thirty years of the century attitudes and policies began to change. Portuguese legislation for the African colonies gradually became tougher, particularly those laws having to do with African labour. With the departure of the Mixed Commission from Angola and with the gradual *rapprochement* in Moçambique over the use of Portuguese African labour for South African enterprise, the Foreign Office took a less stern view of slavery questions in the two territories. The lead here was to pass to other hands. Only in Angola and Moçambique themselves did there seem to be no great change. Conditions stayed pretty much as they had for years before.

In 1869 the state of slavery was abolished in all Portuguese territory,[1] although the slaves were not to become free. Rather they became *libertos,* subject to the rights and duties contained in the Decree of 14 December 1854, until 29 April 1878. Thus the name was abolished and the fact maintained. It had never been Sá da Bandeira's intent that anti-slavery legislation should bankrupt slave owners and estate owners in Portuguese Africa. His fears over the economic collapse of the colonies were groundless, however, because the legislation had no real effect in either Angola or Moçambique. Sá da Bandeira and his supporters still believed that affairs in Portuguese Africa were other than the way they were, and they believed that the spirit which moved anti-slavery legislation in Lisbon would move its enactment in Africa. On the other hand, traditionalists in Africa seemed to believe that there were social and spiritual forces working which would accomplish more than remote decrees. The explorer and Angolan slave-trader Silva Porto wrote in 1869:

It is much to be desired that our legislators had limited their

[1] The Bill had first been introduced by Sá da Bandeira in 1865.

patriotic love to the prosperity of the colonies and not touched such matters as the abolition of slavery, which should have continued at home and in the crown territories where it was needed. Religion, progress, time, and finally the repressive measures of the traffic to foreign lands would have worked its extinction. With civilization both slaves and free men were coming to acquire knowledge of such benefits that a love of work was being created. . . . In the absence of such means and with the law of 29 April 1858 the consequences will be the disrespect of blacks for white people. . . . Present day laws invite such actions.[2]

The attitude was a popular one among a number of Portuguese colonialists, in Africa and Portugal, since it promised eventual spiritual triumphs in lieu of present practical reforms, although its proponents were unable to offer much more historical evidence for the success of their policies than the humanitarians could for theirs.

Stylistically and often textually, anti-slavery laws and labour decrees for Portuguese Africa recapitulated. The Decree of 29 April 1875 was at the same time a synthesis of anti-slavery legislation over the past twenty years, and a model for African labour laws in decades to come. Coming, in a sense, between the past and the future, or what was supposed to be the future, the Decree of 1875 was historically important. Textually, it was even more important, for what it had to say about labour relations in overseas Portugal, really Portuguese Africa, would not be substantially changed for a long time. Most of its provisions were enlightened for Portuguese Africa in 1875—although by the middle of the twentieth century they would seem less so.[3] The purpose of the 1875 decree was to declare all *libertos* free, but its scope went beyond that single declaration. It went into the consequences of the decree and, ultimately, of the final freeing of slaves. Designed to be transitional, the decree took up the matter of contract labour; at that moment it spoke of things permanent.

Article One abolished, effective 1876, the condition specified by the Law of February 1869. Article Two stated that *libertos*

[2] António Francisco da Silva Porto, *Viagens e apontamentos de um portuense em Africa* (Lisbon, 1942), p. 22.

[3] The decree was the product of Sá da Bandeira's influence. Its official patron was João de Andrade Corvo, Minister for Marine and Overseas.

would be subject to government tutelage until 29 April 1878 when they would be totally free. Article Three provided for a magistrate in Angola, São Tomé, and Moçambique, to be called a curator-general, whose duty it was to supervise the care and instruction of the freed men. Article Four declared the labour of all former *libertos* to be free in order to enable them to contract for their services and to receive wages mutually agreed upon.

The substance of the decree had to do with labour contracting, the rights of the workers and the duties of employers, and the role of the colonial government in mediating between the two.[4] The specific provisions were not to be observed by either government or employers. What was to be observed was the sanction given to labour recruiting companies to do business much in the old way, to procure workers where they could and under very doubtful circumstances of legality, and then to ship them to distant places. And, finally, there was the vagrancy clause, under which any *liberto* adjudged a vagrant could be forced to labour two years for the Government or for a private employer. The door was opened for continuing exploitation of African labour.

The 1875 Decree and the 108 articles of implementation published at the end of the year made up the first African labour code. The *Regulamento* of 1878 which abolished the forced labour provisions of the Decree of 1875 and tried to put all colonial labour on some sort of contractual basis, was in most respects a repetition of previous legislation. It did declare a system of free labour, but the belief was that Africans should contract for their services, and most of the articles in the *Regulamento* were concerned with this problem. And the vagrancy section remained.

Although colonial statesmen in Lisbon were becoming wiser about conditions in their African lands, they still believed that good legislation was bound to produce good results. João de Andrade Corvo referred to the 1875 decree as one of Portugal's decisive steps to do away with the clandestine slave-trade and to advance civilization in Africa. He realized, however, that social transformations, even those founded on the clearest

[4] The decree was printed in the *Boletim de governo*, 11 May 1875.

principles of humanity and justice, were often accomplished only with the greatest difficulty. The transition, he hoped, would be brought about without violence and 'without even sensibly affecting the productive activity and wealth of the colonies'. The transition had been made successfully, as he saw it, in São Tomé. In Angola there would be no difficulty, for a programme of public works and agricultural development had been agreed upon to help Portugal participate in the exploration and civilization of the interior of Africa and to wage war against slavery and barbarism. In Moçambique, Andrade Corvo admitted, the extinction of the vestiges of slavery would not be easy. There the populace in the areas where Portugal had no great influence was much addicted to trafficking in slaves. 'It is easy', he wrote, 'for the Muslims to make religious proselytes among the finest and most energetic of the aboriginal races, and in this way they get active and not very scrupulous agents who provide them with slaves.' But the minister foresaw the day when Britain and Portugal together would do away with the remnants of the vicious trade.[5]

British consuls in Portuguese Africa did not share the halcyon view. John Carnegie wrote from Luanda that no one paid much attention to the 1875 decree. 'Advertisements still appear in the journals published here for the sale or hire of the services of *libertos*.' Carnegie himself saw no advantage for the slave or the colony in the abolition decree.[6] Frederic Elton expected no change in Moçambique. Slave-holders were confident of maintaining the old régime by a policy of 'masterly inactivity'.[7]

England remained particularly dissatisfied with what was going on in Portuguese East Africa and continued to say so. On the basis of Admiralty reports and dispatches from Zanzibar

[5] F.O. 84/1448, Andrade Corvo to the Duke of Saldanha (Portuguese minister in London), 11 Mar. 1876. Corvo, in conversation to Lord Lytton, the English minister is Lisbon, spoke of 'vast projects for making roads and canals . . . giving immediate commercial value to recent geographic researches, to lay the foundation for a great African civilization'. Lytton's comment was that 'The Portuguese Government is at present under great illusions as to its own capacity to lead the van of civilization in Africa.' F.O. 84/1411, Lytton to F.O., 4 Dec. 1875.

[6] F.O. 84/1448, Carnegie to F.O., 18 Apr. 1876.

[7] F.O. 84/1448, Elton to F.O., 1 Apr. 1876.

the Foreign Office came to believe that most officials in Moçambique were guilty of complicity, and Sir Charles Murray in Lisbon was instructed to press Andrade Corvo on 'this reprehensible laxity'. He was to tell Corvo that a few miles north of the capital, at Mosembe, slaves were being brought down from Makua country with forked sticks around their necks and shipped, within sight of Portuguese houses, aboard a dhow sent by the King of Johanna from Nossi Bé. At Mokambo, again a few miles from the island, the *Columbine* lay ashore for a month collecting 133 slaves.[8] The most effectual means of suppressing 'the ever increasing traffic' was concerted action by Portuguese officials and British naval officers. If Portuguese officials were to notify British men-of-war and avail themselves of their help when they had intelligence of a shipment of slaves, the ports of collection and the barracoons could be systematically destroyed.[9]

Portugal had, in English eyes, other shortcomings. Transmitting Sir Bartle Frere's report to Lisbon, the Foreign Office suggested that Portugal was letting Europe down in Africa.

> It is evident from these reports that a considerable slave trade is carried on within the Portuguese possessions which the local authorities, though fully aware of, declare themselves powerless to prevent.
>
> This is a state of things which Her Majesty's Government feel convinced the Government of His Most Faithful Majesty does not wish should continue, and it is one which cannot fail to lessen the effect which the representatives of Her Majesty's Government have upon the semi-barbarous Mohammedan sovereigns of Eastern Africa who see that slavery and the slave trade exist with impunity amongst the subjects of a civilized Christian power.[10]

[8] F.O. 84/1354, Sir Charles Murray to Andrade Corvo, 8 July 1872.

[9] F.O. 84/1411, J. Clement Cobbold to Corvo, 15 Apr. 1875.

[10] F.O. 84/1368, F.O. to Murray, 30 July 1873. Frere's report on the slave-trade in East Africa in 1873 was probably the most comprehensive document the Foreign Office had received on the complex of legitimate and illicit commerce in the Moçambique Channel. His collaborator on the Portuguese section of the report was Frederic Elton, a naval officer, who was to become consul at Moçambique in 1875. Frere thought the coastal traffic had declined, Governor Amaral estimating 2,000 slaves a year, while more objective estimates placed the figure at four times that number. There were no longer large cargoes as in former days, but the northern Arab dhows which used to be laid up at Madagascar waiting for a change of monsoon were now

From 1875 on the Foreign Office had a diligent and tactful consul in Moçambique—Frederic Elton, former naval officer and vice-consul at Zanzibar. Shrewd, vigorous, and persuasive, Elton probably understood the slave-trade in Portuguese East Africa better than anyone; he understood as well the limited capacities of Portuguese officials to cope with it. He travelled up and down the coast and into the interior, sending voluminous reports to the Foreign Office which, in turn, sent them on to Lisbon with repeated instructions to its representatives there to make representations to the Portuguese Government on activities in Moçambique. Wylde in the Slavery Department was unrelenting in his efforts to force Portugal to ever greater efforts.

Elton's first journey was up the coast to the district of Mosembe, from the north shores of Conducia Bay to the Bay of Fernão Veloso, territory governed by Abderhaman Seyd Ali, a sheikh nominally subservient to Portugal. Prior to a raid by

seldom lying idle. 'After landing the Indian supercargo with the import cargo of cloth etc. at Madagascar, they stand over to the opposite Portuguese coast, pick up a small cargo of slaves at the outposts with which they return to Madagascar, making sometimes more than one trip of the kind before it is time to return northwards.' Sometimes they carried their slaves on to Comoro, but generally they were sold to the Sakalava of north-west Madagascar. Frere observed that the Portuguese had failed to attach to themselves either the affection or the respect of the Africans of the mainland, with a consequent failure to develop this very rich colony. The sad state would continue until slavery and the slave-trade were extinguished.

The report also described a system of voluntary labour migration from Delagoa Bay to Natal which was the forerunner of the great labour migration from Moçambique to the Rand mines in the twentieth century. Small groups of Africans made the journey overland to plantations in Natal, there to work for one or two years before returning home. Recently Portuguese authorities had imposed a native passport regulation which cost the worker fifteen shillings. Frere suggested that should Royal Mail Line steamers touch at Delagoa Bay, the long overland trek could be avoided and large quantities of workers could be delivered in Natal at the rate of about one pound a head. Over on the French islands, this system was already under attack, labelled as 'forcible migration'. But Frere was told by the governor-general that such stories were not true, and that he could assure the lieutenant-governor of Natal that 'the Portuguese government would in every way aid the colonial government in any endeavor to place this migration on a sound basis for the future'.

F.O. 84/1389, Sir Henry Bartle Edward Frere to F.O., 12 Mar. 1873, 3 Apr. 1873; also Elton to Bartle Frere, 20 Mar. 1873; also F.O. 84/1391, Bartle Frere to F.O., 26 May 1873.

Portuguese forces on Kivolane in September 1874, large numbers of slaves had been shipped from the area to Madagascar. From the Mosembe plateau, south and west, hardly a village was to be found. The Makua inhabitants had all been sold for the Madagascar trade or had fled inland. Any stranger in Arab dress was regarded as a slave-dealer. In recent months no dhows had put in along the coast and the Mujoge (Swahili) traders were forced to legitimate commerce.[11] A year later Elton went inland across the Mosembe plateau. The Tugulu country had been destroyed, and only now were the inhabitants returning to their land. Again Elton was encouraged to find that the Madagascar trade had been dead for six months.[12]

But, as he discovered on a later trip south of the capital, down to the coast between Angoche and Quizungo, Chief Musa of the Makua dealt extensively in slaves. In the Moma River region he sent parties of men into the interior to raid villages and drive the captives to the coast where Musa received head-money on each slave supplied under the agreement he had with the Swahili dealers. Along this section of the coast, Elton was led to believe, incorrectly perhaps, that the Sultan of Zanzibar had more authority than the Portuguese.[13] In the back-country, there was confusion.

> Wherever the Lomwe are found, they enslave the Makuas, the inferior race, whilst the Maviti, further in the interior, of Zulu extraction, with a military organization, enslave both indiscriminately. Hence an important point to gain in the final suppression of the slave trade is to put a stop to a sliding scale of barbarism which leads people, whilst deprecating slave trade strongly as far as their own tribe is concerned, at the same time to traffic in it with their neighbours as victims, and thus perpetuate the wretched hostility and fear prevailing in this part of the coast that prevents men venturing outside their villages without being prepared for warfare.

[11] F.O. 84/1411, Elton to F.O., 21 June 1875. At the end of this, his first long dispatch, Elton added that he hoped his policy of not running full tilt against all the Portuguese slave-holding prejudices and local abuses would be approved. His first task was to do in the export traffic—through representations to the governor-general and by working personally with the petty sheikhs along the coast.

[12] F.O. 84/1448, Elton to F.O., 17 Aug. 1876.

[13] F.O. 84/1411, Elton to F.O., 24 Oct. 1875.

The Portuguese were not guiltless in these depredations. With no force to coerce, the provincial government had fallen back on 'the old Portuguese policy of fostering civil war' and had supplied 'unscrupulous half-caste Arabs and Mujoges with arms, ammunition, and license to destroy'. (These allegations were exaggerated.)

Generally the slaves were run from the rivers and islands of the Moçambique coast to Madagascar and sold to the Sakalava for bullocks (ten bullocks being the price for one slave). The bullocks were then sold at the French islands or on the mainland for one to two pounds a head. The profits of the venture were often invested in another larger shipment of slaves. These slaves might now be sold to French agents and taken under the name *émigrés* on small craft flying the French flag to Mayotte, Nossi Bé, and even Réunion, where they were requisitioned for ten years service. The total was estimated at 7,000 slaves annually, a decline from the 10,000 supposed to have been exported in 1874. Under British pressure, the Hova Queen of Madagascar issued a proclamation declaring all Makua slaves free, but the Sakalava controlled the coast south of Cape St. Andrew, and worked in co-operation with the slave-traders.[14]

On 9 September 1875 the cruiser *Thetis* captured a large dhow standing from Moma River to Cape St. Andrew. Aboard were over 200 slaves (34 men; 16 boys over 10 years of age; 75 boys under 10; 6 boys under 3; 54 women; 19 girls over 3; 7 girls under 3) and 53 Swahili traders and crew. They were stowed 'on two decks squatting side by side in such a position as neither to allow of their standing up, or lying down, or of moving for the purpose of obeying the calls of nature—indeed the stench in her hold showed plainly that the poor creatures were compelled to squat in their own excrement'. After three days out twenty-six captives had died. The traders were mostly men from Comoro. It was the opinion of the commander of the *Thetis* that shipments like this were made with the full knowledge of Portuguese authorities.[15]

At the hearing in the vice-admiralty court at Zanzibar some

[14] F.O. 84/1411, Elton to F.O., 13 Sept. 1875.

[15] F.O. 84/1411, J. Le Houte Ward to Admiral Reginald MacDonald, 17 Sept. 1875.

of the intricacies of the East African slave-trade were shown. Fatima, twenty-three years old, was the slave of a Swahili storekeeper on Moçambique island. She refused his attentions and was taken to Kivolane and sold. Mandowa, a woman of Fatima's age, was sold at Moçambique by one Swahili merchant to another and shipped to Umfusi with seven other girls. Fifteen slaves had been run down at Moma by Selisman, a slave-dealer from Nossi Bé. A woman bought at Moma for fifteen dollars was to be sold at Madagascar for sixty; a man or boy costing seven to fifteen dollars brought forty.[16]

Shortly after his arrival in Moçambique, Elton prepared a confidential report on slavery within the colony. The capital had a population of some 5,000 Negroes and about 800 Portuguese, Goans, and mixed peoples. More than half of the African population was made up of slaves or *libertos*. The difference between the two depended on the master and the remuneration. Portuguese convicts and half-castes were the worst masters. 'They are determined slave holders and live in laziness on what is earned for them by their slaves.' These they sold when they needed to, thus abetting, in Elton's view, the slave-trade. Of the mainland he wrote:

> All the owners of property on the mainland hold *libertos* and slaves. Slave discipline is still carried on. Slave punishments are not discontinued, such as working with a heavy log attached to the leg by a chain. Slaves are let out to work for hire—are lent to foreign commerical houses for a consideration and whether termed *libertos* or slaves fall under the English interpretation of the word slave. For in the case of the *liberto* the equivalent of his labour is never received by him—he is not in the position of a man engaged for a term for certain work. He can be put to work for any person whom his master chooses to hire him, on the terms his master chooses to agree to.

[16] F.O. 84/1411, Elton to F.O., 20 Nov. 1875. By the end of the year Elton was growing impatient with the Moçambique Government's lackadaisical attitude. Of the three ships in the Portuguese naval squadron, only one, the *Douro*, was ready for service and she remained anchored most of the time in Moçambique harbour. Often Elton did not have sufficient time to inform the governor of an anticipated shipment of slaves, obtain his permission for British cruisers to enter Portuguese territorial waters, and then pass the permission on to British naval officers.

Slaves could be bought at many places on the mainland: Delagoa Bay, Inhambane, Quelimane, Ibo, and up and down Zambézia. The slave registration demanded by the Decree of 1854 had never been carried out, one out of fifty, perhaps one out of a hundred slaves having been registered. Some 12,000 had been registered in the capital district, 9,000 in Quelimane, and fewer in the other districts of the province. The promise of indemnification was laughed at. When public officials were eight months in arrears in their salaries, the possibility for public morality was small, and anti-slavery legislation would remain without enforcement.[17]

But all was not darkness. The bishopric of Moçambique had been revived after a lapse of some forty years and an energetic priest, José Caetano Gonçalves, had been named bishop. A determined foe of the slave-trade, he had established a school for African children. The bishop's abolitionist tendencies had won him the enmity of many local citizens, who were set against any education for Negroes or any extension of their freedom. Within months Bishop Gonçalves was under heavy fire, attacked for his school, and condemned in letters to the Portuguese Government.[18]

Along the coast in 1876 the trade to Madagascar continued to decline. The British Navy complimented Governor-General

[17] F.O. 84/1411, Elton to F.O., 21 July 1875. Elton's dispatches were regularly sent to Lisbon for use by the ministry. A draft of a Mar. 1876 dispatch, seen by Queen Victoria and Disraeli, proposed to remind the Portuguese Government that in Natal, England was developing resources without resorting to slavery and that to the north the slave-trade from Zanzibar was being brought under control. Only along the Moçambique coast did the trade continue. Could it be that tariff restrictions were stifling the development of Moçambique and prompting the slave-trade? F.O. 84/1447, F.O. to Lisbon, 1 Mar. 1876.

[18] F.O. 84/1411, Elton to F.O., 21 July 1875. Later in the year Elton himself became involved. On Christmas Day he saw a soldier repeatedly fling a Negro prisoner, whose hands were tied behind his back, to the ground and kick him. Elton's demonstrances were to no avail. 'Whilst he lay groaning and bleeding, a Portuguese in a shirt and trousers and a straw hat . . . , and probably a convict, rushed out of a shop like a mad dog, jumped on the poor wretch's back, kicked him in the face, and hit him with his fist. I have travelled in many countries, but never has it been my chance to witness such an act of disgraceful cruelty, and I am glad to say I gave the actor, there and then in the street, as sound a thrashing with a stick I had in my hand as I was able to administer before he disappeared from the scene.' F.O. 84/1411, Elton to F.O., 25 Dec. 1875.

Guedes de Carvalho e Menezes in his persistence. The governors at Quelimane and Angoche were suspected of connivance, but there was a general belief that Portuguese officials were more alert against the dhow traffic from Moçambique shores. In 1876 only one dhow was captured by British ships and only three were definitely known to have escaped. By the highest estimate thirteen dhows and 1,560 slaves evaded the vigilance of British cruisers and the Portuguese gunboat *Duoro*—a considerable reduction from the estimated 7,000 which were slipped away the previous year. An exodus of Arab and Mujoge traders from the Kivolane–Umfusi delta told the story of what seemed to be a dying traffic in that once notorious area.[19]

Another indication of the decline came from Réunion where Consul Gerald Perry reported that planters were again talking of a treaty to guarantee them a supply of labour from Moçambique. The Convention of 1861, which had permitted planters to recruit in India, had not been successful. Planters in Réunion now wanted an arrangement similar to the one which permitted English planters in Natal to use voluntary workers from Delagoa Bay.[20]

In 1876 and 1877 the French minister in Lisbon approached the government for permission to organize a Negro emigration scheme from Portuguese African possessions. So long as Andrade Corvo was Foreign Minister, such hopes were negligible, but with Foreign Minister António Avila, one could not be so sure. Minister Morier wrote: 'I cannot but think that if he thought he would make himself agreeable to the French Government by according to them what they represent as only an extension to the French colonies of the arrangements concluded with us in regard to Natal and the Cape of Good Hope, he would be inclined to do so.' Morier told Avila bluntly that his government regarded such emigration as part of the slave-trade.[21]

At the end of 1877 Morier again visited Avila to give England's protest on continuing talks of a new emigration

[19] F.O. 84/1479, Elton to F.O., 3 Jan. 1877.

[20] F.O. 84/1471, Gerald Perry to F.O., 24 Feb. 1877, 15 May 1877, and 12 Sept. 1878.

[21] F.O. 84/1477, W. R. B. Morier to F.O., 2 May 1877.

scheme. Avila assured the minister no arrangement would be made which did not provide absolute guarantees that there would be no revival of the slave-trade. Morier pointed out that guarantees in the past had been useless and that French commercial houses had systematically endeavoured to carry on a covert slave-trade. There were no additional labourers available in the Delagoa Bay area, and to acquire them French agents would not be able to distinguish too nicely between free and unfree labour. Morier insisted that there was no proper analogy between the proposed French system and what was permitted under the Moçambique–Natal Convention which regulated and placed checks on a natural and spontaneous labour movement on the part of Africans who sought employment of their own free will.[22]

In 1875 an arrangement had been made between authorities in Moçambique and British officials in Natal and Cape Province to expedite and control a flow of workers from the area in back of Delagoa Bay to South African estates, thus giving formal sanction to an informal migration which had been going on for some years. Ships of the Royal Mail Line made regular calls at Lourenço Marques to transport the workers, about 2,000 of whom made the trip each year. The representative at Lourenço Marques for the Cape was J. J. Monteiro, a British mining engineer who had spent years in Angola and written the study *Angola and the River Congo* (London, 1875). Recruitment was briefly permitted at Inhambane, but was rescinded by the governor-general on the ground that Africans from that region were 'unfit' to work abroad.[23] No sooner were the arrangements completed than the Moçambique Government raised the various fees, including a fifteen shilling passport charge, to twenty-six shillings, an increase of eleven shillings, which gave rise to considerable discussion between London and Lisbon. The authorities in Moçambique were in no way disposed to furnish cheap labour to foreign estates.

The use of Moçambique labour abroad was not then or later

[22] F.O. 84/1477, Morier to F.O., 29 Nov. 1877.
[23] *Boletim oficial de Moçambique*, 15 Dec. 1879.

supported by the majority of Portuguese colonists in the province. An article in an occasional paper, *Africa Oriental*, made pointed reference to the arrangement in an indiscriminate attack on the African population of Moçambique and the metropolitan government. In the article's terms, free Negroes on the mainland lived a life of savagery, pillage, and rioting, while planters were going bankrupt for lack of workers. 'These people who have just left a servile state without being prepared for liberty cannot be permitted to sneer without punishment at the universal law of work.' These hordes of savages, 'unlettered, without education', lived in a reprehensible state of abandonment which foreigners took advantage of.

> We, in order not to wound the sensibilities and liberties of the black race, let them do as they choose, and, full of philanthropic pride, wait for agents of the English emigration scheme to come and take them off to the colonies where they are subject to a most severe and violent regime, while we, with our constitutional law tucked under our arms, bawl in dogmatic tones. 'The blacks are free citizens and for this reason are permitted to do as they choose.'
>
> Let us awake!
>
> Neither constitution nor other laws keep the governor general from making laws necessary to keep the blacks from vagrancy. It is a simple matter of policy which may be settled by administrative action.[24]

(In Lisbon the success of South Africa and the disaster of Moçambique was often laid not to African arrogance but to the venality of Portuguese officials.)[25]

The real cause of the ills besetting Portuguese East Africa was, as it had been for a long time, the failure to extend the authority of government. Elton wrote that laws meant little in remote places where it had long been the privilege and necessity of lesser Portuguese officials or of honorary Portuguese administrators to deal in slaves. In such areas laws were waste

[24] *Africa Oriental*, 11 Dec. 1879. Another Moçambique paper, *O africano* ('Religião, Instrucção, e Moralidade') of Quelimane, 1 Feb. 1880, wrote that Portugal put up too much with English demands. Portugal should remind England of her Irish policy. The editors also said that the 'blacks consider the Portuguese as the only ones with rights in the interior'.

[25] *Trinta diabos junior*, p. 232 (Feb. 1877).

paper. On this point Elton, who was usually dispassionate in his reports, waxed vehement.

> [They] do not secure any amelioration, civilization, advancement, prospects, religious instruction, security, or the slightest good in the least likely to prove of any ultimate or permanent advantage . . . to the unfortunate African races, degraded as they have been by contact with irresponsible convicts, incorrigibles, and their descendants, half-castes, and Goanese, the off-spring of concubinage with the women of Negro tribes, who continue to be freely bought and sold, and who, if misbehaving, are still punished with the scourge, or if favorites are entrusted with unlimited powers over their masters' chattels—over in fact the very people, practically slaves, who because the Law of 1875 so writes and wills it upon paper, we are forsooth to be compelled by such Portuguese protests . . . henceforth and forever to regard as theoretically free.[26]

Elton was in the last years of his life. Before his death he made a careful survey of the coast from Moçambique island to Cape Delgado (in October–December 1876) and a journey up the Zambesi and Shire to Nyasa country (in July–September 1877). Elton died up-country near the end of his second expedition. Along the coast he found news of occasional shipments of slaves, and in the interior he found only scattered signs of an organized traffic.[27] The slave routes still led to Quelimane (Dr. Macklin wrote Elton that a string of slaves in sticks had recently passed down the Shire);[28] recently the governor of the district, under pressure from the governor-general, had temporarily put a stop to the sale of slaves in the vicinity of the town.

Before Elton's departure on his last journey, the dhow traffic had begun to increase once more. Three dhows, one of them arrested by Portuguese forces, were known to be working the Kivolane–Umfusi delta again. Another, flying French colours, was nearly captured by a Portuguese gunboat. Governor-General Guedes de Carvahlo e Menezes issued a proclamation—which

[26] F.O. 84/1479, Elton to F.O., 23 Apr. 1877.

[27] F.O. 84/1479, Elton to F.O., 3 Jan. 1877, 12 Sept. 1877, and 13 Oct. 1877. Of Elton's death, Wylde wrote, 'It will be difficult if not impossible adequately to replace him.'

[28] F.O. 84/1479, The Reverend Macklin, of the Free Church Mission, to Elton, n.d. (Received by Elton at Quelimane on 10 July 1877).

he asked Elton to get translated into Swahili for distribution—informing all the sheikhs and lesser chiefs in the province of Moçambique that his king had determined to put an end to slavery and to 'the illicit and disgraceful traffic in slaves'. The governor announced that he was prepared to pursue and prosecute all those who in any way were 'in the habit of favouring the Arabs and Moors who are in the habit of visiting this coast for procuring people'.[29]

Although Portugal was gradually extending its authority along the coast, or at least was obtaining the allegiance of more coastal chiefs, and the British Navy persevered as always, Henry O'Neill, Elton's replacement who had arrived in Moçambique in 1879, reported that two dhows had just shipped slaves from Kivolane–Umfusi to Comoro to be transhipped to Mayotte and Nossi Bé. A third dhow with 200 slaves and fifty free people had foundered in the bar, only twenty-nine surviving. The governor had agreed to joint British-Portuguese action in Moçambique's territorial waters.[30] It was rumoured that Ibo was in business again, now loading workers for Comoro. Reviewing the events of 1879. O'Neill said that ten shipments were known to have been made during the year: four from Umfusi, three from the vicinity of Ibo, three from the Quizungu River area above Quelimane. Allowing two more shipments for each one that was heard of, O'Neill moderately estimated some 3,000 to 4,000 slaves exported during the year. But O'Neill was hopeful. The anti-slavery law was beginning to have some small effect; and the ivory trade, which was usually managed by slave-traders, seemed to be falling off, and the number of ivory caravans to the interior diminishing.[31] But in Nyasa trade was reported to be flourishing. Arab traders, or their agents, were busy throughout the region. From Nyasa captives were taken down to the coast at Lindi, Kilwa, or Ibo and sold to agents from Comoro or from the Sakalava coast of Madagascar.[32]

In Lisbon the British task for the last four years had been to get a treaty with which to force Portugal to greater efforts

[29] Proclamation of 26 May 1877.
[30] F.O. 84/1539, Henry Edward O'Neill to F.O., 6 July 1879.
[31] F.O. 84/1539, O'Neill to F.O., 2 Dec. 1879.
[32] F.O. 84/1539, O'Neill to F.O., 13 Dec. 1879.

and to permit more freedom of action for British cruisers in Moçambique waters. But the instability of Portuguese Governments thwarted these plans. Morier wrote:

> I know the ways of this government and the very pigeon holes in which they bury my notes . . . the *sine quâ non* condition therefore of any efficient effort to put down the slave trade is to create a new routine establishing a treaty right on our side and a treaty duty on the side of Portugal, to co-operate actively for the purpose of rooting out the slave trade in Portuguese waters. Having worked incessantly in this direction from my first arrival here, I succeeded in obtaining a treaty by which those objects were obtained, and I signed this treaty on the very day that the Ministry [Andrade Corvo's], whom I had educated up to the standard required by Her Majesty's Government, quitted office.

Now Morier saw no hope for ratification and he deeply regretted that it should 'just be this question of the Slave Trade, to which for so many years the Foreign Office has devoted such unremitting attention, that should be the one most seriously affected by the complete derangement of my plans'.[33]

While the coastal slave-trade in Moçambique fluctuated in intensity, an alleged traffic in Angola suddenly came to occupy a furious moment of its own. Vernon Lovett Cameron, a Royal Navy lieutenant, was sent out by the Royal Geographical Society in 1872 to assist in the explorations of Dr. Livingstone. On learning of the death of Livingstone, Cameron had separated from the bulk of his expedition and set off across the continent; after a two-and-a-half-year journey, he reached the port of Benguela in 1875. In his journey Cameron crossed Kazembe and came into Angola through Dilolo in the Katanga and thence down through what was to be known as the Hungry Country through Bihé to the coast. He passed through the slave-trading grounds habituated by the Angolan *pombeiros*, or traders, and along the slave routes down to the port of Benguela. Cameron gave harrowing descriptions of the highlands slave-trade in a letter to Lord Derby, in a lecture to the Geographical Society of Paris, and in his famous account of

[33] F.O. 84/1563, Morier to F.O., 16 Feb. 1880.

his journey, *Across Africa.* His indictment of what he rather freely called Portuguese slave-trading was indignant, self-righteous, and tinged with racist undertones.[34] Cameron's recital of cruelty, brutality, and murder 'by men calling themselves Christians and carrying the Portuguese flag' was of a familiar pattern to readers of Livingstone and anti-slavery literature. Portuguese officials were condemned ('He [João Baptista Ferreira] was openly engaged in the slave traffic, notwithstanding his holding a commission from the Portuguese Government as a district judge, and slaves in chains were to be seen in his settlement')[35] and Portugal's presence in Africa also soundly condemned.

Cameron's philippic and another delivered about the same time by Lieutenant E. D. Young before the Cape Town Chamber of Commerce on conditions in Portuguese East Africa set off a rousing reaction in Portugal, particularly in the press, traditionally more sensitive to slurs on Portugal's honour than the Parliament. But even in the Chamber of Deputies, the incriminations of Cameron and Young took up three full days of debate in February 1877. The speeches of defence in the Chamber had a certain familiarity: both Cameron and Young had enjoyed and profited from Portuguese hospitality; both men were describing conditions in parts of Africa beyond Portuguese jurisdiction; Portugal had made great sacrifice to put down the slave-trade and to advance civilization in Africa; Portugal and England were two proud countries of great honour and dignity.

The burden of the discussion was taken up by Andrade Corvo's long rambling speech, remarkably similar in many ways

[34] In these terms he described Lourenço de Souza Coimbra, a son of Major Coimbra of Bihé, an honorary officer of the Portuguese army: 'His attire and general appearance were worthy of his character. A dirty, greasy and tattered wide-awake hat, battered shapeless and so far gone that a *chiffonier* would have passed it by as worthless, crowned this distinguished person. His shirt was equally dirty, and a piece of grass cloth bound round his waist trailed its end upon the ground. His hair was short and kinky, and his almost beardless face, when not covered with filth, was of a dirty yellow colour. Even had he not been always in a half-drunken state, his bood-shot eye would have told the tale of debauchery. In short, he was, true to his appearance, an unmitigated ruffian.' Vernon Lovett Cameron, *Across Africa* (2 vols., London, 1877), ii. 96–97.

[35] Ibid., p. 217.

to Jose de Lacerda's refutation of Livingstone (*Exame dos viagens do Doutor Livingstone,* Lisbon, 1867), which Corvo freely quoted. Both the minister's speech and Lacerda's book were an example of the Portuguese rhetorical response to English charges of labour malpractice; they were dignified, dense, and largely irrelevant. Cameron had been carried away, according to Corvo, by petty ideas of rivalry, led astray by pride, misinformed by a pseudo-humanitarian fanaticism. For more than a century Portugal had been trying to do away with the slave-trade. Rude Negroes and savage half-castes of the interior, who seemed to be or claimed to be Portuguese, did not represent Portugal. In one burst of misguided eloquence, Corvo averred that there was no slave-trade on Portuguese soil anywhere; there were only free men, and not free men forming a despised caste, but free men as much citizens of Portugal as the honourable deputies.[36]

By the time of the debate, the Foreign Office had received a report from Consul David Hopkins who had been sent to Benguela to look into the charges made by Cameron. In his confidential dispatch of 29 November 1875, Hopkins reported that all the carriers of goods to Benguela were the slaves of masters living in Bihé and beyond; whether Portuguese or not, Hopkins could not ascertain. But it was certain that they could be bought and sold in the areas around Catumbela and Benguela. Most of the workers on the plantations there were slaves, free in name, and all seemed happy and indifferent to having been declared free. He saw no signs of horror; for this, one had to go to the interior. He did not see shackles. He was convinced that Cameron's report of a recent slave shipment from Moçâmedes was incorrect. The native traders of Bihé were described as cruel and aggressive and great promoters of the slave-trade. It was unquestionably true that powerful Africans and mulattoes held commissions in the Portuguese Army and were Portugal's bulwarks against rebellion in the interior. At the end of his dispatch, Hopkins went into a digression on the Negro character, recording 'what years of experience among Negroes' had taught him:

They have neither love, affection, jealousy nor gratitude, and

[36] F.O. 84/1476, Morier to F.O., 27 Feb. 1877.

until they do, the stronger will continue to prey upon the weaker, despite the efforts of all our well-meaning philanthropists. . . .

Valuable lives and much money have been spent on the idea that the Negro could be raised to a civilized state. . . . It is distressing and painful now to find, after fondly cherishing this idea for years, that all our labour has been in vain. He is as he was, and so he will remain, until his country is more fully occupied by a higher type of the human race.[37]

The Hopkins report did not provide much useful information for further representations in Lisbon, and for a little while the offensive passed to Portugal. In a *note verbale* to Morier in December 1876, Foreign Minister Corvo proudly stated 'that the last vestiges of forced labour have disappeared from all the Portuguese colonies, and especially from the islands of São Tomé and Principe'. The regulations respecting labour there were now based upon the identical principles which had been adopted in Britain's African colonies. He was obliged to say, however, that he had received complaints from the curator in São Tomé that conditions on the English packet *Raquelle* carrying workers from Luanda to São Tomé were harsh and inadequate.[38]

The export of Angolan labour to São Tomé remained the issue of contention between the two nations. Ironically, no more enthusiastic defence of the São Tomé system could have been made than the one made by Consul Hopkins. The workers were saved from death in the interior at the hands of their savage countrymen, he wrote in June 1877. They went willingly to São Tomé and willingly stayed there. The introduction of labour to the islands was a necessity. The soil was perfect for growing coffee, and large estates were going to ruin for want of workers. The workers brought in were free men, and any attempt to interfere with their liberty would be severely

[37] F.O. 84/1478, Hopkins to F.O., 6 Jan. 1877. Wylde's conclusion on receiving this report was that Cameron had exaggerated and that Corvo's 'high-blown assertions' were equally wrong.

[38] F.O. 84/1447, Morier to F.O., 28 Dec. 1876. The Foreign Office minute on the dispatch was for an immediate investigation to be made by the Admiralty and the directors of the British and African Steam Navigation Company. Consul Carnegie gave an equally optimistic picture of conditions on São Tomé in his report of 29 Apr. 1876 (F.O. 84/1448).

punished. Hopkins argued that it was more humane under the new laws to let the workers in than it was to block them with British cruisers and condemn them to death in the interior. Slavery now existed only in the minds of the Africans. Although there might still be no difficulty in obtaining a slave in Angola, there would be the greatest difficulty in getting rid of one. He praised the colonial authorities for their efforts to stamp out slavery.[39]

By the end of the year Hopkins, for one reason or another, had changed his opinions completely and was embroiled in a row with Governor-General Amaral. As a result of a trip to Novo Redondo and of conversations with Commander Warren of the cruiser *Swallow* and with European residents in Angola, he had come to see that the free labour emigration to São Tomé was something akin to slave dealing. 'Let them try to blind my eyes,' he told the Governor, 'I still say the people that are being shipped out are not free labourers. . . . They have no will of their own, they cannot go where they like or work when they like or starve when they like. They are nothing more than cattle, and it is a farce after all these years calling slavery by a new name and commencing again.' He regretted having to report such a condition since he had been a strong advocate of the migration of Negroes to São Tomé.[40]

In November 1877, Commander Warren inquired of Hopkins the legality of shipping workers to the islands. He wanted to know if steps were taken to ascertain whether the labourers embarked of their own free will and if the commanders of vessels carrying workers were supplied with documents of sufficient authority that their traffic was lawful. Two weeks later Warren boarded the brig *Pensamento* off Novo Redondo carrying 100 labourers. The workers all had passes stamped by a Portuguese official. Following Hopkins's instructions, Warren did not take the *Pensamento* as a prize. He said that he could not communicate with the workers on board since there was

[39] F.O. 84/1478, Hopkins to F.O., June 1877. Wylde was very upset at Hopkins's dispatch, saying the floodgates for the slave-trade were being opened. Hopkins was to be told his sentiments were not shared by Her Majesty's Government. Calmer heads urged restraint until they had heard from the Law Officers.

[40] F.O. 84/1478, Hopkins to F.O., 22 Dec. 1877.

no interpreter. Conditions were very bad, and the crew of the brig referred to the workers as slaves.[41]

Hopkins visited the *Pensamento* when she docked in Luanda. He also found no way of talking to the workers, who did not understand Portuguese, Umbundu, or the dialect of Novo Redondo. They were wretched and frightened out of their wits, Hopkins wrote Amaral. 'Portuguese subjects are engaged in slaving', he continued. 'The workers were "wild natives", unfortunate and helpless men, women, and children.' No longer was Hopkins sure of their future. 'Although individually the condition of these people may be bettered by the change from their wild life to civilization, yet have we any right to thrust our civilization upon them, and leave, perhaps, wives and mothers mourning the loss of husbands and fathers torn ruthlessly away to satisfy the needy pockets of a few speculators.'[42] No humanitarian could have spoken with more feeling.

Amaral, once again replying through his secretary-general, asked for immediate proof for this slur upon his country's honour. As for the workers, let Warren take possession of any ship he chose, and the courts would decide the legality. The workers were shipped under provisions of Articles 22 and 23 of the Law of 29 April 1875. Bad conditions on shipboard were to be punished by colonial authorities. Labour was as necessary for São Tomé as it was for Natal where some 3,000 workers from Moçambique went every year. Portuguese subjects, just because they were black, should not be denied the liberty of going where they wanted to and contracting with whom they chose. Any African ransomed from a chief in the interior was then as free as all subjects of His Most Faithful Majesty.

[41] F.O. 84/1478, Warren to Hopkins, 29 Nov. 1877 and 17 Dec. 1877.

[42] F.O. 84/1478, Hopkins to Amaral, 17 Dec. 1877. In a confidential dispatch of 27 Dec. 1877 (F.O. 84/1478), Hopkins named the merchants in Novo Redondo who gathered the ransomed slaves. One, Patrício Alvares, was allegedly backed by the Banco Nacional Ultramarino, whose Lisbon manager owned the Monte Café plantation in São Tomé. The workers were purchased for goods valued at three pounds. When purchased they were put in chains until time for embarkation. Hopkins's sources of information were a British subject in Benguela, a Dutch business agent in Luanda, and two British subjects from Luanda who had done much travelling in the interior. As soon as the traffic out of Novo Redondo started to increase, the number of condemned Negroes in the interior began to rise sharply.

Slavery was an element of native society and a punishment for enemies and criminals. So was death. All the people going to São Tomé would have been executed 'if life and liberty had not been guaranteed for them by the men whom you unjustly accuse of being slave-dealers'.[43]

The *curador* and the police chief of Luanda also went aboard the *Pensamento* and found only minor infractions. The following day, 20 December 1877, Curator Troni (soon also to be a deputy for Portuguese West Africa in the Portuguese Parliament), interrogated the workers, 'who had been redeemed on the borders of Novo Redondo by the duly legalized contracting agent August Moreira Patrício Alvares, to work on the plantations of José Ferreira do Amaral'. The questions put were: (1) If they had been enslaved by other natives and ransomed by contracting agents; (2) If the ransom had been made in regions where Portugal ruled; (3) if the contracts had been made in their presence, if they understood the terms, and if they were going of their own free will. The labourers were reported to have replied that they had been enslaved, principally for witchcraft, that they had been ransomed at villages under Portuguese rule, that they understood they were going to São Tomé for two years as agricultural workers and were pleased with their situation. Having satisfied himself on these points and found out that they were not unhappy with conditions on shipboard, the curator closed the case and informed the governor.[44]

Half a year later, John Carnegie, replacement to Hopkins, reported a great improvement. The late Governor Amaral, though a defender of the emigration of workers from 'over-populated Angola' to the islands, was a champion of anti-slavery Carnegie wrote, and had done everything possible to see that the labour was voluntary and the conditions of shipment satisfactory. Carnegie had visited several ships and had found the workers 'well fed, well dressed, and looking forward smilingly to their future home'. Furthermore, he had been assured by all his Portuguese friends in Novo Redondo that the labour was free and not purchased from the interior. A recent famine

[43] F.O. 84/1478, Amaral to Hopkins, 19 Dec. 1877.
[44] F.O. 84/1505, Extract of evidence (n.d.).

back-country was driving many Africans down to the port to contract for their services.[45]

In the meantime the Foreign Office had asked the Law Officers of the Crown for a ruling on whether the boarding of the *Pensamento* was legal under treaty and whether the purchase of slaves for the purpose of enabling them to obtain their freedom in the manner contemplated by the Law of 29 April 1875 constituted a violation of the terms of the Treaty of 1842. The Law Officers replied that the offence named in the Treaty of 1842 (Articles I and II) was 'transporting Negroes by sea for the purpose of consigning them to slavery'. In their opinion the purchase of slaves to enable them to obtain their liberty (which was not, in effect, the case at all) did not constitute a violation of treaty.[46] With this ruling and, in the next several years, with the *rapprochement* with Portugal over sovereignty of the Congo, the Foreign Office no longer pursued the migration scheme with as much vigour as it had. The lead on this issue now passed out of the Foreign Office into the hands of the philanthropists, never to be regained.

Thus the controversy entered a relative period of calm. Angolans continued to be moved to São Tomé under overtly respectable—and acceptable—conditions, and no one was very much disposed to disturb the lull. In October 1880, Morier did write to Foreign Minister Anselmo Braamcamp that reports from Dondo told of a recruiting system to obtain workers for coffee plantations in Cazengo, in Angola, and the islands which in some features resembled the slave-trade. Three traders at Dondo had been appointed by the colonial government as recruiting agents. These men received from chiefs of the neigh-

[45] F.O. 84/1505, John Carnegie to F.O., 30 July 1878. In the 1870's, estate owners in São Tomé and Principe had been recruiting up and down the West African coast. In 1875, fair numbers of men from Liberia and the Kroo Coast were contracted for a year's work by island agents. British subjects were warned by Colonial Secretary J. Kendall in Sierre Leone in Aug. 1877 that they might have difficulty in getting back home. He also advised them of other difficulties in working in the Portuguese islands. One Portuguese ship, the *Ovarense*, carrying workers from Sierra Leone to São Tomé was stopped by a British cruiser, then released. Feeling in Portugal was aroused over the incident, and comparison was made with the facilities given in Moçambique to British agents recruiting for Natal.

[46] F.O. 84/1447, Law Officers to Lord Salisbury, 11 May 1878.

bouring villages youthful workers in return for payments of cloth. The young men were washed and fed, had their heads shaven, and were taken by the recruiter before a government official and registered as free contract labourers. Then they were sent on their way. The age of the young men was generally from twelve to twenty-five, though some children as young as seven were hired. Morier explained that these men were not freed slaves, but simply Africans handed over to Portuguese recruiters for a gratuity. 'This', he said, 'is a disguised slave trade.'[47]

The secret slave-trade continued from Moçambique, although a strengthened Portuguese squadron had begun a new campaign against the dhows carrying captives to Madagascar and the Comores. Acting Governor-General Augusto Sarmento in June 1880 captured three dhows, two with slaves on board, and arrested one Macusse Omar of the Kivolane–Umfusi delta, reputedly the most important slave-dealer in the area. For two years Macusse has led open resistance to Portuguese authority. On his capture he was summarily tried for treason and shipped off to do penal servitude for life in the Cape Verdes. In July 1880 two Portuguese expeditions shelled and burnt to the ground the village slave centres of Umkusu and Kivolane; a force of 2,000 which had gathered to effect the release of Macusse was dispersed. A serious blow had been struck at the most infamous slaving centre in the province. The chiefs of the area had hitherto been semi-independent and derived much of their strength from the liberal supply of money, guns, and powder which flowed into their hands from the slave-trade. All earlier attempts to halt their operations had failed.[48]

Sarmento's predecessor, Francisco da Cunha, had been somewhat indulgent towards slavery in Moçambique and towards

[47] F.O. 84/1563, Morier to Braamcamp, 5 Oct. 1880.

[48] F.O. 84/1565, O'Neill to F.O., 15 July 1880. But the whole of the delta could not be policed. From Mosembe and from Chicoma slaves could be shipped a few miles down to the coast and secretly embarked. The markets remained the same, the sugar plantations of Johanna and Mohilla which were worked by slave-labour. F.O. 84/1565, O'Neill to F.O., 24 May 1880; F.O. 84/1565, O'Neill to F.O., 12 Sept. 1880 and 31 Dec. 1880.

the continuing traffic from the colony.[49] There was strong sentiment, thus described by Consul O'Neill, against the vigorous activities of Sarmento.

> The work of active Slave Trade suppression is not a popular one, nor can it be expected to be amongst those—and they are in the majority—who, a short time since, were slave owners themselves, and who have suffered by an Emancipation Act, which provided no compensation, and who still suffer by the labour difficulties that have followed it. Even amongst the highest class, who feel the slave trade to be a dishonour and a disgrace, there is a very general belief, grounded no doubt partly upon a knowledge of the insufficiency of their means, that the Slave Trade will not be extinguished by these measures. But amongst the mass there is the strongest objection to any such active steps as have been lately taken, which provoke reprisals and emperil the security of their property and trade.
>
> The slave trader does not interfere with the petty trader on the coast, and even when they do not combine and assist each other they work upon a mutual understanding of non-interference, and the latter is too short-sighted to see how injuriously the ravages necessary to sustain the Slave Trade affect his interests. But when the proprietors of land . . . find their properties endangered by such active steps . . . and when all lawful traders find themselves compelled to fly the country . . . then it is not easy to be wondered at that there is a deep-rooted dislike and an opposition to operations of this nature.

O'Neill went on to suggest that the forthright action taken by Sarmento and his subordinates be recognized by the British Government.[50]

In February 1881, Governor Sarmento made two attacks in

[49] Governor-General Cunha had been recalled for consultation. Two of his subordinates were recalled at the same time and indicted for having had Africans flogged. F.O. 84/1564, O'Neill to F.O., 20 Feb. 1880.

[50] F.O. 84/1565, O'Neill to F.O., 8 July 1880. Morier, supporting O'Neill's recommendation, said that Sarmento had done more in a few months than his predecessors in twenty years. A decoration for Sarmento would stimulate national vanity, he believed, and bring dormant forces to the fore. F.O. 84/1563, Morier to F.O., 17 Oct. 1880. The men in the Foreign Office were dismayed by such a suggestion. For one, 'the practice of giving English decorations to foreigners was objectionable'. For another, there seemed no reason to decorate a man who was only doing what his job called for him to do. Yet another suggested the gift of a snuff box or a bit of plate.

force on the Sheikh of Mosembe, who was reportedly responsible for all slave dealings between Conducia and Fernão Veloso.[51] Both attacks were turned back, although the British

[51] In 1880, Consul O'Neill, an even more restless traveller than Elton, made two thirty-five day expeditions along the coast north of Moçambique, the first in May and June to Pemba Bay, and the second in October and November from Pemba Bay to Cape Delgado. His reports, like almost all of O'Neill's accounts, are among the most remarkable descriptions available on Moçambique in the nineteenth century. As he progressed up the coast from the capital, O'Neill was witness to the effects of the slave-trade. The area of Mosembe was ravaged by the sheikh of the district who kidnapped his own people indiscriminately. The area north of Mosembe, in Fernão Veloso Bay, was still underpopulated from the great raids of 1875 and 1876. At the Lurio River, the chief trading settlement between Moçambique and Ibo, O'Neill heard that eleven Mohilla and Johanna men had been trading in the neighbourhood of Ushanga for several months and now had collected over a hundred slaves. The slaves were not from the caravan trade down from the interior, but purchased locally from the headmen of the locality. The chief of the traders carried a letter from the Sultan of Mohilla. In the absence of any Portuguese authority close by, O'Neill had to abandon his efforts to locate the collection and prevent the shipment.

On his second expedition, O'Neill gathered reports of the caravan trade down the Rovuma, a 400-slave caravan having come down the month before and been shipped at Tunghi. The route had been a popular one for years, and neither Zanzibari nor Portuguese authorities had tried to curb it. At Matamba (near Missanji) three caravans had arrived in the last two months bringing about 500 slaves for domestic use and export. Matamba was reported to be the extreme southerly end of the Rovuma route. Most of the captives were Ajawa, Madonde, and Makonde, and they came carrying ivory and tobacco. In back of Kissanga, five days journey, five caravans had arrived during the year, with some 1,200 slaves and ivory (from Ali, a Comoro trader at Kissanga, O'Neill acquired a detailed description of the caravan route from Kissanga to Nyasa). Farms all along the coast, most of them in the hands of 'Mouros', were expanding for the cultivation of gingil seeds. The estates, from 50 to 500 acres, each used from twenty to fifty slaves. The Swahili-speaking farmers of the interior used slave-labour with impunity, while Portuguese owners along the coast were demanding compulsory native labour. Wherever posible, the Portuguese authorities were doing what they could to stop the traffic, but the largest force in the area was the fifty to sixty men stationed at Ibo. F.O. 84/1565, O'Neill to F.O., 3 July 1880, Enclosure No. 1; F.O. 84/1565, O'Neill to F.O., 3 Dec. 1880, Enclosure No. 1.

In September–November of the following year O'Neill made a journey into Makua and Lomwe countries, which still provided a field for 'the supply of slaves which is steadily worked by Arab and other coast traders. . . . The Nyassa districts are not the only source for slaves brought to the coast.' The caravans were now much smaller; sometimes the slaves were incidental to other articles of commerce. But these trickles down to the coast added up to hundreds of people a year. Nowhere did Portuguese jurisdiction extend more than twenty-five miles inland. A hundred miles from the coast the Portuguese were just a name. F.O. 84/1595, O'Neill to F.O., 19 Nov. 1881.

cruiser *Wild Swan* joined in the second attack (her men were forbidden to land).[52] O'Neill was led to comment bitterly, 'A native slave dealing chief, within twenty miles of the capital of Moçambique, twice successfully repulsed the Portuguese forces sent to capture and punish him for that offense. On the second occasion, the force consisted of the whole garrison of Moçambique.'[53]

Possibly more serious than these disasters, however, was the decision taken in April 1881 by the new *Regenerador* Government in Lisbon to recall Governor-General Sarmento in disgrace. According to Morier, Sarmento had fallen victim to the intrigues of Joaquim José Machado, one-time director of public works in Moçambique, and the Geographical Society of Lisbon, because he had not only admitted the existence of a widespread slave-trade in Moçambique, as British consuls had been saying for years, but had also tried to do away with it.[54]

On 22 December 1880, Machado had given a long highly applauded talk at the Geographical Society in which he said that the Moçambique slave-trade was a myth, an invention of the Africans who fooled the British Consul O'Neill. The deception was also manufactured by the governor-general who had purposely misled his own government.[55] What Machado and the Geographical Society were really disturbed about, however, was that a continuing British interest in Moçambique could lead to territorial interests in the area. The Geographical Society in the 1870's and the 1880's was an intensely patriotic organization in so far as Africa was concerned.

Sarmento, in a letter to the President of the Society, accused Machado of either malice or ignorance. Slavery was an institution rooted in centuries of native traditions. An estimated 2,000 to 4,000 slaves a year were still being exported from Moçambique. The population from Cape Delgado to Angoche, a mixture of Mujoge, Banyan, Hindu, and African peoples felt themselves to be an important and idle class; they knew of

[52] Another item in the aborted treaty of 1880 was to permit British sailors to land on Moçambique soil in pursuit of slave-traders.

[53] F.O. 84/1595, O'Neill to F.O., 9 Mar. 1881.

[54] F.O. 84/1594, Morier to F.O., 25 Apr. 1881 and 25 May 1881.

[55] *Jornal da noite* (Lisbon), 24 Dec. 1880, 28 Dec. 1880, and *Diário de notícias*, 27 Dec. 1880.

no other trade and dealt freely with their half-caste brothers in Zanzibar, Madagascar, and the Comores. The governor made a long defence of Elton and O'Neill as men 'who knew the facts', men who went into the interior, men who could talk to the Africans, and men who could find things out for themselves.[56]

Machado's adherents in Moçambique were bestirring themselves. The colonists (either half-castes or degenerate third-generation Portuguese, in O'Neill's eyes) had formed a geographical society in Moçambique. There and in the pages of *Africa Oriental*, O'Neill came under attack. His trips were sarcastically referred to, it being said that native revolts broke out after his visits. It was well known that 'blacks were given up to idleness and drink and would never revolt against the whites unless some other element prompted them to do so'.[57] Much of this sentiment was fostered by the secretary-general of the province, Joaquim d'Almeida da Cunha. This anti-British sentiment was destined to increase for the next thirty years.

One aspect of new African policies being formed in Lisbon was found in the *Portária* of 23 June 1881 which told the governor-general to allow the free emigration of workers from Moçambique to the French colonies of Mayotte and Nossi Bé, subject to various regulations. Workers could be contracted for a period of three years, unless longer contracts were permitted to other nations. A depot was to be set up at Ibo, and an accredited French agent was to supervise all phases of the recruitment. Contracts were to be signed at Mayotte and Nossi Bé and then be sent back to Moçambique. A passport fee of about eleven shillings was charged for each worker. The workers had

[56] F.O. 84/1595, Sarmento to President of *Sociedade de Geografia*, 9 Feb. 1881. Also published under the title, *O governador geral da Província de Moçambique e as conferencias do engenheiro Machado* (Moçambique, 1881).

On 21 May Machado again addressed the Society—this time for three hours. He admitted the zeal of the authorities in Moçambique, but said the slave-trade was almost imperceptible. He quoted an attack by Elton on the Portuguese in Moçambique and referred to false charges made in Natal, Zanzibar, and the Transvaal. He expressed his fear of a British ambition for domination. *Diário de notícias*, 25 May 1881.

[57] *Africa Oriental*, ? Apr. 1881 (Date torn off.)

to be returned in the same manner in which they were brought (sailing vessels could be used). Article XI read hopefully: 'The natives who contract their services are like all other Portuguese subjects, entirely free, and therefore, as such, they are bound to comply with the conditions to which they may have agreed, and said conditions should be clearly explained by means of a competent interpreter to each native.'

The reaction of the Foreign Office was immediate. Throughout 1882 representations were made to Paris and Lisbon that the renewed migration to the French islands would encourage the slave-trade in districts over which the Portuguese themselves did not exercise control. The British minister was to explain to the Portuguese Government 'the extreme improbability of the natives of Ibo or any part of the East Coast of Africa spontaneously desiring to contract themselves for service in the French colonies'. When Foreign Minister António de Serpa Pimental observed that the 1881 arrangement was the same as the 1875 *portária* providing for the migration of workers to Natal and the Cape, he was pointedly told that this migration was voluntary and initiated by the workers themselves. Her Majesty's Government could not be convinced that the migration of workers to the islands could ever be voluntary. When news reached London that a French agent from Réunion had asked for similar permission, the reaction grew sharper.[58] Serpa Pimental said that his government was disposed to reject this proposal and to instruct the governor-general of Moçambique not to allow the migration to Mayotte and Nossi Bé if he had reason to believe it would give fresh impetus to the slave-trade. Although theoretically the Moçambique African was a Portuguese subject free to go and come as he chose, it was believed wise to draw up arrangements for his protection similar to 'ones drawn up in Provincial Portária of 2 August 1875 with respect to the engagement of colonialists for Natal.'[59]

In Ibo the French agent was a certain Gonzagas, an old inhabitant of the region known as the King of Ibo, formerly one of the largest slave owners in the district. A French ship now returned a crew of workers to Moçambique—taken from the

[58] F.O. 84/1616, F.O. to Baring, 20 Aug. 1882, and 11 Oct. 1882.
[59] F.O. 84/1616, Serpa Pimental to Baring, 4 Dec. 1882.

province as slaves years ago—to spread the word of good treatment and to demonstrate the safe return of labourers from the islands. But the effect was lost. A telegraphic dispatch of 16 February 1883 gave the first news of what happened at Ibo when the African population found out about the migration scheme. O'Neill's dispatch later gave the details. On 16 January 1883 a French man-of-war brought a M. Bandromat, planter at Mayotte, to Ibo. He was followed a few days later by the steamer *Emile Eloise* chartered for the conveyance of free emigrants. The arrival of the two vessels caused great excitement among the African villagers who absolutely refused to credit statements that only volunteers would be taken. 'Acting under this impression and determined to resist what they believed to be an unwarrantable encroachment upon the liberty of late years granted them, they assembled in large numbers and (I am told) attempted to disarm the sentries on guard.' The police commandant ordered his men to fire, and some twenty to thirty Africans were killed and many more wounded. Afterwards, most of the Africans fled from the island of Ibo to the mainland. The two French ships thereupon departed.

> This is a sad commencement—if not also the termination—[O'Neill wrote] to a scheme that was worked out . . . under an entire misconception of the native mind . . . the recollection of slavery and the slave trade in that district is far too vivid, as well as the well-known fact that even now it is the terminal point of a great slave route, to permit the native to accept the idea of 'free emigration'.[60]

An infinitesimal number of workers were contracted for the estates of Mayotte. In April 1884 a group of thirty-three were dispatched to Mayotte on short-term contracts, but six months later a chartered steamer had to return from Ibo without a single worker. The governor at Ibo was very strict about having the terms of the contract explained, with the result that most volunteers refused to go through with the arrangement.[61]

O'Neill estimated in 1888 that probably not more than a hundred workers had left the province of Moçambique for all

[60] F.O. 84/1640, O'Neill to F.O., 15 Feb. 1883.
[61] F.O. 84/1671, O'Neill to F.O., 5 Apr. 1884 and 17 Oct. 1884.

of the French colonies in the last six years.[62] The only part of the country where there was any willingness to sign a contract for two or three years for work abroad was at Inhambane and Delagoa Bay. Here Africans knew that they could work for high wages at no great distance from home. O'Neill did not think that de Lesseps's Inter-Oceanic Panama Canal Company would find any workers after it had been given permission to recruit in the territory by a *portária* of 29 December 1887.[63] What was so extraordinary about this unlikely piece of labour business was that it summed up in its ridiculous way what Moçambique meant to both French and Portuguese (and to the English as well): it was seen simply as a labour depot. This was an attitude now so real and so accepted that it would not, could

[62] On his journey to Nyasa in late 1883 O'Neill had encountered a number of traders from the neighbourhood of Ibo collecting slaves and ivory on the eastern shore of Lake Shirwa. 'The traders were not pure Portuguese, but belonged to that caste that go by the name of "Africanos", i.e. Portuguese of colonial descent, in whom may often be found a mixture with native blood. Ignorant . . . many of them criminals and possessing all the vices of the lowest class of whites to be found on this coast, it would be difficult to meet with a set capable of more mischief amongst the native tribes of the interior than they.' These men had come to those parts only in the last several years, and O'Neill supposed it was in connexion with obtaining a labour supply for the French scheme. F.O. 84/1671, O'Neill to F.O., 3 Feb. 1884.

In Lisbon, Minister George Petre continued to deliver his government's complaints about the French scheme. On one occasion Foreign Minister Bocage said he thought the migration was good because the African workers would return to the colony accustomed to regular work and be a valuable addition to the labour supply of the colony. He admitted that the scheme had probably stimulated the slave-trade of the interior, but that the alternative for the unhappy creatures was death and that their lives were saved and their condition improved. F.O. 84/1669, George Petre to F.O., 15 June 1884.

O'Neill was not in disagreement with the Portuguese position that Africans needed to learn to labour. His suggestion was for industrial, not religious missions. 'It is marvelous to see the perfection with which a black will learn to sing a hymn, dress in European clothing, and mimic the manners of his white master, and equally striking to observe the rapidity with which these accomplishments disappear. . . . The one quality most wanting in the native temperament is stability, this want is best met, not by theoretical teaching, but by habits of practical and religious industry.' F.O. 84/1671, O'Neill to F.O., 8 Dec. 1884.

[63] *Boletim oficial de Moçambique*, 3 Mar. 1888. The terms of the decree were about the same as those of previous conventions. A year later the Conseil-Général of Guadeloupe approved the introduction of Portuguese African labourers into that Caribbean island.

not, disappear, and the critical history of Moçambique had to be told in large part in terms of its supply of African workers.

Another *portária*, of 24 November 1887, extended the area of French recruitment to Moçambique island and Inhambane, while a decree of 16 April 1889 opened Quelimane to French agents. In both decrees recruitment for Réunion as well as for Mayotte and Nossi Bé was permitted. At Inhambane, Régis Frères collected some 400 workers, since the cessation of the usual migration to Natal left a surplus of labourers. Natal now relied on workers arriving overland and for two years no ships had touched at Inhambane. But with that single shipment to Réunion, the Inhambane source dried up.

O'Neill was totally satisfied that the regulations controlling the emigration were closely followed. 'There can be no revival in this year of grace 1888 of the manner in which *engagés libres* were collected in the years 1856–1859.' He believed that it was now wrong to speak of the French as engaging in the slave-trade to Réunion, 'while at the same time we take up an attitude of unconcern or inactive disapproval toward the Arab slave trade of the interior, which is root, stem, and branch of the evil'.[64]

The Nyasa trade, a part of the last terrible traffic in humanity from Central Africa, had fluctuated in the last half century. Now it was growing again, at a rate alarming to British missionaries of the region. The trade was principally in the hands of Arab merchants, or their agents, and the Yao, and the participation of Portuguese subjects was limited. But two of the slave routes from Nyasa did terminate on the Moçambique coast, one near Ibo and the other near Quelimane. In 1880 Dr. Robert Laws of the Free Church Mission at Livingstonia reported a caravan collecting at the southern end of the lake. The caravan passed down the Shire and was eventually cleared, according to Vice Consul Nunes at Quelimane, from Quizungo River, some forty miles north of Quelimane. The area between Quelimane and the Quizungo had become an infamous smugglers and slave coast. It had not been visited by British cruisers since 1875. Several Portuguese visitations had

[64] F.O. 84/1901, O'Neill to F.O., 14 May 1888.

accomplished little, and for the greater part of the 1880's caravans of slaves from the lower Nyasa and the Shire highlands were brought down to be traded for powder and guns and shipped off to Madagascar.[65]

Dr. Laws had been in Nyasa for five years and had travelled widely in the region and had a good knowledge of commerce there. In 1881 he wrote to O'Neill from Bandowe on the west shore of the lake that he estimated some 2,000 to 3,000 slaves a year came from that side of the lake and passed down to the coast. At Kota Kota he had seen many people in slave yokes.[66] Two missionaries, Chauncey Maples and A. C. Goldfinch, on a trip in 1881 through Makua and Medo country encountered large caravans from Nyasa, one of not less than 2,000 people on its way to Quissanga (a point on the mainland a few miles below Ibo).[67] For a while this route rivalled the route down the Rovuma and up to Lindi or Kilwa. In 1883 Laws reported the traffic to be even more vigorous. Slaves were being ferried across the lake in large numbers, and the country on both sides of the lake was fraught with warfare.[68]

After 1886 there was a British consulate at Zomba in Nyasa. In one of his first dispatches Consul G. S. Hawes confirmed that the slave-trade was carried on freely in all districts of Nyasa. 'It is unhesitatingly stated by the natives at Zomba that at Luna's near Quelimane, a considerable trade is carried on, and it is an undoubted fact that Matapwiri, an important chief residing near Kulanji, sells slaves freely to the Arabs in charge of caravans proceeding by that route to Quelimane.'[69] Through the last years of the decade small caravans from both banks of the Nyasa made their way down to the Quelimane coast, to Luna's or to the Boror estates. 'The slaves may not be disposed as slaves,' wrote Acting Consul John Buchanan, 'though to all intents and purposes the system adopted meets the requirements of slavery.' Whether the slaves were 'ransomed' or not was of no concern to the traders who had their ivory

[65] F.O. 84/1564, O'Neill to F.O., 12 Jan. 1880.

[66] F.O. 84/1616, O'Neill to F.O., 12 Jan. 1882.

[67] Chauncey Maples and A. C. Goldfinch, 'Makua Land between the Rivers Rovuma and Luli', *Proceedings of the Royal Geographical Society*, iv (February, 1882), 79–90.

[68] F.O. 84/1640, O'Neill to F.O., 30 Apr. 1883.

[69] F.O. 84/1751, G. S. Hawes to F.O., 27 Jan. 1886.

carried to the coast and then sold the porters.[70] Most of the traders were from the Zanzibar coast who came to Nyasa with a supply of goods. These were bartered among the Ngoni for slaves and ivory which were then taken in a quick journey to the Quelimane coast and sold. The profits in the transaction were large; they went into the pockets of the traders or his agent who returned up-country, bought the goods commissioned by the coast merchants, who had first advanced the trading stock.[71] Slave-traders from Zambézia, who had twenty years before followed Livingstone up the Shire, were no longer very active.[72]

Portuguese authorities were at last in a position seriously to curb—and finally to curtail—the export trade. Administrative or military posts were being set up at points where the dhow traffic had shipped slaves, and a strengthened naval force was patrolling these sections of the coast. At Umfusi, at Boror, at Musimbwa, and at Cape Delgado new posts were established. An attempt to occupy Quizungo, however, had ended with the annihilation of the Portuguese force. No longer was any attempt made to hide or deny the existence of the slave-trade. The *Boletim* for 1887 and 1888 was filled with accounts of raids on suspected inlets, descriptions of slaves in sticks, and of small expeditions marching off to cut caravan routes from the interior. The governor-general's decree of 22 October 1887 creating a military post in the district of Boror read in part:

> In consequence of the absence of any government authority in that district, caravans arrive there from the interior to barter, not only the ivory they carry, but also children of both sexes who are

[70] F.O. 84/1889, John Buchanan to F.O., 10 Jan. 1889.

[71] F.O. 84/1889, Buchanan to F.O., 29 Jan. 1889.

[72] The traffic from the northern end of the lake and westward continued into the early 1890's, but few caravans passed down to Quissanga, most of them going along the upper route to the Zanzibar coast. Some renegade Portuguese subjects participated, but the burden of the activity was borne by others. O'Neill's dire predictions that the human plundering would spread south along the lake or down toward the coast failed to come true. F.O. 84/1901, O'Neill to F.O., 31 May 1888.

This dispatch is perhaps the best description available of the forces and people involved in the Nyasa trade. To read O'Neill and Hawes and Buchanan at the same time is to realize again the extraordinary capacities of the consul at Moçambique.

bought by certain traders in the town of Quelimane. These abuses do not immediately reach the ears of the government which is unable therefore to punish or suppress them. It is imperative that this state of things should cease, for it is a disgrace to us, and it discredits us in the eyes of foreigners, chiefly English, who often make use of this route going to and from the stations of Mandala and Blantyre.[73]

By 1890 Portugal was embroiled with England in Central African territorial disputes, and the purpose and continuity of slaving reports were broken. With the appointment of H. H. Johnston as consul at Moçambique in 1889, a new order came into the Anglo-Portuguese relationship. Elton and O'Neill had been, in a sense, slave officers; Johnston was a consular officer. Nor was Johnston so much concerned with the Nyasa slave-trade as his predecessor. Although more friendly to Portuguese pretensions in Africa than most British consular officers, Johnston was now in favour of reducing Portuguese territory in East Africa to the narrowest dimensions, but only because of alleged incompetence, not because of native policies.[74]

A trickle of traffic still ran from Moçambique. In 1892 Acting Consul William Churchill received direct intelligence of two dhows shipping slaves at the Likuga River, some twenty-five miles north of Quelimane, and from the Ligonia River, a few miles further north. Other dhows were seen at Moma. The slaves had been brought down by the south end of Lake Shirwa and taken to several spots north of Quelimane. They were to be carried to Madagascar coast. Churchill's informant, the

[73] At this time in Lisbon at a meeting of the Geographical Society, at which were present Foreign Secretary Henrique Barros Gomes, former Foreign Secretary José Barbosa do Bocage, and the explorer Alexandre de Serpa Pinto, a committee was appointed to establish an Anti-Slavery League under the patronage of the King of Portugal. The Society stated that in creating the League they would be reasserting Portugal's constant adherence to the cause of humanity and civilization in Africa. In supporting the mission undertaken by Cardinal Lavigerie, the Portuguese were joining in the action of the whole civilized world. On the dispatch to London from the British minister George Petre announcing the League's formation, an under-secretary made the comment (initialed by Lord Salisbury): 'They have discovered that the suppression of slavery is the traditional policy of Portugal. They have no sense of the ridiculous.' F.O. 84/1965, Petre to F.O., 28 Mar. 1889.

[74] F.O. 84/2051, H. H. Johnston to F.O., 17 Mar. 1890.

English trader Frederic Gardner, blamed the traffic here on 'the disgraceful way the Portuguese allow all these things to continue'—by not asserting their authority on the section of coast between Moma and Likuga rivers.[75] Churchill passed the intelligence on to officials in Moçambique, who did not seem much interested. The *Clamor africano* confidently stated that the coastal slave-trade had ceased, and where it lingered it was on such a small scale that its occurence was rare and exceedingly difficult to discover. All civilization could do now was to demonstrate to the people of Africa how wrong it was to trade their fellow beings and relations.[76]

Two years later Consul Carnegie Ross, who had for a time been vice-consul at Quelimane, could not verify a report by H. H. Johnston that Quelimane was still the centre for a slave-trade towards which all Yao and Arab traders directed their steps. Ross had visited the alleged trading centres and had found nothing to indicate a slave-trade there. In Quelimane itself a mild form of domestic slavery prevailed which 'involved little hardship on the natives'. As for the rumoured dhow traffic from the coast between Angoche and Quelimane he had no knowledge to confirm or deny.[77] Consul Ross was no more interested than, according to Churchill, Portuguese authorities had been. Portuguese armed forces occupied the larger part of the province in the next ten years. The last trickle of the slave-trade dried up. On this issue there would be very little more controversy. With the growing needs of the Rand mines for Moçambique labour, it even came to be that the moral advantage in this long dialogue passed—almost imperceptibly perhaps —to the Portuguese.

In Portuguese East Africa, then, the problems of slavery and the slave-trade, dominant though the issue was in Anglo-

[75] F.O. 84/2225, William Churchill to F.O., 3 Aug. 1892. The Gardner dispatch, undated, is included.

In August the governor-general complimented the Governor of Ibo on his energetic work against the slave-trade, which led Churchill to wonder just what had been done, since Portuguese gunboats and provincial governors were virtually powerless to cope with the silent dhow traffic. F.O. 84/2225, 29 Aug. 1892.

[76] *O clamor africano* (Quelimane), 19 May 1892.

[77] F.O. 63/1280, A Carnegie Ross to F.O., 14 June 1894.

Portuguese discussions, was a diminishing one. In Portuguese West Africa the same issue was now only of occasional importance, but it did not disappear. The problem grew in importance, quietly to be sure, but none the less seriously.

São Tomé continued to demand Angolan workers. Cocoa was now becoming an important crop and was soon to be an abundant article of export. Labour shortages were as acute as they had ever been. After the abolition of indentured slavery in 1876, many of the African cultivators on the island took themselves into the bush where they formed villages and tended small farms of their own. They refused to work on the *roças* (estates) and the planters began once again to try to recruit in Liberia and on the Kroo coast, but the previous bad faith of employers who had made it difficult for workers to return home after the expiration of their contract was a serious obstacle. For want of workers many plantations had to be abandoned.

A decree of 1878 permitting the introduction of Angolan labourers into the island under more lenient conditions,[78] gave an impetus to agriculture. In 1879 and 1880 some 3,000 workers were brought in. Captured in the interior, brought down to Novo Redondo and Benguela, sold to agents of planters at prices ranging from four to six pounds sterling, registered and contracted by government authority for a five-year period—a steady stream of African men and women were sent off to permanent labour on the islands. By general reports they were well fed, well cared for, and well housed. But they were never to be allowed to leave. Most workers were locked up at night to prevent their running away. The mortality rate was high, running in some years close to 20 per cent., and was attributed to damp climate, different food, and, most often, to homesickness. Illegally caught and immorally retained, the São Tomé worker passed into a condition of life little differentiated from slavery.[79]

[78] *Boletim oficial de Angola*, 27 Mar. 1880.

[79] F.O. 84/1616, Consul A. Cohen to F.O., 16 July 1882. Cohen had recently visited São Tomé. This is the first really substantial report of the São Tomé labour system. The Foreign Office's reaction to Cohen's report was one of indifference. Believing that the Law Officers' ruling of 1878 cut off any British intervention, the Foreign Office was concerned only with what example this emigration scheme might offer the French in their search for labour.

In search of workers for the islands' expanding plantations, the officials of São Tomé and Principe concluded a treaty with the King of Dahomey in 1885 (which Portugal said she would submit to the Great Powers for approval), making the Dahomey coast a Portuguese protectorate. The king promised to give up his yearly slaughter of sacrificial slaves for compensation and to give up 200 labourers instead for the plantations. Foreign Minister José Barbosa do Bocage was at great pains to convince England the arrangement would not encourage the local slave-trade. The Negroes would be free from the minute their feet touched Portuguese soil, and a labour contract would be made with them for a period of three years, at the end of which they could either remain on the islands or leave. 'No one could deny', Bocage said, 'that the gain to humanity would be cheaply purchased if these poor slaves were to be rescued from their shackles at the cost of three years labour under proper treatment and restrictions.'[80] The arrangement lasted into the 1890's,[81] drawing some humanitarian fire in England where by some remote association Portugal was held responsible for outrages in Dahomey, but it was never very successful in providing a secure source of workers.

In fact the *only* reliable source was Angola, and this is where they came from, more in good years, fewer in bad, but steadily they came. Their passage had become an accepted aspect of

[80] F.O. 84/1708, Petre to F.O., 24 Sept. 1885. The Decree of 29 Dec. 1885 gives the modest details of the Portuguese protectorate but makes no mention of the gift of slaves. When questioned on the subject in the Chamber of Deputies by the foremost Republican colonialist Consiglièri Pedroso, Minister for Overseas Manuel Pinheiro Chagas said the treaty was both useful and necessary. 'There was a dearth of labour in the province of São Tomé, and the treaty permitted this to be supplied by means of contracts under the shadow of the Portuguese flag, which precluded the possibility of any resemblance to slavery.' F.O. 84/1766, Petre to F.O., 11 Feb. 1886.

[81] Each year Portugal was more assured of her contribution to African dignity. Now that African colonies gave a distinction and prestige, Portugal saw herself as a considerable European power and a great moral force. At a solemn meeting of the Geographical Society to welcome home the explorers Serpa Pinto and Augusto Cardozo from an expedition to Central Africa many pious pronouncements were made, one of them being that of the Society's president. Turning to the king, he said: 'In North America, a great statue of liberty has been recently inaugurated, but you, sir, have raised a far nobler statue, not made of bronze and marble, but of human flesh by the freedom you have granted the Negro race.' *Jornal do comércio*, 14 Dec. 1886.

Angolan life. For the last twenty-five years of the century, the following are the statistics of *serviçaes* engaged for the islands of São Tomé and Principe.[82]

1876–1884	10,535	1892	1,409
1885	2,066	1893	2,130
1886	1,468	1894	2,223
1887	1,681	1895	2,173
1888	1,664	1896	2,691
1889	1,425	1897	3,786
1890	8,066	1898	3,131
1891	3,191	1899	3,510
		1900	4,740

During the decade the traffic seldom was an important consideration in Anglo-Portuguese discussions. For about a year in 1894–5, however, the Angola–São Tomé migration scheme came under particular scrutiny, foreshadowing the polemical decade ahead. In June 1894, Joseph Pease, M.P., sent a letter to Sir Edward Grey, Under-Secretary of State for Foreign Affairs, asking if the conditions described in enclosures represented any breach of the Brussels Act. The first extract was by a representative of a well known but unnamed Liverpool firm [presumably John Holt's]. It said that slaves were being constantly bought in the hinterland of Angola and brought down to Benguela and Novo Redondo for shipment to Luanda, thence sent up-country to Cazengo, or on to the islands. Of late years the supply of able-bodied men was insufficient and scores of little children were being carried off to the plantations. The second enclosure was a letter from Captain (Retired) Algernon Littleton, R.N., who told a story about the same. When he was on the coast, some ten years or more ago, the system was regarded as just so much slavery, and he had no doubts that it remained pretty much as it had been, 'since the Portuguese are not progressive'.[83]

In response to the Foreign Office's request for an explanation of the Pease correspondence, Acting Consul W. S. R. Brock, a British merchant, gave *his* view of the system based on 'practical knowledge gained . . . over the last eight years'. He began

[82] From *Diário de notícias*, 4 Nov. 1904.
[83] F.O. 63/1447, Pease to Grey, 5 June 1894.

by saying that the Liverpool letter talked of slaves, which conjured up in the popular British indignation visions of traffic in human flesh. 'The essential difference between slavery and contracted labour is that whereas the former *is* slavery pure and simple, the latter is hired labour under Government supervision. To assume therefore that they are one and the same is to try and fit facts to a theory and prejudice a good cause by taking for granted what is to a great extent hearsay.' It was nonsense about the children, since they would be useless on a coffee plantation. A few children might go with their mothers, but only in order not to be separated from them (what happened to children who didn't go with their mothers, Brock did not say). Cohen's report of 1882, according to Brock, was more the work of a prosecutor than of a judge. Climate on the islands was as good as in their own country, and the food was better. As for *mal du pays*, that could 'be translated into a feeling of regret for having been so foolish as to have so far committed themselves as to be obliged to work'. Death rates were closer to 3 per cent. than 19 per cent. Brock then proceeded to attack the *Anti-Slavery Reporter* and Lord Mayo (see the following chapter) for peddling misinformation. He closed his report with a stirring defence of the system.

My opinion is that, taking it all round, the *serviçaes* are well treated and well cared for, that they are not unhappy, and that there is no hardship in the way they are worked.

It must be remembered that they are drawn from the lowest types of humanity, and have none of the instincts of civilization; and that morally they are improved rather than deteriorated by their more regular life and work.

The labour question is far too complicated to discuss here. . . . The native hates work and cannot be got to see the necessity of it. The climate is such that the white man cannot long sustain manual labour under the burning sun. . . .

On how the problem is to be solved depends much of the future of Angola. One thing is certain, that the provinces of Angola would suffer immense damage by the abolition of the present system and that it would mean absolute ruin to the island of São Tomé.[84]

[84] F.O. 63/1447, Brock to F.O., 28 Aug. 1894.

In earlier years such a dispatch would have drawn a quick rebuke, but the Foreign Office concluded that the report contained much controversial material—which it would be better not to show to Pease.

But if the Foreign Office did not rise to the familiar bait, Clayton Pickersgill, British Consul at Luanda, did. In his dispatch of 15 December 1894 Pickersgill said that he had now had a chance to examine the evidence which Brock exerted himself to explain away. The Pease correspondence was true in all its important features. The burden of the blame lay with the *curador dos serviçaes* who promoted the export trade. The question was not how the workers were treated on the island but how they were obtained. In the last twenty-one months, Pickersgill had travelled three times on steamers carrying *serviçaes*. He had talked to some of the workers: one had been traded by his village chief to a Portuguese trader for goods; another had been given to pay for a debt; a woman had been given in exchange for a woman stolen from her people, made a slave, and finally handed over to a Portuguese trader. Had the curator gone among the workers with an honest interpreter and asked whether they had engaged to work for five years of their own free will, he would have received a negative answer in every case. But had he done this, there would have been a storm of complaints and he would have been dismissed. In Benguela, Pickersgill had talked with the agent of a European trading station about prices and supplies of different types of workers. At Cazengo the manager of a coffee estate told him that when the time expired for 500 *serviçaes*, they could be recontracted for another five years without their consent, or knowledge, by taking the list of their names to the nearest magistrate. 'Contract labour is simply a form of the Slave Trade.' What was the cure? 'As long as there is a wilderness with creatures in it who are no man's care, so long will they be regarded as game, and the only sure way to put a stop to poaching is for the government to occupy the country it claims to possess.'[85]

Pickersgill wrote a supplement in 1897 to this report. He had then made an extensive visit to São Tomé. The *serviçal* system,

[85] F.O. 63/1447, A. Clayton Pickersgill to F.O., 15 Dec. 1894.

he admitted, was tempered by the humanity of the Portuguese character and by good treatment. But the wrongs were glaringly evident. Taken as a slave, sold as a slave, the worker was kept in servitude to the end of his days. There was a native song common among the workers. 'In São Tomé there's a door for going in, but none for going out.' Pickersgill estimated that 20 per cent. of the *serviçaes* died the first year, 50 per cent. the first five years. The obligation of the Portuguese Government was clear, to forbid further export and to repatriate gradually the workers from the islands.[86]

The Foreign Office gave momentary consideration to Pickersgill's 1894 report. 'The question is whether', one minute read, 'we should now in any form renew our efforts in favour of the natives. Slavery is nominally abolished in the Portuguese colonies, and I think for the present we had better leave it alone.' Lord Kimberley's opinion was, 'I agree.' The dispatch of 1897 touched no conscience at all: 'No action. Leave it alone.'

[86] F.O. 63/1447, Pickersgill to F.O., 16 Mar. 1897.

CHAPTER V

Voices of Protest

By the 1850's English anti-slavery militancy had lost some of its vigour. The major battles against the slave-trade and against slavery had been won, and there was disagreement now on how the remaining tentacles of the traffic should be cut off. The movement itself, as it became smaller, seemed to grow less militant, more conservative. In the 1850's and 1860's into the 1870's the policies pursued by the British Government against the scattered vestiges of the African slave-trade were usually more active, more purposeful than were the courses of action advocated by popular and even philanthropic opinion in the country. But on two points the Government and philanthropists were generally agreed: conditions in the Portuguese African territories, particularly Moçambique, were disgraceful and the restrictive tariff policies of Portugal, which denied the formal functioning of legitimate commerce, perpetuated these conditions. Toward the later years of the century philanthropic opinion moved ahead of official British representations in denouncing alleged outrages in Angola and Moçambique.

The *Anti-Slavery Reporter*, whatever the other vagaries of the British and Foreign Anti-Slavery Society, followed a clear and consistent direction on Portuguese Africa. Introducing an article reprinted from the Liverpool *Albion*, the *Reporter* commented in October 1853:

> We take occasion to call the attention of our readers to a subject which can never be worn out, a subject the oftener it is mentioned the more it excites the indignation of the philanthropist, while it awakens all the sympathy of our nature in favour of those unfortunates who are the victims of its horrors: we mean the Slave-Trade!

The article itself was a recitation of incidents and rumours having to do with the traffic from Moçambique to Cuba. The attack centred on the corruption of local officials without whose participation the export of slaves would have been impossible. In 1853 there were still hopes in England for the regeneration of Portuguese Africa. The *Albion* was encouraged that a society had been formed, headed by Sá da Bandeira, 'a philanthropist of Portugal', to lease the province of Moçambique, then to colonize it, work its mines, and introduce a system of trade with the interior, thus 'gradually removing the chiefs from the practice of slave dealing'. Moçambique was expected to become a second Brazil, another Australia, and could afterwards regenerate the home country.[1]

The following month the *Reporter* reprinted a letter to the *Daily News* from a correspondent in Lisbon who felt it 'his public duty to lay the facts before the British public'. He described the coastal operations in Moçambique: 'The slave trader goes there in two characters: the first is as a contrabandista, with an immense cargo of goods, upon part of which he pays a duty; these goods are then put into exchange for slaves; now commences the character of the dealer, and having had his manacles etc. conveyed to the spot, proceeds to his shipment.' Now that Governor Alfredo Pinto de Magalhães was to be removed, humanity could be congratulated, but unhappily he was to be replaced by a callow youth unfit to govern the province (Vasco Guedes).[2]

The *Morning Herald*'s Lisbon correspondent wrote to describe the *furor* created in the Chamber of Deputies by the alleged out-fitting in Oporto of two slavers for Angola. Adding his commentary on the situation, the correspondent said that hopes for the extinction of the slave-trade were baseless, since as soon as vigilance was relaxed, slavers returned in droves. Nor should his English readers take seriously the furious nature of the debate. It did not reflect any genuine philanthropic sentiments. 'The indignation expressed by Count Thomar, and

[1] The *Anti-Slavery Reporter*, 1 Oct. 1853, pp. 230–1. The extract was from the *Albion*, 18 July 1853.

In my references to the *Reporter*, I will identify the issue by date, not by volume number. The *Reporter* went through three series, changing its volume number each time. There are, in addition, inaccuracies within each series.

[2] *Reporter*, 1 Nov. 1853, p. 252.

re-echoed by all the journals adverse to the government, is all pure humbug. Nobody here feels the least horror of slave trading.'[3]

It remained for David Livingstone to give English impatience, contempt, and self-righteousness their final form. Livingstone's influence on the Foreign Office's policy towards Portugal in Africa was probably negligible, given the coincidence of his and their attitudes, but his influence in giving a colour and cast to what were essentially anti-Portuguese sentiments in the breasts of English philanthropists was great. In terms of popular opinion Livingstone reached a wide audience. His views were dominant in much of the press and many of the pulpits; English opinion on Portuguese Africa in the 1860's came pretty close to being Livingstone's opinion. Livingstone's sentiments were also sympathetic to commercial interests in the country.[4]

Bemused by the commerce in ivory, beeswax, and palm oil in Angola, Livingstone found the slave-trade there spoken of in the past tense. In a letter to *The Times* he gave a rosy picture of the colony's future and the near extinction of the slave-trade.[5] But in the face of stagnation along the Zambesi he began to believe that only sturdy English enterprise would save the day for moral decency and progress. Until his second expedition, however, Livingstone—and his audience—could have some expectations for a Portuguese resurgence.[6] After the Zambesi expedition, whose unhappy outcome the Portuguese in Moçambique had virtually nothing to do with, Livingstone's

[3] *The Morning Herald*, 16 and 24 Jan. 1854.

[4] Ironically, Livingstone's basic quarrel with the Portuguese in Africa was probably not over the slaving issue at all, but over the priority of exploration in Central Africa, a subject on which Livingstone's and Portugal's vanities collided head-on. But the outlet for most of the missionary's exacerbation was in fulminating against the slaving habits in Portuguese Africa and the moral delinquency of its inhabitants.

[5] *The Times*, 24 Dec. 1856.

[6] On presenting Livingstone with the key to the City, the Chamberlain, Sir J. Key, perorated: 'The African mind is awake. The Portuguese colonies are casting off their jealousies. The slave traders, taught by your wise counsels, are turning their thoughts to the prospect of a more lawful commerce, insomuch that it seems not too much to expect, that if a ship were to sail up the Zambesi river tomorrow, not only might it soon be filled with the most valuable materials for our home manufacturers, but every facility for international barter would be afforded by the natives themselves.' *The Times*, 21 May 1857.

temper snapped. From then on he had few kind words for Portugal's Africa and even modified some of his earlier generous remarks.[7] In a lecture before the British Association in Bath in 1864, Livingstone recounted the familiar tales of slave-dealers (some of them only remotely Portuguese) dogging his tracks up the Shire, 'now a valley of dry bones'. In one hut he came upon two skeletons, and a little one rolled up in a mat between them. This was the result of slave raiding forays by Portuguese Africans among the Nyanja. Thereupon Livingstone launched into an assessment of conditions in Moçambique and England's responsibility. He hated to put the blame for being baffled on anyone else and he did not want to cast a slur on the Portuguese in Europe where men like Count Lavrádio and Sá da Bandeira were as anxious to see the abolition of the slave-trade as anyone else. But there was an evil done by the assertion in Europe of dominion in Africa, when that dominion was asserted by only a few half-castes, children of convicts and black women, by people who had to pay tribute to the Africans. How could this sort of dominion benefit Portugal? Portugal gained nothing but a bad name as the first nation to take up the slave-trade and the last to relinquish it. It was time for England to take new and vigorous action. England could not forget her obligation to the great community of nations.[8]

Three years before Livingstone's return from the Zambesi, the British and Foreign Anti-Slavery Society had noted the 'venality of the Portuguese officials' in Moçambique and the lack of hope for improvement unless the metropolitan government chose to deal summarily with the evil. According to the *Reporter*, England permitted Portugal to exercise sovereignty over a great extent of the East African coastline only on the understanding that the ports there be thrown open, 'thus practically laying down the principle that freedom of commerce is

[7] In a letter from the Shire cataracts, 6 July 1863, to Horace Waller, Livingstone wrote: 'I regret ever believing that Portuguese statesmen had any desire for the civilization of Africa, but I did so for the best.' The letter is in the archives of the Society for the Propagation of the Gospel, to which I am indebted for making a copy available to me. Professor I. Schapera gave me the reference to the letter.

[8] *Reporter*, 1 Oct. 1864, pp. 221–5. The speech was given 19 Sept. 1864.

one of the most potent means of suppressing the slave trade'. Livingstone's expedition had really been to open up the entire Zambesi to trade, but the Portuguese had thwarted him.[9]

Parliamentary opinion on the subject was at first more sympathetic, even kindly. In a debate in the House of Lords in 1861 on establishing a consulate in Moçambique Lord Stratheden supported the measure in order that England might 'assist Portugal in repressing the slave trade'. He believed that if the governor-general honestly performed his duty, anti-slavery efforts would be successful, but so long as functionaries connived at the trade, it could not be put down. Lord Wodehouse, opposing the establishing of a consulate, said a consul would only get bogged down in tiresome correspondence and remonstrating with Portuguese officials. Lord Brougham was inclined to the belief that the Portuguese Government had been most zealous in their desire to abolish the slave-trade. According to the Bishop of Oxford, a staunch humanitarian, a consulate at Moçambique 'would result in light being thrown on deeds of darkness', and if the light of civilized Europe were thrown on Portuguese activities in eastern Africa, official connivance at the slave-trade would be prevented. What was needed was a moral presence. Men like Dr. Livingstone could not serve humanity in Africa so long as under the shadow of a Christian power 'the abomination of the slave trade was suffered to continue'.[10]

In Commons, on 26 July, Mr. Buxton allied himself with the bishop, Lord Brougham, the Anti-Slavery Society, and *The Economist*. A consul and a couple of ships of war might just be able to do the job. At the end of an indecisive debate, Lord Palmerston rose to explain the difficulties of colonial administration in Moçambique, the great distances between centres of authority, and the remoteness of Lisbon from scenes of local corruption. He did not despair either of seeing the export trade restricted or slavery itself abolished in Moçambique. The colony needed its labour for its own purposes of cultivation.

[9] *Reporter*, 1 Jan. 1861, p. 13. Sources for the *Reporter*'s attacks on Portugal were varied: clippings from English and continental papers, letters, lectures, articles, and books.

[10] *Hansard*, Third Series, v. 164, 855–75, 15 July 1861.

He really saw no immediate need for a consul in such an unhealthy station.[11]

A year later Palmerston was somewhat less bland about the state of affairs in Portuguese Africa. In response to a question about the migration of workers to São Tomé and its legality under the Treaty of 1842, Palmerston said that Her Majesty's Government had received repeated reports that a slave-trade was being carried on under the pretence of a free labour migration and that the Government was making inquiries. 'I am sorry to have to add to this statement that the love and habit of the slave trade have been so ingrained in the Spanish and Portuguese nations that, in spite of all the efforts of their respective governments, the colonial authorities . . . do perseveringly violate the orders of their governments and the treaties by which Spain and Portugal are bound.'[12]

In 1867 the Anti-Slavery Society took direct action. With the Comité Français d'Emancipation, the Society had a delegation visit the King of Portugal at the Tuileries on the occasion of his visit to Paris in 1867. The English delegation drew a deplorable picture, using mostly Livingstone's words, of conditions in Moçambique: deserts where gardens had been a short time before, villages destroyed, and the people terrorized by slave-traders. 'The Committee trust they will be pardoned if they venture to insist upon the principal remedy which that good man suggests as being the most effectual means of putting an end to this hateful and dreadful traffic in human beings. He [Livingstone] asserts that the slave traders deal in Negroes because the Portuguese ports are closed to legitimate commerce.' In the discussion the delegation also brought up the matter of the *liberto* migration to the islands. They were then assured that the king was deeply interested in their petition, and in an ante-chamber following his visitation, Foreign Minister José Ribeiro informed the English gentlemen that the traffic to São Tomé was being restricted and that the slave-trade in East Africa was practised only by Arabs.[13]

[11] *Hansard*, Third Series, v. 164, 1641–9, 22 July 1864.

[12] *Hansard*, Third Series, v. 168, 1744, 18 July 1862.

[13] *Reporter*, 15 Apr. 1867. The English delegation was made up of Joseph Cooper, Arthur Albright, Edmund Sturge, R. I. Fowler, J. Wilson, and John B. Hart.

At two meetings afterwards, the delegations from America, England, France, Holland, and Spain—making up the Paris Anti-Slavery Conference—asked the study committee to draft a letter to the Portuguese monarch. The bluntness of the text probably meant that Joseph Cooper, of the British and Foreign Anti-Slavery Society, wrote most of it. The letter, sent on 5 December 1867, read in part:

Your Majesty is aware that your African possessions are the scene of a most frightful Slave-Trade, extending over the whole of the East Coast, and that in the provinces of Angola and Benguela, the habit of indolence, the cruel practices, and the debauchery which always accompany slavery, render all civilization impossible and spread amongst the heathen population a horror of the Christian name.

If, in the present century, and notwithstanding their possession of every element of greatness, the noble Spanish and Portuguese nations appear to be deprived of that glory which not long ago they had achieved in both hemispheres, it is impossible not to believe that the Divine favour has been turned aside from them in consequence of their perseverance in maintaining the Slave-Trade and Slavery, after setting European nations the wicked example of instituting these crimes.[14]

If there came to be a sameness in the nature of the English protest, it was not only because there was a sameness in the slaving practices of Angola and Moçambique, it was because the sources of information publicly available were limited. Bluebooks, containing dispatches received by the Admiralty and the Foreign Office, were the most reliable sources for information and indignation. Not until the 1880's and the 1890's would there be more than a modest bibliography of accounts by travellers and residents in the Portuguese territories. Until then, the public had to rely on the published or lectured commentary of Livingstone, MacLeod, Captain Sullivan, Lovett Cameron, Young, Winwood Reade, and Monteiro. The literature was not unprejudiced.

Captain G. L. Sullivan's *Dhow Chasing in Zanzibar Waters and on the Eastern Coast of Africa* was the narrative of five

[14] In *Special Report of the Paris Anti-Slavery Conference* (London, 1868). The report was published by the Anti-Slavery Society.

years service in the suppression of the slave-trade, one of the best published accounts of how the Indian Ocean Slave traffic worked. Sullivan did not have anything original to write about the Portuguese participation in the trade—in fact most of his material was borrowed from other sources for the long section. 'Portuguese Possessions', but Sullivan became a much quoted authority in the humanitarian arsenal. The fault lay, as always, with Portugal's excessive claims to territory in Moçambique, in the venality of her officials there, and in the corruption of the population. Even these comments were second hand; only when he anchored in Moçambique harbour did Sullivan write from his own observations. In this case a group of sixteen Africans sought refuge on the *Daphne*, some with lacerations on their backs, another with an iron ring around his leg, others with tales of brutality and murder. Told that they were free Negroes, Sullivan replied that they were slaves. 'Ask any of the ten thousand Negroes that crowd the streets of Moçambique where they are from, and the reply is the same as that of the slaves captured on board the dhows: stolen, dragged from their homes and families, sold and bought, sold and bought again, and brought from the markets on the mainland to this place where they are worse off that they were before.'[15]

E. D. Young, though he never achieved the distinction of either Livingstone or Cameron, was a more polemical figure than either, and his descriptions of the slave-trade from Nyasa down the Shire, thence to the coast, were the most useful accounts available outside of the consular reports of Elton and O'Neill. In a series of speeches, or lectures, interviews, and in his book *Nyassa*, Young told the well-known harrowing story of the slave-trade in East Central Africa. Even Young admitted that the Portuguese responsible were few in number and that the responsibility for the outrages was not predominantly Portugal's, but Young could not find an occasional kind word

[15] Afraid that they would be flogged to death if he returned them to Portuguese authorities, Sullivan carried the runaways with him for two months. On his return to Moçambique, most of them chose to go ashore. G. L. Sullivan, *Dhow Chasing in Zanzibar Waters* (London, 1873), pp. 235–45.

Sullivan's action caused a lengthy discussion in London between the Portuguese minister, the Viscount of Seisal, and the Foreign Office. See *Slave Trade No. 1* (1876), pp. 38–47, for some of the correspondence.

for Portugal, as Livingstone had done, and he was frequently abusive in his characterizations.

> In the year 1864 when the Livingstone Expedition and Universities Mission withdrew from these parts, the country was in the last stage of ruin and destruction. A hideous tribal war was raging between the Ajawa and the Manganja, at the instigation of the Portuguese, who had their emissaries everywhere, and led off tens of thousands of captives to Tette, where they were despatched to be sold to the warlike tribes south of the Zambesi. There these people were drained of their women and children, for the slave driver only required these, and not the men, for this purpose. So long as we were there in the land, the horrid trade was checked here and there. When we left, no witnesses could report their doings. . . . No tongue can tell the amount of bloodshed and misery that has sprung from the deeds of these few Portuguese who have conducted this business at Tette. . . .[16]

Young, like Consul MacLeod, had an hysterical edge to his denunciations and a hyperbolic view both of himself and of the slave-trade he attacked.

> It is a hideous story to repeat, and one now well known in England, however ignored in Portugal. For two or three yards of calico-a-piece, these poor Manganja and Ajawa women and children have been led away. Thousands after thousands—not to draw forth eventually congratulations between Lisbon and English cabinets, when detected and liberated on the coast—but to pass away into

[16] E. D. Young, *Nyassa, a Journal of Adventures.* Revised by Horace Waller (London, 1877), p. 170. On page 194: 'Perhaps never was the memory of Alphonse de Albuquerque and Camoens subsidized to greater advantage than in the speeches that were made . . . against Dr. Livingstone, Captain Cameron, and myself. Wading through the speeches, one is painfully conscious of the crass ignorance which exists in Lisbon concerning matters in East Africa. It seems utterly impossible to break in upon this ignorance.'

And on page 198: 'Here the speaker [Manuel Pinheiro Chagas] disappears very suddenly into the arms of Sir Walter Scott, Shakespeare, and Byron, and, as if he were not quite safe, he leads his listeners on to the deeds of the Invincible Armada and to the spire of the Kremlin. The Olympian Eagle is summoned to the rescue; King Dom Duarte, the princes Henrique, Don Fernando, and Dom Pedro all come to the call! I trust I may not appear very rude if I express the opinion that Senhor Chagas would do well to stimulate his countrymen to raise up from amongst themselves, just now some one who, by taking these matters to which I allude practically in hand, may claim from future orators a place on the illustrious master-roll. . . . It is rather hard upon the glorious dead to attach them by the thread of history to the Governors who represent Portugal in Central Africa at present.'

lands yet *more distant still,* and *further removed from the inquisitive eye of philanthropy.* Just as the lapwing stumbles and tumbles about before the village lad, till she leads him away from her young ones concealed in the grass, so have these excellent senators and ministers combined to draw off their countrymen from the great iniquity which lies crouching in a country they have hitherto known little of, and cared less about . . .

How few have passed into the wilds whence these poor slaves originally came! But when the few report what they find there—simply because they happen to be like Livingstone and his followers, or like Capt. Cameron . . . are they therefore to be dubbed liars to a man, because to them has fallen the task of telling the Portuguese what goes on in their own possessions.[17]

A permanent seethe of English, and Scottish, protest was in the Nyasa missionary communities. Another dimension of contempt was added to Anglo-Saxon indignation—that of the righteous Protestant for the depraved Catholic. No one spoke more forcefully in this vein than Henry Rowley, of the abortive first Universities' Mission. In a book on his travels with Livingstone, Rowley gave an indignant picture of slavery in Moçambique, a picture of cruelty and perversion not unlike that in *Uncle Tom's Cabin.* Masters with whips, children in chains, pastoral innocence violated. To defend such conditions, Rowley let a Portuguese slave-master speak.

You see, in order to live out here, I must have slaves, and in order to keep slaves, I must have a whip. My whip is no worse than any other whip I know of, but I do not justify it as a right, I simply defend it as a necessity. Wherever slavery exists discipline must of necessity be brutal. You English, because you do not keep slaves, take the philanthropic, the religous view of the question; we, who do keep slaves, take the material view, which regards the man as property. . . . I admit the philanthropic view is the best, for in the eyes of God all men are equal; and, though the African be a degraded man, I know enough of him to be sure that he can be raised by kindness and religion into a position not very inferior to our own. But, if you keep slaves . . . you must degrade them by the whip . . . until, like dogs, they are the unhesitating servants of your will. . . .[18]

[17] Quoted in the *Reporter,* May 1878, p. 35.

[18] Henry Rowley, *The Story of the Universities' Mission to Central Africa* (London, 1866), pp. 64–65.

Ten years later Rowley, again in ironic recapitulation, ridiculed Portuguese pretensions and actions in East Africa. Now he had joined the mounting English attack on the Portuguese Government, and he mockingly charged the last, hitherto sacrosanct, stronghold of Portuguese integrity—their legislation for the African territories.

The instructions which these governors, major and minor, received from the home government are admirable. The blessings of civilization and Christianity are set forth in eloquent phraseology, and the duty of extending such blessings urgently enforced. Slavery, it is true, is recognized, or was until the other day, as a necessity for the well-being of the colonies, but the slave trade is denounced, and the laws which regulate the conduct of the master toward the slave are so honourably framed, that, studying them alone, it would be difficult to escape the conviction that the Portuguese slaves in Africa are better off in every way than their free brethren. Theoretically, nothing can be better than the position, the policy, and the character of the Portuguese in Africa. It represents a highly civilized Christian people using their superior knowledge and capacity to develop the resources of the land and to raise from degradation the barbarous races that have been brought under their power, or within the scope of their influence. Practically, nothing can be worse or more humiliating. . . .[19]

To describe the actual state of affairs, Rowley claimed both vital experience and abundant information. He himself had witnessed scenes at Tete, Quelimane, and Moçambique, The depravity of morals was indescribable. The cruelty surpassed imagination. Many stories could be told, but one or two would have to suffice.

As I was leaving Quelimane for Moçambique . . . a slave was brought down to the whipping post, which was close to the river, by four men (soldiers), each of whom was armed with a rod made out of hippopotamus hide. A civilian, dressed daintily, and who used an umbrella to shield his person from the rays of the rising sun, and who smoked cigarettes meanwhile, accompanied them and looked on at the proceedings. He was, I was told, the master of the slave. The slave was bound by his feet and wrists to the whipping post, and then two soldiers commenced to beat him, two on and two off as they grew tired, and they continued until I had

[19] Henry Rowley, *Africa Unveiled* (London, 1876), p. 75.

counted more than five hundred strokes. 'He is dead,' was the careless remark of a Quillimane man, who stood close to me on the deck of the vessel. . . . He may have been for he had long ceased to show signs of life, and when he was untied from the whipping post he fell down as one that was dead. Then the man with the umbrella, still smoking a cigarette, strolled away towards the town.

'What was the man's offence?' I asked of the men about me. A shrug of the shoulders, as though that was of no consequence, was the only reply . . .

The more vile effects of slavery amongst the Portuguese . . . will not bear publication.[20]

From the particular condemnation of policy and practice Rowley moved on to a general condemnation of character.

The slave trade and slavery has been the curse of the Portuguese in Africa. Everywhere one goes one sees amongst them that deterioration of character. . . . On God's earth I believe it is impossible to find amongst Christian men a worse state of things than you meet amongst the Portuguese in Africa. . . .

The condition of the Portuguese colonies both in Western and Eastern Africa is most degraded. . . . Such towns as are inhabited have a miserable population of Europeans and half-castes, and natives who are heathens and slaves.

This seeming blight of a curse is not only in the possessions of the Portuguese, but upon themselves also. They appear to have lived in an atmosphere of depravity until it becomes part of their very nature. . . . A few ignorant and generally immoral priests . . . are still to be found amongst the Portuguese in Africa . . . I fear they are a shame to humanity—to say nothing of Christianity. As one of their own countrymen said to me, 'Virtuous precepts from their lips are a perfect mockery'.[21]

By 1885 such commentary as Rowley's was commonplace; by then it was the justification for urging British territorial action in East Africa and was not really concerned with the remnants of slavery or the slave-trade.

The anti-Portuguese quality of English humanitarianism was

[20] Ibid., pp. 186–7. Presumably the unmentionable vileness had to do with sexual outrages. The alleged incidence of homosexuality in Zambézia offended sturdier English sensibilities through the rest of the century.

[21] Ibid., p. 158, p. 228, and p. 230.

largely formed out of the Moçambique experience, but it found ready application in Angola in the first years of the 1880's when it seemed that an Anglo-Portuguese Treaty was going to give control of the great Congo waterway to England's oldest ally.

There had not been much said, apart from diplomatic reports, about Portuguese activities in West Africa; most of what was said was favourable. Livingstone himself had been reassured. Cameron was vehement, of course; but he was talking about areas remote from Portuguese jurisdiction and about people who were Portuguese only for reasons of their own. In addition, there was no Zanzibar, no Natal, no Nyasa, no centre of English interest nearby from which Angolan deficiencies might be more easily seen. Not until the arrival of English missionaries towards the end of the century did Angola come under humanitarian scrutiny.

Winwood Reade (by his admission, 'The first young man about town to make a *bonâ fide* tour in Western Africa . . . to travel with no special object and at his own expense, to flirt with pretty savages, and to smoke his cigar among cannibals') found Angola an agreeable place to visit, although inhabited by two somewhat inferior races of people, Africans and Portuguese. But, apart from general misrule, corruption, brutality, and the use of the pressgang to get African porters, the Portuguese in Angola conducted themselves as genial slave masters. It was true that the colonists of São Tomé had a bad reputation and that runaway slaves worked in chain gangs, but Reade never witnessed a case of corporal punishment. 'Those who know what slaves are will immediately infer that those of Angola are really the masters, and not only masters, but tyrants. Such is unfortunately the case with Negroes, school-boys, and all inferior beings. It is useless to appeal to anything except their epidermis.'[22]

[22] W. Winwood Reade, *Savage Africa*: 'Being the Narrative of a Tour in Equatorial, Southwestern, and Northwestern Africa, with Notes on the Habits of the Gorilla; on the Existence of Unicorns and Tailed Men; on the Slave-Trade; on the Origin, Character, and Capabilities of the Negro, and on the Future Civilization of Western Africa' (New York, 1864), p. 257.

In his chapter 'Black Ivory' (pp. 237–44), Reade made such statements as: 'It is to the slave-trade that we owe the first spirit of enterprise in Africa.' 'The African slave-trade has done its work in assisting the progress of civiliza-

The best English account of Angola in the half-century was quite matter of fact about slavery in the province. J. J. Monteiro, author of *Angola and the River Congo*, was an Englishman of Portuguese origin, who spent fifteen years in the territory; engineer Monteiro was of about the same persuasion on Africans and slavery as Arbitrator Huntley. He regarded Negroes as inferior beings, humanitarians as fools, slavery in Angola as not such a bad thing, and the Portuguese administration there as totally bankrupt—a familiar enough set of prejudices in any number of practical English travellers to Portuguese Africa in later years.

It is not my intention to deprecate any efforts for the benefit of the Negro race, but simply to show that good seed in Africa *will* fall on bare and barren ground, and where weeds *will* rise and choke it; and I must warn philanthropy that its bounty is less productive of good results on the Negro of tropical Africa than perhaps on any other race. . . . It is heartrending to see money, lives, and efforts squandered and wasted under the misguided idea of raising the Negro to a position which, from his mental condition, he cannot possibly attain. . . .[23]

Having this view, Monteiro was not upset by slavery in Angola. All labour was slave-labour, but Africans were well treated by their masters. 'Public opinion is strongly opposed to ill treatment of slaves . . . and I never heard of slaves being worked or treated in the hard and cruel manner. . . .' The system of making *libertos* from slaves had never taken hold in Angola, and the authorities had not bothered to enforce liberation after the given number of years. The complete abolition of slavery was going to create great economic hardships—to Africans as well as to Portuguese. 'It is a pity', wrote Monteiro,

tion.' 'By means of the slave-trade, the dangerous classes of Africa, the destitute and the criminal, were carried off to the New World.' 'The blacks have already become the bugbear of the New World.'

Reade was for slavery and against philanthropy. But the time had come to keep the labour in Africa. He said it would be impossible to prove to savages that the slave-trade was inhuman; nor could Europeans be converted to that belief. 'Portugal, the valet of England, affects an enthusiams [for suppression] she does not feel.' British squadrons along the coast were useless. The book is dedicated to several English consuls in West Africa and to the memory of Edmund Gabriel.

[23] Joachim John Monteiro, *Angola and the River Congo* (2 vols.; London, 1875), i. 240.

'that philanthropy should blindly put so sudden a stop [after twenty years!] to a custom that has existed from time immemorial, and of which the evils are, in a country like Angola, exceedingly slight. . . . Let slavery be abolished by all means, but only in the most gradual manner, and in proportion to the industrial and moral advancement of the race.'[24] Monteiro's feelings for Portuguese slavery, however, did not blind him to an absurd tariff policy and the despotic oppression of an administration whose misrule had kept the colony at a great industrial and economic disadvantage.

A change in British policy in the Congo brought humanitarian suspicions and resentments into focus. Since the Portuguese occupation of Ambriz, at 8° S. Latitude, England had for twenty years resolutely refused to recognize Portuguese sovereignty above that point. But in 1876 England began to reconsider her Congo policy, and over the next seven years uncertain and sometimes desultory negotiations took place between the two nations, culminating in the draft treaty of 1882–3. Britain would recognize Portuguese sovereignty up the coast to Cabinda (5° 12′ S. Latitude), freedom of navigation on the Congo and Zambesi was specified, joint suppression of slavery would be carried out, and freedom, more or less, of evangelization in the region was provided for. But effective control over the Congo waterway was to pass into Portuguese hands, and on this point humanitarian and commercial interests in England were outraged.

The argument against an Anglo-Portuguese treaty on the Congo was an argument in principal not, in specifics. Apart from the shipping of Angolan workers to São Tomé under dubious auspices, the Portuguese in West Africa had not been visibly active in the slave-trade. But there remained the possibility—and now were joined the two halves of the humanitarian proposition—that where Portuguese high tariff policies kept out legitimate trade, the slave-trade was likely to flourish in its place. Early in 1883 the Anti-Slavery Society took up the fight against cession of the Congo to Portugal. Church groups, missionary societies, chambers of commerce and the like were

[24] Joachim John Monteiro, *Angola and the River Congo* (2 vols.; London, 1875), ii. 41.

urged to tell Her Majesty's Government that the people of England would never approve of such a disposition. In a memorial to Lord Granville:

> The committee cannot but view such a measure with the gravest apprehensions, whatever the amount of sincerity which may be credited to the Government at Lisbon in respect to the suppression of the Slave-Trade. It has been proved by a long and painful experience that its inadequate, feeble, and corrupt Execution in Africa has both given a covert protection to the Slave-Trade, and, at the same time, interposed the most vexatious obstructions to the extension of legitimate commerce, by which that traffic might be superseded.[25]

The *Daily Telegraph* and *The Times* questioned placing the mouth of the river in the hands of a weak and impecunious state with a corrupt colonial administration. *The Times* was also fearful that missionary activity in the Congo Basin might suffer, it 'being well known within what narrow limits toleration of religion exists in the States of Southern Europe . . .'. The English press generally supported the Government on the treaty negotiations, but not because of any trust in Portugal's colonial capacities.[26] In Commons, on 3 April 1883, the member for Manchester, Jacob Bright, made a sharp attack on Portugal. Any guarantees given regarding slavery or slave-trading given by that country would be a delusion. Bright had talked with Lord Mayo, recently returned from Angola, who told him startling stories of a slave traffic between Angola and the islands of São Tomé and Principe. The slaves were *sold* in São Tomé, with good-looking girls fetching a high price. There was too much credulity in the Foreign Office if they believed anything on paper was likely to enable England to get Portugal to discourage slavery. Mr. W. E. Forester, a member of the Anti-Slavery Society, pointed out that the Portuguese Government was not accessible to public opinion with regard to keeping its treaties; their own slave-trade treaties were a mockery to the world.[27]

[25] *Reporter*, Mar. 1884, p. 69.

[26] Anstey, pp. 113–67, and Ruth Slade, *English Speaking Missions in the Congo Independent State* (Brussels, 1859), pp. 66–74, deal in great detail with English opinion on the treaty.

[27] *Hansard*, Third Series, v. 277, 1284–96, 3 Apr. 1883.

According to the *Spectator*, Granville had erred in not taking into account the 'horror with which Portuguese dominion is regarded by the trading classes and the philanthropists of Great Britain. . . . Portuguese statesmen are the worst colonial administrators in the world. . . . They regard their colonies as estates . . . they crush trade with taxes . . . they evade all the Anti-Slave-Trade treaties.'[28] To a lengthy Portuguese pamphlet defining—and defending—Portugal's role in the Congo (*Portugal and the River Congo*), a hastily published *Short Reply* put together a number of commentaries, practically all that were available, on Portuguese policy in West Africa. Livingstone, Cameron, and Ritter furnished most of the substance. Monteiro and the Portuguese explorers Capello and Ivens were also included, their remarks on Portuguese slavery given drastically out of context or in mutilated form.[29]

In the mounting opposition to the treaty, the question of slavery—or even freedom of commerce and evangelization—was directly of minor importance. There were other international considerations which were more decisive—French competition on the Niger and fear of German interference—in the abandonment of the treaty, but where the matter touched Portugal directly it was apparent that there was a profound distrust of Portugal, and implicit in the view of Portugal as a backward impotent colonial power was the conviction that slavery was a way of life in Portuguese Africa. In another memorial to the Foreign Office, in April 1884, the Committee of the Anti-Slavery Society emphasized that in Portugal's extensive African lands either Portuguese or Arabs had been practising the slave-trade for ages. The feeble character of her home government made any control over these activities unlikely. The traffic to São Tomé was offered as 'unquestionable evidence' of a continuing slave-trade. Such corruption would in the Congo restrict commerce and Christianity.[30]

When Granville asked to be furnished with any information

[28] 'Sovereignty of the Congo,' the *Spectator*, 7 Apr. 1883, pp. 441–2.

[29] *Reporter*, Apr. 1883, p. 107. In extracting quotations from the *Reply* the editors remarked that they did so 'to show the condition of this country into whose blood-stained hands it was coolly proposed by our Government to deliver the key of the vast territories of Central Africa'.

[30] *Reporter*, Apr. 1884, pp. 84–88.

the Society had to prove the charges, a series of documents were got together for the Foreign Office. They included: extracts from Lord Mayo's *De Rebus Africanis*; a letter from a Congo merchant ('Slavery does not exist *de jure* . . . but *de facto* it exists under the appellation of *engagement livre*, and it is carried on with the full knowledge of the Government. . . . The Negroes of Cabinda are so demoralized they sell each other. . . . All factories purchase their labourers and domestics. . . . The Portuguese, both officials and merchants, are totally demoralized and have the worst influence over the natives'); a letter from a 'Gentleman recently returned from the Congo' who described a shipment of workers to São Tomé and his conversation with four Angolans being shipped to Guiné who told him they were slaves; a letter from Sir Frederick Goldsmid, who had also travelled on a ship carrying labourers to São Tomé ('My impression of the poor creatures was thus noted at the time in my diary: "If this is not Slave-Traffic, I know not what it is." ')[31]

The voice of the Reverend Holman Bentley, of the Baptist Missionary Society, back in England in 1884 after five years in the Congo, was added to the chorus. In letters to the *Daily News*, *The Times*, and the *Pall Mall Gazette* he berated Portugal. In the letter to *The Times* he wrote:

As for Slavery, its remains are now very short-lived in the Congo, while if the Portuguese come into power it will be revived everywhere under specious forms, such as interminable ten years' contracts, perhaps even not so decently covered as that. Lord Mayo has just thrown light on Portuguese doings. He has told us how Slaves are being shipped monthly to San Thomé with scarcely any attempt at concealment. . . . By a simple change of name, by the simplest maneuvre, slavery becomes lawful. . . . Will the Christian

[31] *Reporter*, May 1884, pp. 92–96. When, in June 1884, the British Government said it would not seek ratification, the Society blithely assumed for itself no small share of the credit: 'Our readers will remember that the Anti-Slavery Society has not only taken a very prominent part in opposing the treaty with Portugal but was almost the first public body to enter a protest against handing over the mouth of the Congo . . . to that power. . . . The efforts of the Anti-Slavery Society were not confined to the mere sending in a protest to the Foreign Office, but have continued during the last sixteen months, with scarcely any intermission, and in conjunction with Chambers of Commerce the Society was mainly instrumental in raising an important debate in the House of Commons in April last year.' Ibid., July 1884, pp. 155–6.

churches and philanthropic bodies allow the door to Central Africa to be closed without protest? Will our men of business allow this immense field now so rapidly opening to commerce to be blockaded by such a power as Portugal?[32]

In the course of the debate, neither the treaty nor Portugal was without defence. W. C. Cartwright, M.P., writing in the *Fortnightly Review*, made a spirited riposte to both the Anti-Slavery Society and the Baptist Missionary Society. He noted that peculiar forces had combined to defeat the treaty, the sentimental forces of the Society, 'whose members had inherited from the olden days a distrust of Portugal', and the religious prejudices of the Baptist Missionary Society who were jealous of the jurisdiction of a Roman Catholic power. As for the question of indentured labour to São Tomé, it was no different from the coolie system.[33]

By far the most important and formidable spokesman against Portuguese rights in the Congo was H. M. Stanley, who had been retained by Léopold II. Speaking at the Jubilee Anti-Slavery Meeting in Manchester in late 1884 (to a crowd of 5,000 in Free Trade Hall and another 1,500 in the neighbouring Y.M.C.A. Hall), Stanley gave an extraordinary recital of Portuguese cruelty and venality in West Africa. From the engaging start of his talk ('How do you get the nigger to work? If you are Portuguese, you force him'), Stanley drew upon the now familiar sources—the dispatches of Consul Carnegie, Lord Mayo, Goldsmid, and the anonymous 'Congo Gentleman'. Stanley, too, had travelled with the 'colonials' on their way to the islands from Luanda.

It [the migrant system] is called legitimate by the Portuguese; it is legalized by outward forms, ceremonies, and processes. It may be legitimate according to the unfortunate manner that the Portuguese define words which have very different meaning to us. It is convenient when speaking to English people to have such terms as civilization, colonization, legitimacy, but their interpretation of such terms could never find place in an English dictionary. To

[32] *The Times*, 14 Apr. 1884. In his book, Bentley had very little that was harsh to say about the Portuguese in West Africa. W. Holman Bentley, *Pioneering in the Congo* (2 vols.; London, 1900).

[33] W. C. Cartwright, 'The Congo Treaty', *Fortnightly Review*, 1 July 1884, pp. 88–107.

me it appears that whatever is legitimate should not be unjust, immoral, or unlawful. Civilized communities cannot therefore commend this trade in colonials, or compulsory expatriation of one innocent unoffending citizen or subject of a State, because it is unjust, it entails misery, unhappiness, breaking up of home, family ties; there is a moral wrong in it. . . .

At the end of the harangue, Stanley spoke of the legacy of Portugal in the Congo, 'the vitiated morals of the inhabitants of the lower river and the general evil effects of that close intercourse they had maintained with the natives—an intercourse tainted by crime, misery, and murder'.

There are a few whites who still remember those strange old times, when the Slave-Trader, after disposing of a shipful of unfortunates, resorted to the gambling table to try his fortunes, and drank royally of champagne or Rhine wine after a sumptuous banquet with *bon* companions of the same order. I saw some of them in 1877, and I remember too well the conscious feeling of horror and disgust that possessed me, as with a morbid feeling of curiosity I slowly studied their physiognomies, and tried to divine in what part of their heads was developed that bump of destructiveness, and hate of their kind, that marked them destined for such a trade.

But the local history of the lower Congo must not be studied too closely . . . as it is altogether too befouled with crime, unnatural sin, and nameless atrocities for repetition. It is enough that it kindles us to persevere in the new and self-imposed mission of endeavouring to rescue the Congo from the chance of such a great misfortune as Portuguese rule would be to the region to which the International Association has attracted the attention of united Europe. If Europe judges wisely and well at the forthcoming conference [The Berlin Conference of 1884–1885], we may mark its date down as an Era of Expansion and Growth that perhaps shall go on unchecked to the end of time.[34]

The best example at hand of Portuguese slaving ways in West Africa was the São Tomé migrant-worker system. The most recent public statement on that was in Lord Mayo's *De Rebus Africanis*, a little book published in 1883, a year after Lord Mayo had visited Angola, accompanied by H. H. Johnston. The intent of the book was 'to lay before the public . . . the actual

[34] *Reporter*, No. 1884, pp. 203–21.

state of trade on the coast, to show them how great the commercial interests existing there are, and on what grounds Portugal and its Government base their claims to rights over territories in which . . . they now possess no real power whatever'.[35] Only a few pages had to do with the São Tomé system, but they remained one of the sources for humanitarian attacks over the next thirty years.

With regard to the much-vexed slavery question it may be stated with truth that slaves can be bought and sold still in the provinces of the Portuguese colonies . . . They [the planters of São Tomé] have got over the difficulty [absence of labour on the islands] by importing what they call 'colonials'. At Catumbella, some seven miles north of Benguella, the natives are brought down by agents from the interior, the agents stating that they are natives freed from the slavery which they were in to their own chiefs, the retail price being about seven pounds each. They are brought in lighters to Benguella from Catumbella, and then taken to Loanda in the Portuguese mail steamer, where a certain form is gone through. Their names, ages, and descriptions are taken down by the Government officials and they are asked a number of silly questions such as 'Are you hungry?' 'Have you had anything to eat?' or 'Do you want any food?' in order that the affirmative 'Yes' may be solicited and put down as declaring their willingness to go and labour at St. Thomas for five years. The Government officials, of course, get their fees for each contract. Then the agent proceeds to ship these niggers by Portuguese mail boats from Loanda to St. Thomas on the Line. The Negroes are provided with a wooden spoon, and, I believe, some tin platters and a certain amount of cotton stuff for clothing. Then they are examined by a doctor and shipped off as deck passengers to St. Thomas . . . If the women are good looking, they become the mistresses of the Portuguese planters; if they are ugly, they go to the fields. They are paid about two pence a day and provided with food and lodging. The great curse of the system is that any planter, after he has received his consignment of black labourers, can . . . re-contract these natives, without consulting them, for another term of five or seven years. That this is virtually slavery cannot be denied. The natives, when labouring at St. Thomas, are treated well, but none of them ever sees Africa again. It is not exaggeration to say that this rule is invariable. They suffer very much from nostalgia (home sickness),

[35] Lord Mayo (D. R. W. Bourke), *De Rebus Africanis* (London, 1883), p. 1.

and go to St. Thomas only to work and die. These are the bare unvarnished facts.[36]

The solution, according to Lord Mayo, was for British gunboats to board the lighters and steamers before they got to Luanda and demand papers for every African on board.

Cheered by what it considered its contribution to frustrating the Anglo-Portuguese treaty, the British and Foreign Anti-Slavery Society now began to give Portuguese Africa its unrelenting attention. The time was propitious. British interests in Africa were beginning to coalesce, often at the borders of Portuguese territory, and a vigilant eye and a strong voice could serve the cause of commerce and Christianity. Portugal was the enemy over the next twenty-five years in what, in retrospect, seems to have been the Society's last great campaign. And to the extent that humanitarian opinion against Portugal had, or needed, leadership, this could usually be found at the Anti-Slavery Society.

There was at times a spitefulness and at other times a pious casuistry in the Society's anti-Portuguese campaign. Commenting on the results of the Berlin Conference where Portugal lost territory to which she had at least as good a claim as Leopold II, the *Reporter* wrote, 'We cannot pretend to be pleased at the large extent of territory given over to Portugal. . . . We think this will produce some difficulty hereafter as regards the Slave-Trade.'[37] The pages of the *Reporter* were uncritically opened to cranks and vested interests.[38]

Any club was used to beat Portugal with. The *Reporter* printed excerpts from an article in *Neueste Nachrichten und Münchener Anzeiger*.

It is a fact that the Slave Trade puts forth its most vigorous shoots under the glorious banner of Portugal. . . . One sees on the African coast many black men, both of whose ears are wanting. These are mostly slaves who, having attempted to escape by flight

[36] Ibid., pp. 25–26. H. H. Johnston had generous remarks about Portuguese race relations in Africa.

[37] *Reporter*, Mar. 1885, p. 318.

[38] *Reporter*, Apr. 1885, pp. 342–4, prints an anonymous letter received from the west coast of Africa which was nothing less than libellous.

from the amenities of Portuguese civilization, are thus marked by their humane masters in order that they may know them again! Certainly nine-tenths of the plantation labourers on the island of San Thomé are slaves, the greater part of whom have been brought from San Paulo de Luanda and San Salvador. From the latter place they were brought a year ago, chained together, *viâ* land route, from Nokki to Mboma, and then shipped to their destination. Even Portuguese gunboats, under the pretence of sounding the Congo River, anchored off the factory of a certain Rosa—in order to take on board a cargo of *black ivory* for San Thomé.[39]

Consul O'Neill was quoted from an address given to the Scottish Geographical Society: 'We must not shirk, we cannot, indeed, escape from the duties and responsibilities that the enterprise of our race and our vast wealth throw upon us. Let us only take care that civilization, commerce, and Christianity shall truly and honestly go hand in hand.'[40]

A letter from F. S. Arnot, a Brethren missionary who had travelled much in Angola and Barotseland, told the story of a small African boy he left behind at Bihé who was sold by one of the Silva Porto's slaves to traders who carried him off to the coast. 'I at once sent off to the coast for particulars about him, as slaves are shipped from Benguella every month, in large companies, to Portuguese colonies elsewhere.'[41] In the same issue was reprinted a lurid story from South Africa.

A correspondent of the *East London Despatch*, who had recently been at Delagoa Bay, writes: —The 'Slave-Trade,' or black ivory business, seems to flourish as well as could be desired here. This afternoon (November 30) I saw a Banyan swaggering along the street with four native girls in his wake, and on asking the 'boss' of the 'central' what that meant, was informed that the girls were Slaves of this rascally yellow-coloured gentleman, that is, they were his by right of purchase. The fathers of these poor creatures, and certain others (Europeans) whom it would not be hard to trace, I am informed, sell them to whoever will buy, for from ten to

[39] *Reporter*, Oct. 1885, p. 460. The date of the article is 8 Oct. 1885. The author is anonymous, but 'easy to recognize as a distinguished African explorer'.

[40] *Reporter*, Mar.–Apr. 1886, p. 38. O'Neill was urging support for British enterprises like the African Lakes Company.

[41] *Reporter*, Mar.–Apr. 1886, pp. 54–55.

twenty pounds each; the same as they would sell an ox. A pretty state of affairs to be sure. . . . A certain business house in Delagoa have their agents—I am informed—in the Kambane country to purchase these captives. After purchasing some are sent here and there to black friends, to be disposed of in the usual way, others are kept in the house of this human flesh-dealing firm. . . . When the new Governor came into office, in July 1885, he gave a slave girl to the 'Delgado' as a present. These are facts that it would be well for some of our philanthropists to investigate.—*Daily Argus*.[42]

In the late years of the 1880's, the Society gave its full attention to the growing crisis in East Africa between Portugal and British economic and evangelical interests there—although the Committee did find time to protest particularly the arrangement by which planters from São Tomé got slave-labour from the King of Dahomey. In company with the foreign mission agencies of the Church of Scotland, the Free Church of Scotland, the Universities' Mission, and with the African Lakes Company and the Royal Scottish Geographical Society, the Anti-Slavery Society sponsored a public meeting on 24 April 1888 to protest at the anticipated expansion of Portuguese influence in East Africa. On 18 May 1888 the same organizations sponsored another meeting in Manchester Town Hall, where Horace Waller told the audience that 'the criminals of Portugal, when they reached the penal settlement, turned their attention to the slave trade, and here, in a nutshell, was the history of the demoralization of the natives'. W. H. Wylde, now in retirement from the Foreign Office, the man probably more responsible than any other for the British Government's determined resistance to Portuguese slaving in the 1850's, 1860's, and 1870's, urged that Portugal's claims in Nyasa were absurd and that every pressure should be brought on the Foreign Office, which only moved when there was a sufficient public feeling.[43] Charles Allen, Secretary of the Society, wrote to Lord Salisbury stressing the inadvisability of granting any of Portugal's territorial claims. Portugal had never kept any of the anti-slave-trade agreements. It was well known that the Portuguese in

[42] *Reporter*, Mar.–Apr. 1886, p. 55.
[43] *Reporter*, May–June 1888, pp. 65–69.

East Africa were hostile to the missionaries because they interfered with the slave-trade. Familiar stories were used to demonstrate the allegation.[44]

Portugal, even if she chose, could not hope to answer the barrage of English charges, many of which were either irrelevant or exaggerated. She had neither the facilities nor the audience. Portugal's defence was perhaps best made in 1889–90 at the Brussels Anti-Slavery Conference. The conference grew out of the campaign of Cardinal Lavigerie to suppress the slave-trade in Africa—and out of the machinations of Leopold II. The British Government had been interested in the proposals from the beginning, recognizing that most attention should be paid to the so-called Arab trade, 'from the Portuguese possessions in the Mozambique'.[45] In Portugal the conference was looked upon with a certain amount of mistrust. Only on 29 September 1889 did Portugal receive a formal invitation to a conference beginning on 15 October.[46] Portugal accepted the invitation and sent as delegates Henrique de Macedo, Portuguese minister in Brussels, the explorer Hermenegildo Capello, former Governor-General of Moçambique Augusto Castilho, and Portuguese consul to Newcastle, Jayme Batalha Reis. The king of Portugal observed that his nation was pleased to participate, for the theme was attractive to a nation like his, 'which long ago abolished slavery in all its territories, and in them and beyond them, on sea and land, has pursued slave traders with all its vigilance'.[47]

At the proceedings Portugal was content to play a secondary role.[48] Her important contribution to the conference was a document prepared by the Ministry for Marine and Overseas,

[44] Charles Allen to Lord Salisbury, 27 June 1889 and 16 July 1889. In *Reporter*, July–Aug. 1889, pp. 176–8.

[45] F.O. 84/2010, Salisbury to Lord Vivian (British Minister in Brussels), 17 Sept. 1888.

[46] F.O. 84/1966, Petre to F.O., 29 Sept. 1889.

[47] *Jornal do comércio*, 3 Jan. 1890. From a speech made the previous day.

[48] In the early days her delegation had tried to get established certain posts in the interior as being within Portuguese jurisdiction (The conference disavowed any approval or disapproval of territorial questions), and on the question of the alcohol traffic took the position that it was not relevant to the slave-trade. Britain refused to budge an inch on the first point, and on

the *Mémoire sur l'Abolition de l'Esclavage et de la Traité des Noirs sur le Territoire Portugais.* Perhaps no modern nation has used the historical past with such feeling (and generally with so little success) to defend and explain the continuity of present policies. The *Mémoire* was a noble example of this genre of Portuguese literature. 'Portugal presents herself', it began, 'before the nations of Europe as one who has earned by ancient right a debt of universal gratitude through the priority of her discoveries, the sincerity of her efforts, and the grandeur of her sacrifices.'[49]

Portugal, the *Mémoire* argued, was no more responsible than any other European country for instituting the slave-trade. Its origins were shrouded in antiquity. Portugal had from the fifteenth century sought to save the African slave from a primitive moral and spiritual degradation, to civilize him, to make him a Christian. England was the country with whom Portugal had most in common in her African policies, both in the days of slaving and in the century of repression and abolition. An assembly of decrees from the early sixteenth century down to the present was used to prove the humanitarian purity of Portuguese intent in overseas conduct. A dispatch of 16 December 1841, for example, to the commander of the naval station in Angola telling him to spend as little time as possible in port and as much time as possible as sea looking for slavers was submitted as proof of Portugal's anti-slave-trade sentiments.[50] After 1854 the flow of legislation reached the proportions of a tidal wave. In conclusion:

> The great work of generous civilization, which Portugal freely imposed on herself, and in which, in concert with England, she co-operated loyally and selflessly, has been concluded in a brilliant and humanitarian manner...

the second the president, Baron Lambermont, replied that the question *was* relevant in a broader context. 'In the present state of affairs', he observed, 'the African races are not capable of assisting in their own defence. It is nonetheless desirable that steps were taken to prepare them for that duty by gradually raising the standard of their intelligence and morality. Strong drink is one of the chief causes of the degradation and destruction of the Negro race.' F.O. 84/2102. Protocol for sitting of 24 Feb. 1890.

[49] *Mémoire sur l'Abolition de l'Esclavage et de la Traité des Noirs sur le Territoire Portugais* (Lisbon, 1889), p. 23.

[50] Ibid., pp. 30–31.

All the indigenous people of Africa have been definitely emancipated there by our laws, and they have come to enjoy the same rights, advantages, and priviliges as citizens of the metropolis.[51]

As for the present, the members of the conference were assured categorically that in Angola the slave-trade was dead these many years. Not only were there no longer any marches to the sea of Negroes for export, but the coast itself was dotted with factories and towns all engaged in licit commerce. In the interior the spread of agriculture and Portuguese influence had destroyed the last vestiges of the infamous commerce. On the other hand, the east coast did, admittedly, still present a problem, since Islam with its 'cortege of retrograde, sensual, and anti-civilizing customs' was dedicated to extending the traffic; but here Portugal was making heroic efforts to chart the coast and rout the slavers. Military posts were being established on the sites of the most notorious slave-shipping centres. Naval patrols had been increased. The memorial then liberally quoted Elton and O'Neill to prove Portugal's good intent in Moçambique. As for the allegations of Lovett Cameron, he had been implicitly rebuked by the British minister in Lisbon. The greatest explorer of them all, Stanley himself, had written on 11 May 1878 to the Secretary of the American Anti-Slavery Society that the Portuguese African provinces were governed by men motivated by humanitarian sentiments as sincere as those of Englishmen or Americans. There was, of course, some trade carried on out on the Portuguese African frontiers by Portuguese subjects, but it was impossible always to distinguish between Portuguese Africans and Portuguese Europeans.[52] As for São Tomé, British consular officers were unanimous in their praise of conditions on the island and the zeal of local authorities in protecting the workers. For its work, past and present, in abolishing the slave-trade Portugal deserved a place of honour.[53]

By 1890 the focus of English criticism was the Portuguese presence in East Africa. Slavery was now only a convenient club,

[51] *Mémoire sur l'Abolition de l'Esclavage et de la Traité des Noirs sur le Territoire Portugais* (Lisbon, 1889), p. 35.

[52] Ibid., p. 49.

[53] Ibid., p. 50.

one aspect of a larger problem, a problem of general mismanagement and immorality which made the cession of some or all of Moçambique to England a humanitarian necessity. Miscegenation and its evil effects became an issue with as strong an emotional appeal as slavery. (But by the end of the century when England needed Moçambique ports and Moçambique labour, these intemperate attacks declined, and Angola and the cocoa islands again became the object of philanthropic attack.) Most of the literature on East Africa written between 1885 and 1900 was not the work of humanitarians, but in sentiment and substance it was freely used by philanthropic critics.

The *Cape Times*, which probably did not represent entirely selfless interests, was particularly pleased to record examples of Portuguese misbehaviour.[54]

In February 1891 the newspaper printed a long, curious

[54] In mid-Sept. 1890, some fourteen African draftees slipped off the *Rei do Portugal* when she docked at Cape Town. They were pursued down the street by Portuguese marines with sabres drawn ('enough to make one wonder where is the boasted anti-slavery policy of England'). A hearing was held, at which several of the runaways testified that they had been seized, kept as prisoners, then sent aboard ship in irons to be taken to Luanda as military recruits. The men were not turned over to the ship and remained in Cape Town. *Cape Times*, 22 Sept. 1890.

Roger Casement described the practice. 'During my residence at Lourenço Marques in the years 1895 and 1896 frequent assertions were made to me that on the departure of each troopship returning to Portugal from the Moçambique coast, it was a practice of the authorities in that town to seize any stray natives who could not produce immediate evidence of their being in the employ of white men, and to ship them by these vessels to Angola as military convicts.

'So widespread was the belief in this custom that it is certain for some days before the sailing of each transport Lourenço Marques was practically emptied of its usual hundreds of unemployed or partly employed natives. . . .

'The local authorities more than once volunteered to me the unsought declaration that the practice of so seizing men, although once in force, had long been discontinued.

'These disavoways were at the time not accepted by the merchants of Lourenço Marques who complained that their work was seriously hindered by the periodic panic and exodus of their workmen. . . .'

F.O. 2/230, Roger Casement to F.O., 19 July 1899. Casement said that the practice was still continued.

Colin Harding met some of these Delagoa men at the fort of Mosiko in deep Angola. They would remain there, he wrote, until too old for service. They complained to Harding they had been brought there against their will and were not allowed to go home. Colin Harding. *In Remotest Barotseland* (London, 1905), p. 208.

interview with H. C. Moore, an American arrested for a short time in Zambézia on charges of being a British spy.

'Do not the natives cry out against the Portuguese domination?' 'Yes, the Portuguese treatment of the natives is most cruel. . . . When I was in the fort at Tete, a prisoner, I had a daily opportunity of seeing Portuguese law enforced. The poor black Slaves, for they are nothing more, are strapped on to a board, fixed up in the court, and flogged mercilessly. . . . There is no law, simply the enforcement of brutal power.'

'Which must sooner or later succumb to European advancement?' 'Yes, and the natives know this.'

'Practically a system of slavery exists throughout the whole territory?' 'The farms all the way up the river are worked by slaves, and the social position is judged by the number of slaves a man owns. . . . The slavery of a past generation still exists in Portuguese Zambézia. All the carriers for natives, or Portuguese, as they call themselves, are slaves . . .

'These so-called Portuguese are almost as black as Negroes, are they not?' 'There is no distiguishing between. And all the officials have black wives, even the Governor of Zumbo.'[55]

The following year the *Natal Advertiser* printed a letter from P. D. Dangerfield on conditions in Quelimane district. Mr. Dangerfield said that slavery in its worst days could not compare with the atrocities and the barbarous manner with which it was allowed nowadays. Each district had a 'manawombo', a chief of chiefs, and under him the 'inhaquava', or head of district, whose job it was to supply field labour. This he obtained by raiding villages with a force of sepoys. When captured, they were driven to Mapanda, housed in open sheds, and worked in the fields from sun-up to sunset without break. The worker was obliged to furnish his own food. Runaway workers were mercilessly beaten. 'Their condition was abject slavery without any of its redeeming points. . . . The poor wretch is kidnapped, forced to labour against his will without any reward, and beaten and starved. This is not conducive to peace and prosperity.'[56]

[55] *Cape Times*, 20 Feb. 1891. According to Moore, most of the Africans of Zambézia were 'hard and willing workers'. They were just waiting for the Chartered Company to give them a freedom it had not been their lot to have before.

[56] Quoted in the *Reporter*, Mar.–Apr. 1893, pp. 74–75.

A similar tale was told by Sir John Willoughby in three articles in the *Graphic*. Describing the *prazo* system as it extended from the mouth of the Zambesi up to Zumbo. Willoughby condemned the whole region as a den of iniquity, crime, and extortion. Human life had no value or meaning to a half-caste *prazo* owner. African workers (or slaves) were shot daily for the slightest offence, particularly in the remote *prazos* above Tete.

At Matakania, sixteen miles below Zumbo, I spent one night at the *prazo* of Araujo Lobo [a sergeant-major and chief officer of the district under the governor at Zumbo], and just as I was leaving next morning, I saw two gangs of slaves, each consisting of a dozen women, mostly with little children on their backs, and all chained together by means of heavy lengths of chain attached to iron rings around their necks. They were being employed in porterage between the stockades and the river, and I was informed they were the result of Araujo Lobo's latest raid up the Zambesi for men and women. I lay stress on this fact, for the Portuguese Government, both at home and on the coast, have openly asserted there is no such thing as slavery now.[57]

Montagu Kerr had mixed impressions of Zambézia, but they did not all favour Portugal's presence. Like almost every Englishman in East Africa, he was obsessed by a colour consciousness. On learning that a man he saw lying in the shade was regarded as a *mzungo* (white man), 'Merciful powers! Had my vision been deceived for a lifetime? If this was white, where under the heavens could black be found?'[58] Up the Zambesi he saw great numbers of slaves, although slavery did not flourish as it did in days gone by. Kerr speculated that to eradicate it completely in this part of the world would be very difficult. 'The people have been brought up in the atmosphere of slaving and cannot understand any other form of existence. . . . From what I have seen of the Portuguese, they are good masters and possessed of great patience.'[59]

In his travels in Zambézia in the 1880's, Frederick Selous formed a similar opinion of conditions there. The blight of

[57] The *Graphic*, 27 Feb. 1892. The piece is illustrated with drawings of a string of slave women in chains.

[58] Walter Montagu Kerr, *The Far Interior* (2 vols.; London, 1886), i. 286.

[59] Ibid., ii. 47, 53.

slavery and miscegenation lay upon the land. In 1882, he remembered, slave-hunting on the central Zambesi was a common thing, and Selous saw strings of slaves which told him that 'slavery was by no means dead, as some people would have one believe'.[60] Selous was disappointed to see that the administration of the country was in the hands of men 'as black as any of my crew'. At Zumbo 'all the Portuguese were mere wrecks of men—frail, yellow, and fever stricken—and offered a strong contrast to the robust and powerful figure of the natives'.[61] Visiting Tete in 1889 he observed that though the native population of the lower Zambesi might not be slaves, 'they certainly do not seem to be free men in the English sense of the word'. He went on to describe the indignities of the *prazo* system.[62] And he discussed the relative merits of English and Portuguese *vis-à-vis* the peoples of East Africa.

> I do not think that the natives of South East Africa who have been accustomed to the Portuguese like working for Englishmen: we are too energetic for them. Many of my countrymen believe the natives despise the Portuguese, and admire the superior strength and energy of the North Europeans, but I think there is a good deal of misconception on the matter. . . . In my opinion the more mean-spirited and cowardly reverence nothing but wealth, and where they see an Englishman, Scotsman, German, or Swede—for all North Europeans I have observed have the same pride of a dominant race that forbids them to show any signs of effeminacy before an inferior people—walking in the sun, bare-armed and often bare-legged, carrying his own rifle and running after game, they think he is only doing so because he is poor and cannot afford to pay men to hunt for them, and porters to carry him in a *palanquin* . . . and they despise him accordingly and contrast him unfavourably with the more effeminate and luxurious Portuguese whom they respect more than the British because they think he is rich enough to afford comforts which the latter cannot command.[63]

In the same year, 1893, David Rankin's *The Zambesi Basin and Nyasaland* was published. The middle portion of the book

[60] Frederic Selous, *Travel and Adventure in South-East Africa* (London, 1893), p. 57.
[61] Ibid., p. 62.
[62] Ibid., p. 273–5.
[63] Ibid., p. 285.

had to do with life in Zambézia in 1890 and before. Rankin was personally generous to the Portuguese there, saying that in ten years of association he had received nothing but the greatest courtesy and kindness from them. Of domestic slavery at Tete, Rankin said that it was the custom of Africans voluntarily to make themselves slaves, since they were kindly treated, had plenty of food and very little work to do.[64] Labour conditions in the region were something akin to slavery, but worse than the remnants of slave-trade was the low state of morality in Zambézia. 'To recount what happens at the present day on the upper waters of this great river would be a history so revolting and repugnant to every instinct of humanity, or even of savagedom, that it can have no place in these pages. The wildest flights of delirium could hardly conjure up the brutalities possible to a negroid Portuguese unbridled by any control or restriction to the exercise of the most infamous and degraded passions.'[65]

The unbridled immorality was most noticeable in the half-caste world of Moçambique. The offspring of the intermixture between Portuguese and African was 'a well defined class, the self-styled *muzungus*. . . . The characteristics of the men evince a much lower moral type. They are conspicuous for callousness and a predilection for the grossest forms of brutality, dishonesty, and sensuousness. . . .'[66] Tens of pages heaped scorn on the *muzungus*. They revealed as much of a particular British prejudice as they did of alleged characteristics of the Zambesi population.

> A half-caste Muzungo imagines that a white man never works, and that idleness is the escutcheon of nobility and civilisation. It has often caused me mixed amusement and pity to come accidentally across one of these would-be representatives of our own civilisation seated in a bottomless chair, with five brawny valets around him, no blacker than himself, one brushing his teeth, another washing his face, another vainly endeavouring to get out the spirals of his woolly hair, another cleaning his nails, and the

[64] David Rankin, *The Zambesi Basin and Nyasaland* (London, 1895), pp. 110–11.
[65] Ibid., p. 116.
[66] Ibid., p. 233.

fifth holding a cracked mirror, in which his Negro features are somewhat reflected and distorted.[67]

In his diary Lugard recorded scenes of Africans tied together and referred to as slaves. Up the Zambesi slaving was laughed at by everyone, and the methods of Portuguese administration there needed investigation. The slave-trading Portuguese half-caste—'the worst of European productions'—had spread desolation over a thousand miles of the Zambesi Basin and turned it into a 'pestiferous' region.[68]

More forthright was Lionel Decle, an Anglicized Frenchman. The *prazo* system permitted a kind of legalized slavery; the lessee could requisition native labour without payment and could rent it out to other employers.[69] The Portuguese *capitão-mor*, an honorary title given to strong men in the remoter areas of Moçambique, generally used his irregulars for the purpose of slave collecting and brigandage. The Jesuits (who had returned to the colony in 1881) 'were perpetually buying young slaves for a couple of pieces of cotton "to save them from slavery".'[70] According to Decle, slavery was universal; though slaves were no longer branded by their captors, as they were ten years ago, conditions were on the whole worse. And worse than slavery was miscegenation.

Another feature of society in the Portuguese Zambesi is . . . without any parallel in the world. All the white men established there have one, two, three, or four native wives, with whom they live openly. . . . They are in fact servants. . . . They live with the servants, and yet whenever they bear their master a child he takes it publicly to the church to be baptized. . . . There are few men I met at Tete who had not two or three half-breed children. . . . This state of things is found not only among private residents, but also among the highest officials and military officers. In this kind of relation affection seems to play no merit. The woman has not much more place in the family than a dog in England. They eat on the floor after their master has finished; indeed they are simply machines for the manufacture of mulattoes. . . . The Portu-

[67] David Rankin, *The Zambesi Basin and Nyasaland* (London, 1895), pp. 198.

[68] F. D. Lugard, *The Rise of our East African Empire* (2 vols.; London, 1893), pp. 16–29 *passim*.

[69] Lionel Decle, *Three Years in Savage Africa* (London, 1898), p. 241.

[70] Ibid., pp. 245–6.

guese in this colony live under a state of morality which they have made for themselves, and which is quite different from that of any other European society I ever heard of.[71]

The bluntest accusations, the final racial rejection of Portugal in East Africa, came from Rhodes's companion de Waal, spokesman for the Nordic *herrenvolk*. Of the Portuguese at Inhambane: 'They are not white at all, their colour corresponding with that of the coloured people of Cape Town; the latter, however, are more civilized. Not only are these Portuguese ugly, thin, weak, and narrow-shouldered, but judging from the little I saw of them, they have fallen to such a low grade of animal life that I feel ashamed to describe their mode of living.'[72] He thanked Providence that Portugal had not settled the southern shore of Africa but left it to the Dutch 'who turned the Cape into a very useful country for the white man'. At Neves Ferreira, sixty miles from Beira:

> The Portuguese there, like the natives, dwell in huts; and there is no difference between the hut of the Portuguese and that of the Kaffirs, and not much distinction between the two races. The Portuguese wear clothes and the Kaffirs do not, the Portuguese are yellow, the Kaffirs, black; the Portuguese are physically weak, the Kaffirs, strong—those are the only striking differences. . . . They mix with each other, take each other around the waist, and talk one language when together—Kaffir. *This* is certain though: the natives are more cleanly in their habits than their yellow masters. The latter are as thin as dried fish, and they die like rats.[73]

The Portuguese in West Africa would not be judged so harshly until the late violent years of the cocoa islands scandal, for this was the issue which would not die. Missionaries and travellers who sailed up the coast from Luanda saw the familiar sight of African deck passengers in their new striped cotton clothes. Heli Chatelain, linguist, scholar, and one of the best known of Protestant missionaries in Angola, travelled, from 19 May to 21 May 1890, with some 200 contract workers on the royal mail steamer *Moçambique*. They had come from all along the coast

[71] Ibid., pp. 249–50.

[72] D. C. de Waal, *With Rhodes in Mashonaland*, translated by Jan H. Hofmeyer de Waal (London and Cape Town, 1896), p. 129.

[73] Ibid. p. 148.

and from the far interior in back of Luanda, Benguela, and Moçâmedes. They were men and women between the ages of fifteen and fifty. Around the neck of each was a tin tag with a number and the name of a São Tomé estate owner punched on it. Some looked healthy, others tired and bewildered, and some 'were starved to skeletons, and had the ghastly, feverish, piercing, half insane look that is peculiar to this condition. The most of them had the hard, vacant, indifferent expression of men who know they are going to what they most dread, while they are ignorant of where and in what shape their sad destiny awaits them'. But all of them, Chatelain supposed, were externally improved on what they were in their homes.

Food was given them in a large common barrel. In the struggle at mealtime much of the food was wasted and only the stronger obtained their portion. The sad spectacle was an amusing sight for the passengers and crew who looked down on the 'black swarm, saying in the happy feeling of their superiority, "What beasts and brutes these slaves are" '. When Chatelain thought that these people would never see their homes again, whether in Luanda, the Zambesi headstreams, or the coastal south, he could not keep the tears from his eyes.[74]

Even Mary Kingsley, Portugal's best English friend in Africa, told of Krumen who had worked out their contracts and were not repatriated; many had set out in small boats across hundreds of miles of open Atlantic, almost all never to arrive. 'My Portuguese friends assure me that there was never a thought of permanently detaining the boys and that they were only keeping them until other labourers arrived to take their place. . . . I quite believe them, for I have seen too much of the Portuguese in Africa to believe that they would, in a wholesale way, be cruel to natives. But I am not the least surprised the

[74] In São Tomé plantations, government buildings, and hospitals were springing up with youthful vigour. The island population was made up of a few Europeans and two classes of Africans, the São Tomistas born on the island and the unfree imported labourers. During his walk around the city, Chatelain talked to some of them. They all said, 'Oh take, do take us back to our country, or some other place!' The whites spent their days complaining of the climate and the worthlessness and corruption of the Africans. *Reporter*, Jan.–Feb. 1891, pp. 34–35. The extract is from the *African News*.

poor Krumen took the Portuguese *logo* and *amanhã* for Eternity itself, for I have frequently done so.'[75]

If the procedures by which labour for São Tomé was acquired were well known, as were the details of the workers' passage to the islands and their life on the estates there, relatively little was known or said about the source of the labour. Much of it, in fact, came from within easy distance of ports and was simply acquired by purchase or bribery from village chiefs. But in the 1880's and the 1890's the caravan routes from the deep interior, Katanga, Kasai, and Barotseland, were bringing slaves down to Catumbela,[76] and by the end of the century most of the workers being shipped to São Tomé came through Catumbela, many of them from far beyond the Angolan frontier. This trade was managed by Ovimbundu traders, the *mambari*, and except for their failure to curtail it and for their willingness to buy slaves that came to the coast (rather large conditions, perhaps), the Portuguese in Angola did not have a great deal to do with the inland traffic—which may be one reason why the humanitarians kept their attack within familiar boundaries.

Another reason was ignorance. Livingstone and Cameron had touched upon the activities of the *mambari*, but it was not until Colin Harding's account of the traffic out of Barotseland early in the twentieth century that English philanthropists had a text for this aspect of the trade. Earlier information was scattered and not directly related to the São Tomé traffic. Letters from the Brethren missionaries F. S. Arnot and C. A. Swan appeared more or less regularly in *Echoes of Service* in the last fifteen years of the century.[77] Arnot's remarkable account of his first seven years in Central Africa (1881 to 1888), *Garenganze* (London, 1889) had much information that would later be useful to those humanitarian investigators Henry W. Nevinson and Joseph Burtt. Arnot travelled from Benguela up-country along slave routes with Ovimbundu traders. François

[75] Mary Kingsley, *Travels in West Africa* (2nd edition; London, 1898), pp. 41–42.

[76] See Jan Vansina, 'Long-Distance Trade Routes in Central Africa', *Journal of African History*, iii (1962), 375–90, for a background to the function of these routes.

[77] See Robert Rotberg, 'Plymouth Brethren and Katanga, 1886–1907', *Journal of African History*, v (1964), 285–97.

Coillard's *On the Threshold of Central Africa*, translated and published in London in 1897, was the record of twenty years of missionary pioneering among the Barotse and gave more details of the extent of the Angolan slave-trader's activities.

There were serious distractions in the 1890's for the English humanitarian protest. Events in East and South Africa and the shocking exposés from the Congo took some of the attention away from Angola. But the spirit would return, with force redoubled, in the last great crusade against a European slave-trade.

CHAPTER VI

Labour from Moçambique

By the end of the nineteenth century Portuguese African labour legislation was coming closer to the reality in the colonies. Twenty years of exploration, negotiation, and failure had brought the home government to a sensible, from the imperial view, attitude towards the African peoples in the colonies. If Portugal was to succeed in Africa, it seemed that she had to succeed materially, and that meant that the African population had to be put to work—for themselves and for others. The problems of Portuguese Africa in 1900 were not, of course, even remotely the result of the relatively tolerant labour codes of earlier decades, and the tough labour code of 1899 did not produce any noticeable amelioration of Portuguese Africa's practical difficulties. The realities of life in the two territories continued to be but little altered by legislation, for they derived from attitudes which had grown out of Portuguese-African associations over the centuries. What was significant about the new policies was that they told the eclipse of humanitarian considerations in Lisbon's colonial plannings. Only in the early days of the Portuguese republic which came into being in 1910 did the spirit of Sá da Bandeira briefly awaken.

The *Regulamento de 1899* was rhetorically of a piece with earlier African labour legislation; substantially it was different. It freely admitted the principle and necessity of forced labour for Africans. A committee had been formed in 1898 to study the problems of Portuguese Africa. Dominated by António Enes, former royal commissioner of Moçambique and a forthright imperialist, the committee determined that muddled liberal ideas should not be carried into the new legislation. Taking the arguments once used to defend slavery and clothing them with the language of the new colonial sociology, the committee decided that 'the state, not only as a sovereign of semi-barbarous populations, but also a depository of social authority, should have no *scruples* in obliging and if necessary forcing [italics the committee's] these rude Negroes in Africa, these ignorant Pariahs in Asia, these half-savages from Oceania to work, that is to better themselves by work, to acquire through work the happiest means of existence, to civilize themselves through work . . .'.[1] Enes believed that although to transfer a slave into a free man was a good thing for him and for society, laws that then let a worker become a vagrant cancelled out the benefits. Only silly liberals and humanitarians would take a contrary view.

Thus the Decree of 9 November 1899 stated in its first article that 'all natives of Portuguese overseas provinces are subject to the obligation, moral and legal, of attempting to obtain through work the means that they lack to subsist and to better their social condition'. The worker had full liberty to choose the method of fulfilling the obligation, but if he failed to do so, the colonial authority could intervene. Africans who had sufficient capital to maintain themselves or who had a paying profession or Africans who farmed a plot of land deemed satisfactory by local officials or Africans who produced goods for export were to be exempted from the requirement, as were women, men over sixty, boys under fourteen, the sick and invalid, policemen, chiefs, and prominent African leaders. All others had to work. The services of Africans forced to do labour could be requisitioned by the Government or by private individuals. A number of articles in the *Regulamento* specified minimum wages, health services, and good and honest treatment by the employer. Another article forbade contracts ex-

[1] From a section of the 'Relatório da Comissão', published in *Antologia colonial portuguesa* (Lisbon, 1946), pp. 25 et seq. In the instructions given to the committee, one may read: 'Considering that no other nation can be compared with advantage to ours in the application of humanitarianism and liberal principles in its colonial domain . . . but [considering] that we should not think that we have completed our civilizing missions with the honourable series of measures which from 1836 to 1878 gave the most remarkable testimonial of our will to expell all forms of slavery from our overseas possessions.

'Considering that the period of slavery produced a lasting influence of moral and intellectual backwardness on the populations, most of them of primitive rudeness, who do not therefore understand the benefits of liberty which may have been extended to them . . . since they continue acting as if they were still under the absolute and unconditional yoke of the stronger and more powerful. . . .'

tending beyond five years. And, as always, a curator who received a payment for each contract expedited, was provided for to supervise the contracts and the fulfilment of the terms.

The application in Moçambique of the Regulation of 1899 could only have been visionary. Zambézia was still in the hands of *prazeros*, two-thirds of the province had been leased out to the Moçambique Company, the Niassa Company, or the Zambézia Company, and, in real terms, most of the province was unoccupied by Portuguese authority and even 'unpacified'. Only in the vicinity of Lourenço Marques and Beira were there development projects of sufficient size to demand a consistent flow of labour. Such a labour policy was, in the Moçambique of 1900, almost irrelevant.

Many years earlier Moçambique had found her vocation, and whatever progress the province was to make over the next two decades could be largely measured by the use of Moçambique's labour outside the territory, not inside it. For half a century workers from Moçambique had gone to the French islands, to Madagascar, to Natal, to the diamond mines in Kimberley. Now, towards the end of the century, the flow to the gold mines in the Rand began. 'Between 1890 and 1899 the total number of natives employed on the gold-mines rose from approximately fourteen thousand to ninety-seven thousand. Native labourers went to the gold mines from all over Southern Africa. The most important source was Portuguese East Africa. In 1897 it was estimated that half of the labour employed came from there. . . .'[2] By 1910 over 60,000 Africans from Moçambique were working in the Rand mines. Portuguese East Africa was the most important pool of labour available.

By the Decree of 18 November 1897 the royal commissioner of Moçambique, Joaquim Mousinho de Albuquerque, hero of pacification—a man whose views on forced labour were somewhat more conservative than those of António Enes—established regulations for the recruiting of labour in Moçambique. The regulations contained in the decree and the regulations applied by the Chamber of Mines were to be the basis of a

[2] Sheila T. van der Horst, *Native Labour in South Africa* (London, 1942), p. 136.

modus vivendi which was to lead finally into the Moçambique–Transvaal Convention of 1909.

No one could recruit for labour in Moçambique without legal authorization from the South African Government and a licence for the district governments of Moçambique province. The licence was to be renewed annually and could be cancelled at the discretion of Portuguese officials. Chapter II of the regulations provided for the manner of recruitment and the transport of the workers, while Chapter III defined the activities of the Portuguese Curator of Natives in Johannesburg. The recruiter was responsible for the African workers from the time they were contracted until they reached their destination; they were further obliged to present them to the curator on the expiration of their contracts. Article 39 defined the obligations of the workers: to accompany the recruiter to the place of employment, 'to perform for the employer . . . all work consistent with his strength, wages, and treatment received', and to present his signed pass as prescribed by laws. Workers who ran away or otherwise violated the contract were to give sixty to ninety days of their labour free. At each stage of the procedure the colonial government charged certain fees, both of the recruiters and the workers. The total of these charges was an important contribution to the colonial budget.

The arrangement of 18 December 1901 for a *modus vivendi* made between the high commissioner for South Africa and the governor-general of Moçambique provided that the procedures set out in 1897 be continued. Contracts were to be made for not more than one year and could be renewed. For the expenses of fiscalization, contracts, passports, and registration the Government of Moçambique was to receive the sum of thirteen shillings per contracted worker. The Transvaal Government would use its best endeavours to discourage or prevent 'the clandestine immigration of Natives from the Portuguese territory'. In another direction, tariffs and the classification of goods passing over the Lourenço Marques–Johannesburg railway line which were in force before the Boer War were to be re-established; whatever modifications occurred in tariffs and classifications in goods from South African ports to the Transvaal would occur also on the Lourenço Marques–Johannesburg run.

The *modus vivendi* had been the result of extraordinary bargainings between Governor-General Manuel Gorjão and British consul Fritz H. E. Crowe on behalf of South Africa's High Commissioner Lord Milner. After the war the mines were in desperate need of labour, and the permission to recruit in Moçambique had been rescinded.[3] Gorjão was particularly anxious to curb the actions of foreign recruiting agents who had flooded into the province. In September 1899 a decree had been issued to the effect that future recruiting would be permitted to only one accredited agency for the Chamber of Mines, but with the war's outbreak the decree never came into force. As Crowe wrote the Foreign Office:

The native labour supply from this territory was almost entirely in the hands of some adventurers and unscrupulous Englishmen who made it their business to ingratiate themselves with and to know the natives willing to work in the Transvaal. The consequence is that these men have a very large number at their call—and even if the Portuguese prohibit these men from recruiting, they have so well established their association with native leaders of gangs and the natives themselves, that without appearing to they could cause the natives to flock across the border in large numbers....

The governor general has consistently assured me of his desire to see the mines amply supplied with native labour, but it remains to be seen if the new system will be up to the demands of both the Transvaal and Rhodesia:—behind these amicable expressions I notice a desire to get something in the way of tariff concessions from us in return. . . .[4]

After many preliminaries Crowe met with Gorjão on 15 October 1901 to begin to work out definitive arrangements. The governor had these comments: The emigration of 30,000 Africans a year from the districts of Lourenço Marques, Gaza, and Inhambane would be prejudicial, if not ruinous, to agriculture in these areas, and the compensation should be adequate. The old system of recruitment which had led to much abuse and many deaths had to be done away with, and Africans had to be recruited under the superintendence and protection of

[3] F.O. 63/1449, Lord Kitchener to Colonial Office, 31 May 1901.
[4] F.O. 63/1449, Fritz H. E. Crowe to F.O., 15 Apr. 1901.

Portuguese authorities. 'It also being an ascertained fact that many natives were compelled by native chiefs to accept the contracts with licensed engagers as well as and principally with illicit dealers, it is understood that Portuguese authorities will facilitate the engagement of all natives who wish to go voluntarily in the Transvaal. . . .'

The governor was also deeply concerned about the problem of alcoholism, because experience had shown that emigration to the Transvaal had encouraged the vice of drunkenness. The only practical way to curb the vice was to emphasize the prohibition of the sale of alcohol to miners—and to let them have a moderate quantity of wine, whose effects were not very noxious. A small ration of Portuguese wine could be served with their food. Crowe commented that

> His Excellency . . . does not deny that this being Portuguese wine will be advantageous to Portugal; but it is certain the preference for alcoholic drinks is above all a question of habits, and it is of the utmost importance for the general object that the governor general has in view—the deterioration of the native race and the diminution of the native population when they return—that they should renounce the use of alcohol, which would be much easier if they were already accustomed to Portuguese wine, and had not lost their taste for it from having used other wines during their stay in the Transvaal.

The governor then submitted his basis for a *modus vivendi*, the salient article being that the contracting, transporting, and feeding of the recruits be under Portuguese supervision, that wine be served in the mines, that special authority be allowed the curator in Johannesburg, and that the colonial government receive 41*s*. 6*d*. for each worker delivered at the frontier.[5]

Milner could not agree that the migration was at all detrimental to Portuguese interests. The African worker always brought home a large sum of money which tended to encourage local trade and industry. This was a sufficient compensation for recruiting privileges. An improved system of recruiting was

[5] F.O. 2/789, Crowe to Milner, 17 Oct. 1901. This volume of correspondence is one of the most valuable collections of papers in the whole Anglo-Portuguese labour discussion.

needed, yes, but it had better be left to accredited agents of the Witwatersrand Native Labour Association which was recognized by the Transvaal Government and supported by the Chamber of Mines. Wine could not be dispensed in the mines. Even if the proposal were sound, the force of public opinion and the policy of the British Government would forbid it. As for the recruitment and transportation under Portuguese management, this the Chamber of Mines flatly refused to accept. The mines would never engage Portuguese Africans under these terms; they would only recruit through their own agency, which would undertake to follow Portuguese regulations and to employ a certain proportion of Portuguese subjects as its agents. To stop this illicit migration and recruitment the mines would agree not to hire anyone not contracted by the Association. On most other points the two governments were in agreement.[6]

In the telegraphic exchanges which followed the discussions came down to the matter of recruiting. The Moçambique Government wanted to take over the task—under the guise of humanitarianism, although a growing xenophobia and thoughts of economic gain were far more important. But the Chamber of Mines refused to yield. 'Since the Portuguese have nothing else to give us except recruiting facilities, there is no inducement for us to conclude an agreement at all if we cannot get what we want on that head.' Gradually the governor's position gave way, and the final agreement provided for licensed W.N.L.A. recruiters contracting under strict Portuguese supervision.[7]

The reaction in the Portuguese press to the negotiations was not sympathetic. The Witwatersrand Native Labour Association was not a popular organization in Portugal, and when the question was raised about recruiting privileges in Zambézia for the Association, the cry went up that Portuguese agricultural interests had to be protected. Sharp comparisons were made between the labour scarcity in the islands of São Tomé and the glut of Portuguese labour in the Transvaal. The *Século*

[6] F.O. 2/789, Milner to Crowe, 30 Oct. 1901.

[7] F.O. 2/789, telegram, Crowe to Milner, 14 Nov. 1901; telegram, Milner to Crowe, 16 Nov. 1901; Crowe to Milner, 27 Nov. 1901; Milner, memorandum of 5 Dec. 1901.

demanded that the migration from Zambézia be stopped.[8] The next day the *Popular* reiterated the demand.

There was no question of the value of the *modus vivendi* to Moçambique. In a report to General Gorjão, now briefly minister for the colonies, Joaquim Machado stressed the advantages of the arrangement. In addition to the railway receipts on the traffic through Lourenço Marques to the Rand, which the *modus vivendi* guaranteed, the influx of money into the province was considerable. Africans could now pay their hut tax. Only twenty years ago Africans from Lourenço Marques and Inhambane would not work and had no desire for the necessities of civilization; now a number of them dressed in the European manner, wore shoes, owned houses, drank tea, coffee, and wine, in short, consumed some 600,000 pounds sterling worth of articles a year. In Manica and Sofala district the value of African purchases had risen to 450,000 pounds. Any dislocation of the arrangement would bring hardship to Moçambique, since labour was really the only valuable asset the province had to offer in return for trade advantages, transit guarantees, and the railway tariff. Lourenço Marques was not indispensable to the economic development of the Transvaal, for other southern ports could carry the traffic. Machado calculated that the population of Moçambique, an estimated 2,000,000, could produce 200,000 workers a year for the Rand mines; calculating the wages of each worker at fifteen pounds a year, such a migration would mean about 3,000,000 pounds a year brought into Moçambique, a return that would far exceed anything yielded by agricultural operations, whose success Machado rather doubted. And, finally, there was the incalculable benefit that Africans would be educated, taught the value of money, and, most important, taught how to work.[9]

[8] *O século*, 28 Oct. 1901.

[9] F.O. 2/769, Joaquim Machado to Gorjão, 12 July 1903. Sir Harry Johnston testified twice to the advantages which Africans from Inhambane had obtained from going to work in the Kimberley diamond mines. Prosperity and civilization existed there, because the men had come home with their wages, built houses, and cultivated tidy gardens. *The Times*, 22 Dec. 1902; also, F.O. 2/789, Sir Harry Johnston to Lord Landsdowne, 17 Nov. 1901. Both of these dispatches are concerned with African labour problems, particularly in the British protectorates.

Moçambique labour was not enough. In his letter to *The Times* H. H. Johnston had expressed surprise that recruiters had not gone to Portuguese West Africa where there was a good supply of diligent workers. In 1903 the Foreign Office, which was extremely solicitous throughout the decade in trying to help the Rand mines solve their labour problems, instructed Sir Martin Gosselin, the minister in Lisbon, to urge the Portuguese Government to permit the W.N.L.A. to send an agent to Angola to enter into negotiations with local authorities. The Foreign Office knew it was not likely that the Portuguese Government would agree, 'but nothing must be left undone to obtain labour'.[10] Two weeks later the Foreign Office recommended Colonel Barrett Leonard, Secretary of the Niassa Company—which had chartered a vast tract of northern Moçambique—to Gosselin on his visit to Lisbon. The London directors of the chartered company had come to an agreement with the W.N.L.A., on recruiting in the company's lands, but the Lisbon directors did not view the prospect with favour. If Leonard were not successful in his private talks with members of the Government, could Gosselin intimate to the Portuguese that the British Government approved of the transaction and the British Government would be pleased if the royal commissioner of Moçambique, who had a seat on the company's Lisbon board, were instructed to urge on his fellow members 'the desirability of sanctioning the agreement already arrived at in London'? Gosselin was told for his personal information that the subject was one to which the British Government attached a very great importance.[11] British concern was gratified when Portuguese Niassa was thrown open to labour recruiters from the Rand—thus instituting a series of labour scandals in northern Moçambique.

While recruiters for the mines sought further afield for Portuguese African workers, closer at home Rhodesia was demanding labour from southern Moçambique. Once again the Foreign Office was called in to help British economic interests in southern Africa, this time the British South Africa Company, which was lamenting Portugal's refusal to allow the export of

[10] F.O. 2/769, F.O. to Sir Martin Gosselin, 9 June 1903.
[11] F.O. 2/769, F.O. to Gosselin (confidential), 20 June 1903.

workers from the Delagoa Bay region to Rhodesia. In response to the British minister's observation that there existed in Rhodesia a labour shortage which only African workers from Moçambique could alleviate, Foreign Minister João Arroyo apologetically refused. In the first place, there simply weren't enough workers available; in the second place, as soon as High Commissioner Mousinho had by local decree sanctioned the exportation of workers to Rhodesia, the French Government had claimed a similar concession for Madagascar and French Somaliland. 'Senhor Arroyo also observed that a further exportation of labourers from the Districts of Lourenço Marques or Gazaland would . . . have to be sanctioned by Cortes, and he doubted whether Parliament would be prepared to sanction the almost wholesale removal of the native population, the more as by so doing it would inevitably be considered here as a sort of revival of the slave trade under cover of paid labour.'[12] Why the deputies should reach that conclusion, Arroyo did not say.

As became obvious during the discussions for reviewing the *modus vivendi,* the exclusive recruiting agency for the mines—the ubiquitous Witwatersrand Native Labour Association—did not inspire either confidence or affection in Portuguese colonial officials. As one of the major recruiters in Moçambique from 1895 to 1900, the Association had not acted with restraint; to get workers its agents had engaged in a shameless free-for-all with other labour touts. By its own admission, 'In Moçambique the services of "every Labour Agent in Portuguese territory whose opposition was of any moment" were secured at a cost which did not "materially affect the price of natives landed on these fields".'[13] The Association had been reorganized in 1900 with a view that it should be the sole buyer of labour for the members of the Chamber, but it could only maintain its monopoly in Moçambique. The behaviour of the Association's agents improved, but Moçambique officials were distrustful of its procedures, especially since the colonial government was convinced that it could do the job better—and for a greater profit—than the Association.

[12] F.O. 2/508, Hugh MacDonald to F.O., 1 Feb. 1901.

[13] From an Association report of 1898. Quoted in van der Horst, *Native Labour,* p. 135.

In 1906 the W.N.L.A. found itself in the middle of a complicated wrangle over its recruiting monopoly. The labour pool from Portuguese East Africa was not sufficient when it was distributed among the various members of the industry making up the Chamber of Mines, and early in the year the J. B. Robinson group, whose mines made up one-fifteenth of the industry, began to manœuvre for a privileged position. Robinson set up a separate recruiting company, the Transvaal Mines Labour Company, to apply for recruiting licences—though later the applications were to be made by agents directly nominated by Robinson. Tentative permission was granted by the Moçambique Government, which said the final decision had to be made in Lisbon. Robinson thereupon approached the British Government to use its influence in Portugal. The Chamber of Mines and the Witwatersrand Native Labour Association opposed any private arrangements.

They were joined in their opposition by the Earl of Selborne, Governor of the Transvaal. On receiving a communication from the Colonial Office that the Government favoured Robinson's petition and that it seemed desirable to have competition in the recruiting of native labour, Selborne wired Elgin:

> How many recruiters of native labour there may be is a matter of perfect indifference to me, but if you take a hand in this matter I warn you that you will, I think, live to regret it.

The matter was for the Portuguese Government to decide. If they permitted Robinson to recruit, they would be inundated with requests. The moving spirit of the Transvaal Mines Labour Company 'rejoices in the name of Kaffir Wilson and he has one of the most unenviable reputations in all South Africa'. Selborne was concerned about the workers, and he hated to restore the old order of things. The labour touts who used to swarm about in free recruiting days were a 'crowd of ruffians'.[14]

[14] F.O. 367/19, Elgin to Selborne, 7 May 1906; Selborne to Colonial Office, 10 May 1906. In a later communication Selborne sent an extract from Consul-General J. G. Baldwin in Lourenço Marques. Baldwin said that before 1900 recruiting in Moçambique was the most profitable industry in South Africa as far as the recruiter was concerned. When restrictions were brought about by the formation of the W.N.L.A., recruiters were furious and set about maturing their plans for a return to the old system. F.O. 367/19, Baldwin to Selborne, 5 July 1906.

But British intervention in Portugal had its effect, and Robinson got his licence to recruit—or so it seemed. In the meantime, the Moçambique authorities had moved to exploit the ambiguous situation. There was much feeling in Lourenço Marques that if new licences were handed out, a Portuguese company should have preference. If this should fail, a pleasant alternative, favoured by Governor-General Alfredo Freire de Andrade, was for all licences to be cancelled and the recruiting of workers to be carried on by a specially formed government department with salaried government officials as recruiters. The *curador* in Johannesburg had drawn up a detailed plan which Freire de Andrade had sent to Lisbon. For the Transvaal the plan had dangerous implications. 'With only one recruiting agency and that in the hands of the Portuguese Government, and with the power such an agency could give to regulate the number of natives recruited, the governor-general would possess a powerful weapon which could be easily used in connection with the railway and other matters.'[15]

In Lisbon the Overseas Ministry had issued only *one* recruiting licence, to Robinson's man Holmes, who had been chosen to take charge of the recruiting in Moçambique. Robinson sent a furious telegram to the Foreign Office demanding parity with the Witwatersrand Native Labour Association. A personal recruiting licence was useless; what he wanted was an organizational licence permitting large-scale recruiting.[16] Once more the Foreign Office began to apply pressure on the Portuguese Government, but Portugal did not yield. In mid-November, Foreign Minister Luis de Magalhães wrote Minister Villiers that the Government in Moçambique had had a satisfactory relationship with the Association and had at the beginning of the year got from them an improved system for repatriating workers. In return for this the governor had told the W.N.L.A.

[15] F.O. 367/19, Baldwin to Selborne, 18 Aug. 1906. No other arrangement could have upset the Chamber of Mines and the British Government more; although the latter was perfectly willing to run the risk of being party to a situation of anarchy in Moçambique, it could not be Portuguese anarchy. It is likely that the Association, knowing that nothing was more calculated to restore its monopoly than the threat of a Portuguese-controlled recruitment, encouraged these aspirations in Moçambique.

[16] F.O. 367/19, J. B. Robinson to F.O., 15 Sept. 1906.

that he would grant recruiting licences to no one else without denouncing his agreement with the Association at least three months in advance. The Portuguese Government wanted to allow only one major recruiter in Moçambique; an occasional private licence to recruit could be granted, but nothing would be done to give equal opportunity with the W.N.L.A.[17]

A week later Villiers met with Magalhães who told him the whole matter had been handled by Minister for Overseas Ayres de Ornelas, a former governor of Moçambique district and a man whose word carried weight. The overseas minister felt that the pressure of rival agencies 'tended to unsettle the mind of the natives and to cause disturbances, whereas under present arrangements the work of recruiting was conducted in an orderly manner'. Holmes had been granted what he asked for, personal facilities for recruiting. Villiers then added that 'some resentment has no doubt been aroused by the enquiry conducted by Consul Nightingale into the conditions of labour in the islands of São Tomé and Principe and by the terms in which public mention has been made of the matter'.[18]

Portugal's position was now very strong, and she willingly agreed to the formation of a commission of inquiry to look into the whole subject of labour for the Rand mines; during the period of inquiry no new licences for recruiting were to be granted. By now the need for labour was acute. British policy now forbade the use of Chinese labour in the mines, and the Robinson group's talk of importing white workers for the mines was seen to be the bluff it was intended to be. What Portugal most wanted, the control of the labour monopoly in Moçambique, she would not get, but the bickerings in London and in Johannesburg made it clear she could drive a hard bargain.[19]

[17] F.O. 367/19, Magalhães to F. H. Villiers, 12 Nov. 1906. In response to this, Grey wrote on 22 Nov. 1906: 'The unaccomodating attitudes of the Portuguese on the recruiting question is very unexpected and is producing a very unfavourable impression here. The issue of an effective license to the Robinson group is, however, the urgent matter for the moment. . . .'

[18] F.O. 367/19, F. H. Villiers to F.O., 18 Nov. 1906.

[19] The British Government had made a bad case in its open favouritism of the Robinson interests. To a question of 17 Dec. 1906, Under-Secretary Winston Churchill denied any preference for the Robinson group, but he did affirm a prejudice against the Witwatersrand Native Labour Association. '. . . We could not view without anxiety the concentration of the whole black

But nothing was regarded as more sinister, by both mine owners and politicians, than Portuguese control over the labour supply, and undoubtedly this consideration, as well as the failure of recruiter Holmes to get workers, drove Robinson into making his peace with the Association and the Chamber even before the commission of inquiry met. For the Earl of Selborne, now representing all the mining interests, the terms of reference for the commission should be 'what system of recruiting and distributing natives from Portuguese East Africa will ensure the largest and most continuous supply of labour to the Transvaal'. Other considerations should be provisions for the humane treatment of the workers and the satisfactory and economic working of the mines. As for a Portuguese monopoly. 'You will see at once that such a solution would be fatal. In that case the Portuguese Government would in every point of railway negotiations have a complete and permanent squeeze over the Transvaal. . . . It is quite certain that the recruiting would not be always voluntary as we understand the word.'[20]

The commission functioned in a desultory manner. Consul Baldwin reported regularly from Lourenço Marques on the unhappiness in Moçambique over the lack of Portuguese participation in the recruiting of labour. Constant pressure was being put on the Association to take on Portuguese agents whenever a new licence was granted. The Association would not 'object to comparatively honest and efficient individuals, but in the case of the people they are generally asked to employ, the request is only a species of blackmail'. Baldwin saw the campaign as part of a deliberate plan to get rid of the foreign element and to introduce Portuguese men into that part of the Association's work which took place in Moçambique. He did not believe that the W.N.L.A. could operate much longer under such harassment.[21] Towards the end, sentiment had become

labour supply in the hands of the Witwatersrand Native Labour Association—that powerful body which exerts such immense influence on local politics and which in a hundred ways has woven itself into all the apparatus of economic and social life in Johannesburg. This body . . . has a tremendous and sinister influence. . . .' *Hansard*, Fourth Series, v. 167, 1135–6, 17 Dec. 1906. [Quoted in telegram from Elgin to Selborne, 19 Dec. 1906, in F.O. 367/47.]

[20] F.O. 367/47, telegram, Selborne to Elgin, 8 Jan. 1907.

[21] F.O. 367/47, Baldwin to Selborne, 5 Feb. 1907.

more spirited against the Association, principally because it was believed that the organization made enormous profits, none of which remained in Moçambique. The three newspapers in Lourenço Marques, one of them semi-official, attacked the Association. The governor at Inhambane had submitted a remarkable report purporting to show the disastrous effects of Rand recruiting in his district. No industry would flourish in Inhambane until there was labour, he wrote, and there would be no labour until foreign recruitment was curtailed. Nor would trade increase, because the workers brought back more merchandise (125,000 pounds sterling worth) than was imported by local traders (25,000 pounds worth) each year. To some extent these losses were offset by the gold brought back, part of which went to pay the hut tax, but the workers were reluctant to spend the rest of their earnings. To enable commerce of the district 'to wrest from the hands of the natives a portion of their accumulated savings', the governor had issued an edict that all Africans be properly clothed. These had resulted in issuing licences for twenty more clothing stores in the interior, 'but even if the natives were obliged to wear polished boots and top hats, only a hundredth part of their savings would pass into circulation'. Once it had been easier to pry their savings loose.

> There existed formerly a magnificent vehicle for the transfer of money from the hands of the native to those of the general community. It consisted in the distillation and sale of fermented kaffir beverages. In those times the Europeans and Asians lived in comfort, agriculture progressed, and the native returning from the Transvaal quickly used the money he had saved in satisfying his vice in drink, he then had to look for more work, either in his district or in the Transvaal to obtain the necessary means for purchasing more. In this way there was abundant and cheap labour for agriculture, and the economic life of the district was being steadily developed. . . . But this magnificent device for circulating money was rendered ineffective by the law which prohibited the use of fermented drinks, which was passed with a view to protecting the Wine Industry of Portugal.

And from the point of political influence, the provincial governor distrusted the emigration. Africans, in comparing the materially rich Saxon race with the somewhat less affluent Latin race, might be led to the incorrect conclusions. Within the province the Association was a state within a state: its headquarters were better constructed than administrative offices, its runners were better uniformed and better paid than Portuguese African sepoys. To the unsophisticated mind it must seem that English employees came to provide money and clothing while the Portuguese employee came only to collect hut tax, 'to order him to do agricultural labour or to clean up the roads gratuitously or to construct bridges, also gratuitously'. Thus the Africans of Inhambane respected the English rather more than they did the Portuguese. The governor suggested several improvements in the terms of the recruiting, *viz.*, that no African could go to the mines unless he had previously worked for two years on an agricultural or industrial project in Moçambique, that no workers could go until they had registered at a local Portuguese administrative office and obtained permission, that the W.N.L.A. should not be allowed to dress its runners in any distinctive way, and that no worker be allowed to bring back any merchandise with him from the mines.[22]

Foolish though the report may have been, it was none the less typical of much of the argumentation which went on in Moçambique and Portugal from the early days of the Rand recruitment down to the middle of the twentieth century. Few of the critics of the arrangement were offended morally, though there could have been a strong humanitarian protest in Portugal against a colonial system which so bluntly used Moçambique's one important asset, African labour, to enrich a handful of foreign capitalists. The arguments, however, were economic and nationalistic, the one maintaining that the development of Moçambique was stunted through lack of labour and the other that Moçambique Africans were being denationalized. Both proposals begged the question and were devoid of any real substance.

The Moçambique–Transvaal Convention of April 1909 and all subsequent conventions provided for labour recruitment privileges in Moçambique for the Rand mines in return for the guaranteed passages of about 50 per cent. of all traffic to the

[22] F.O. 367/47, Baldwin to F.O., 19 Oct. 1907 (enclosure).

competitive area (the Johannesburg, Pretoria, Krugersdorp industrial region) through Lourenço Marques and over the Lourenço Marques Railway. Moçambique profited from the railway traffic and rates, from the service charges on each worker leaving the colony, and from the constant influx of wages into the territory. The recruiting was entrusted to the Witwatersrand Native Labour Association which remained responsible for the worker from the moment he signed the contract until he was returned to his village. In Moçambique the Association maintained fifteen to twenty recruiting stations and a small army of African and European recruiters.

In 1909 about 75,000 workers were contracted in Moçambique. The figure in following years would fluctuate between 65,000 and 100,000. After 1913 workers could not be recruited from north of the twenty-second parallel, because of the high incidence of tuberculosis and pneumonia among workers from the tropical zone. In the first decade of the century the mortality rates in the mines was sixty-seven per thousand, which gradually declined. The 1909 Convention provided for a maximum two-year contract, unless the curator in Johannesburg approved of an extension, which he usually did. A 1912 amendment to the convention provided for deferred pay, and the door was opened to considerable corruption and chicanery by colonial officials.[23] The recruiting of the workers was not always above reproach, and there were many cases of coercion by local chiefs in return for some gratuity, but the recruiting processes were fundamentally correct. Given the labour laws in the province, there was a greater disposition among African men to work voluntarily for higher wages in the Rand than to be coerced into a job with little or no pay at home.[24]

[23] In Dec. 1913 Consul MacDonell reported serious abuses to the Foreign Office. At the same time he wrote a private letter to Under-Secretary Tilley. Both the deferred pay and death benefits were regularly siphoned off into official's pockets. F.O. 367/344, MacDonell to F.O., 2 Dec. 1913.

[24] In a speech before the Portuguese Anti-Slavery Society on 31 Dec. 1910, Governor-General Freire de Andrade spoke on the convention. He recognized that 'the native is today the most important element in the development and progress of our Colony of Moçambique, for he brings the greater part of the gold with which we meet our liabilities'. The governor estimated that some 300,000 pounds sterling a year were brought back each year by workers from the Rand. No Africans were recruited against their will, and colonial authorities were vigilant that all the conditions of the contract were fulfilled.

From the beginning of the century Southern Rhodesia had also attempted to relieve its pressing labour shortages with Moçambique workers. In 1900 the manager of the Rhodesian Labour Board went to Lourenço Marques to arrange for the recruitment of workers. In order to avoid competition the Labour Board agreed to withdraw from the province and to allow the W.N.L.A. to do its recruiting. In return for this concession the Association agreed to stay out of Rhodesia and Zambézia, and to deliver to the Labour Board 12½ per cent. of all the Moçambique labour it recruited. The Board was also to pay a share of the general administrative expenses of the Association. In 1902 the administrator of Southern Rhodesia demanded that the labour promised now be delivered. When the W.N.L.A. declared that it had been impossible to contract workers for Rhodesian mines, since Africans refused to work there, the agreement was terminated six months hence, in June 1903. Two years later Rhodesian authorities again proposed to recruit for themselves, according to the terms implicit in the *modus vivendi* of 1901 which applied both to the Chamber of Mines and to the Southern Rhodesia administration.[25]

The workers were well treated, although mortality among workers from north of the twentieth parallel was 10 per cent. and south of the parallel only 7 per cent. The clandestine sale of alchohol *was* detrimental to their health, and it would be advantageous to serve the miners allowances of weak but pure Portuguese wine. Workers from Moçambique made up 60 per cent. of the miners on the Rand and 80 per cent. of those working underground. But there were many disadvantages, in the governor's opinion, in the convention. Moçambique annually lost an important part of her most robust population, many of whom died in the mines or returned home diseased. They learned a different language and tended to look with disfavour on agricultural work, which had suffered greatly from lack of labour. For the present the convention should be continued, 'but the only way to prevent the difficulties which have arisen is to develop the province gradually until it may be possible to dispense with the profits which the emigration brings'. In concluding, Freire de Andrade told the Anti-Slavery Society that 'it would do a noble work if it were to take these millions of natives under their care and secure for them the attention which should be bestowed on those for whom the Portuguese nation is responsible'. F.O. 367/234, Villiers to F.O., 16 Jan. 1911 (enclosure).

[25] F.O. 367/47, W. H. Milton (Administrator) to Selborne, 5 Mar. 1907. At about the same time the secretary of the British South Africa Company wrote to the Colonial Office that the available labour was insufficient for the expanding industries of Southern Rhodesia. He requested licences for the Rhodesia Native Labour Board to recruit in Moçambique. F.O. 367/47, D. E. Brodie to Colonial Office, 15 Mar. 1907.

The difficulty was basically that not enough workers could be obtained to satisfy both the Transvaal and Rhodesia. The W.N.L.A. had no intention of sending labourers contracted in Lourenço Marques, Gaza, and Inhambane districts to Rhodesia, and it had made no great efforts to recruit in those areas contiguous to Rhodesia. And there was another difficulty. The whole of that territory was under the administration of the Moçambique Company, which refused to grant recruiting licences in spite of Portuguese requests that it do so. The Transvaal ministers, in discussing the Rhodesian proposition, made it plain that they would oppose any petition unless Rhodesia lifted its ban on recruiting there by the Chamber of Mines; if the ban were rescinded, then the ministers would support a request for Rhodesia to obtain licences to recruit in the Tete district of Moçambique and would even extend the use of the facilities of the W.N.L.A. there.[26]

In 1909 Administrator Milton again tried to get Moçambique labour. He wrote to Selborne that the shortage was acute in both fields and mines and that he hoped the high commissioner would address the governor-general of Moçambique for permission for Rhodesia to recruit in two areas of Moçambique, the Barue district, which had recently come under Portuguese administration though still a part of the Moçambique Company's lands, and in the region south along the Zambesi opposite Zumbo.[27] Selborne replied that the Barue district had only recently been pacified by Portuguese forces, and almost immediately thereafter an agent for the Association had set up a station there. 'The probability, therefore, is that the Transvaal Government, to whom the supply of labour for the Witwatersrand mines is a matter of great importance, would object to the Rhodesia Native Labour Bureau getting similar facilities there and starting a rival recruiting organization. In the second of the districts referred to . . . the Witwatersrand Native Labour Association also has its recruiters, so here again the Transvaal Government would probably object. . . .' Selborne suggested the tactic of friendly discussions with the Transvaal Government,

[26] F.O. 367/47, Selborne to Colonial Office, 27 May 1907 (Encloses minutes of Transvaal Ministers' meeting of 11 May 1907).

[27] F.O. 367/47, Milton to Selborne, 5 Feb. 1909.

involving certain accommodations, one of which might be that the Association would be permitted to recruit in Southern Rhodesia.[28]

Finally, by the beginning of 1913, Rhodesia could contemplate getting Moçambique labour. The opposition of the Union Government had been withdrawn, and the Colonial Office asked the Foreign Office to support in Lisbon the request of the Rhodesia Native Labour Bureau for recruiting licences.[29] What had happened was that the W.N.L.A. was no longer recruiting from north of the twenty-second parallel because of the high mortality rate among Africans from those regions. 'In these circumstances it would appear that if the Rhodesia Native Labour Bureau can obtain the permission of the Portuguese authorities to recruit in this area it will not come into competition with the Witwatersrand Native Labour Association, so that no objection on the part of the Union Government to the grant of such permission by the Portuguese authorities is now to be apprehended.'[30] In September, H. W. Kempster, Managing Director of the Labour Bureau, had gone to Lourenço Marques to begin direct negotiations. At the end of his visit, British Consul-General MacDonell and Kempster were inclined to believe that the licences would be granted. The Bureau requested permission to recruit in the districts of Zambézia and Tete up to about 15,000 workers a year. The terms of the agreement were close to those of the Moçambique–Transvaal Convention of 1909, though the fees collected by Moçambique on

[28] F.O. 367/47, Selborne to Milton, 19 Feb. 1909. A clandestine recruitment for the Transvaal was going on practically at the Rhodesian–Moçambique frontier, near the juncture of the Save and Lundi Rivers. The Portuguese commandant of Mossurise, who had been trying to put down the recruitment, sent two letters to Lourenço Marques which purported to be from labour tout W. E. McKechnie to a Mr. Ledeboer, Makulabe, Transvaal. In the first letter, Aug. 1909, from Lesongwa, McKechnie said he had great hopes for recruiting if there were no interference. He also referred to an illicit traffic being carried on by Boer policemen, who were employed in that section of the province. In his second letter, of 3 Sept., McKechnie was more optimistic and asked for food for thirty to fifty men to be sent up to him. The Portuguese were causing trouble, but 'as long as the big native population is in their territory, just so long shall the recruiters go on, and as long as the recruiting stays here, so shall I; it is the best recruiting ground I have struck'. F.O. 367/89, *varia*.

[29] F.O. 367/340, Colonial Office to F.O., 8 Jan. 1913.

[30] F.O. 367/340, D. E. Brodie to Colonial Office, 30 Dec. 1912.

each worker were somewhat higher. Even the deferred pay clauses, which was proving so distasteful to the managers of the W.N.L.A., were part of the terms. In the years ahead the numbers of workers going to Rhodesia would sometimes equal those of workers going to the Rand.

English humanitarian opinion was not over-attentive to the migration of Moçambique Africans to the mines, although there had been strong protests against the use of Chinese labour. In fact the system was often recommended by philanthropists, who seemed to have no sense of the moral ambiguity of what they proposed, as a procedure to be followed by plantation owners in São Tomé. It was enough that the system was for the most part voluntary, that Portuguese participation was kept to an acceptable minimum, and that the Moçambique worker, it was believed, could obtain cultural and economic advantages by contracting to work abroad. There was also the distraction of the rather more flagrant misuse of African labour, exclusively by Portuguese, in West Africa. An occasional missionary protest, a stray remark in Parliament, and a vaguely questioning attitude in the offices of the Anti-Slavery Society or the Aborigines Protection Society made up the sum of protest.

The *Anti-Slavery Reporter* had only the remotest interest in Moçambique. It did print an extract from an article in the *Westminster Gazette*, wherein the correspondent implied that the greater part of the labour for the mines was there under compulsion,[31] as well as selections from an indignant account in *Central Africa*, the journal of the Universities' Mission, on how agents for the W.N.L.A. and Portuguese officials worked hand in hand in Portuguese Niassa.[32] H. R. Fox Bourne,

[31] *Reporter*, Jan.–Feb. 1903, pp. 27–28. The article is from the 28 Jan. issue of the *Westminster Gazette*.

[32] The Reverend H. Barnes wrote: 'Picture the pair working the lakeside together—the Portuguese sergeant asking for four shillings [the hut tax] or the equivalent in work at Mtengula, and side by side with him a smooth-tongued agent of the Rand offering the four shillings on the spot plus a small sum in cloth to console the wife or mother. All perfectly fair and straightforward, and I suppose any man would prefer to have his tax paid for the year even at the cost of exile for an uncertain period rather than stay at home and see the hut burnt as a penalty. So of course some people went from nearly every village. . . . They supposed they would have to sweep

splenetic secretary of the Aborigines Protection Society could only comment, 'the whole system of labour-recruiting for the supply of Kafirs for the Transvaal mines is, albeit a mild one, a form of slave-trading'.[33]

In legal terms there could have been no serious quarrel with what went on in the name of the *modus vivendi* or the Convention of 1909 or the Moçambique–Rhodesian agreement. The issue was not slavery, or even the cheating which went on under the system by which the worker was sometimes gulled into signing a contract and other times deprived of his earnings; the issue was the essential function of African labour—and this was not a consideration of any overriding importance in colonial Africa or the humanitarian conscience of the early 1900's. Implicit in the arrangements was an innocence of concern for the people involved, who were bartered as commodities for traffic and tariff advantages; but, again, this was a judgement for a later day. A certain amount of harm was done as a result of the migration system but, ironically, it was done indirectly, in West Africa where the Foreign Office, because of its close participation in securing workers for the Transvaal, could bring no diplomatic or moral pressure to bear on Portugal during the crisis of the São Tomé labour scandals.

Apart from Rand recruitment, however, there were labour conditions in Moçambique and stories of domestic slavery and perverse brutality which drew the rebuke of both the Foreign Office and the humanitarians. Progress had been slow in Portuguese East Africa. The most successful action in the long history of struggle against the dhow traffic was reserved for the

and hoe, but they did not suppose they would be sent underground. The agent was telling all the villagers positively that they would not be set to work in the mines but on the surface. Pressed for the ground of his confidence, it proved to be nothing more than the fact that the Central African labourers of last year's recruiting had been a failure, and a costly failure, underground. Pressed further to say whether there was anything in the terms of the engagement expressly forbidding their employment underground, he was obliged to admit there was nothing. Pressed further to give me grounds on which to base a happy confidence like his own . . . I was entreated to take it on my informant's personal word of honour. . . .' *Reporter*, Nov.–Dec. 1904, pp. 142–3.

[33] *The Aborigine's Friend*, Mar. 1907, pp. 19–20.

year 1902. On 12 March of that year the following telegram, dated the same day, was read to the Portuguese *Cortes*.

725 slaves have been liberated, 12 slave dhows have been captured. Not a single shot has yet been fired. The *San Rafael* entered the port of Simuco [about halfway between Moçambique island and Pemba Bay] piloting the ships of the naval division, a magnificent port which up to the present has only been used by slave dealers.[34]

Subsequently fifty slave-traders were killed and 106 were taken prisoner. The same year seventeen traders were captured at Moma River in Angoche. In both places the Arab traders were mostly Suris, trading for captives to supply the Persian and Arabian markets.

The Government had much more difficulty in putting down the abuses carried out in the name of contract labour and seemingly sanctioned by the Regulation of 1899. In forwarding a copy of a provisional order by Governor-General Gorjão barring the *chibalo* (forced labour) system in the districts of Gaza and Lourenço Marques, Consul-General Baldwin wrote that it had been the custom of contractors, industrial concerns, and large employers of labour to arrange with the commandants of sub-districts for periodic supplies of labour. The Africans were indentured for fixed periods at wages set well below the market rate. The commandant received a capitation fee; it was his custom to order each chief in the region to hand over a certain number of men, who had no say whatsoever in the choice of job or employer. The system was much abused, particularly by lesser officials who thus supplemented their salaries. While the Provincial Decree of December 1906 did not set aside the obligation to work, it did bar the use of forced labour by private employers, thus leaving the government as the only user of forced labour in the province.[35] The decree was ineffective and did not remain long in force.

At Inhambane it was common talk in the town that local authorities, acting under orders from the governor-general, had forcibly taken Africans from their homes and sent them off to L. Cohen and Company, agents in Lourenço Marques for the

[34] F.O. 2/638, Erroll MacDonell to F.O., 15 Mar. 1902 (enclosure).
[35] F.O. 367/47, J. G. Baldwin to F.O., 15 Dec. 1906.

Lewis and Marks mines. 'It is, of course [Vice Consul Neel wrote], no uncommon thing in the Inhambane district for natives to be seized in this manner, and sent away to work for the Portuguese Government in some other portion of the Province, but it is an entirely new departure on the part of the Authorities to force natives to go to a non-Portuguese territory.' While he was in Inhambane, Neel saw Africans brought into town with their hands tied behind their backs, destined, he was told, for Cohen and Company. On the steamer down to Lourenço Marques were a group of workers who were met on the docks by an armed escort of police and marched up the hill, 'a somewhat unnecessary precaution if the natives in question had volunteered their services'.[36]

The one area in which the British Government showed its old-time firmness in dealing with Portugal was Zambézia. Sir Edward Grey would keep coming back to the question, 'What about Zambézia?' In 1910 reports of outrages against the native population, including a neo-slave-trade in workers to São Tomé and Principe, had trickled into the Foreign Office, and Consul-General R. C. F. Maugham was instructed to go up the river to make investigations. Maugham, one-time consul at Beira and a resident of Moçambique for a number of years, was generously predisposed toward Portugal's African policies—as they were practised, not legislated—and his report had much more value than the Foreign Office, expecting something more sensational, believed. The Foreign Office was particularly unhappy that Maugham had used only African sources of information, who were 'notoriously unreliable'.[37]

[36] One of the reasons why it was difficult to get satisfactory information on what was going on was that ' . . . Forced labour is the birthright of natives living in Portuguese territory, and natives who have been seized for forced labour, and who find that their forced labour has to be performed in Johannesburg or elsewhere under British rule, where good wages are earned, and where they are not robbed of their earnings by a swarm of officials, native police and caçadores [runners] are too agreeably surprised to say a word against the methods by which they were "recruited", and thereby run the risk of being sent away to perform forced labour elsewhere, viz, Portuguese territory.' F.O. 367/29, Selborne to Colonial Office, 4 Aug. 1906 (enclosures).

[37] See R. C. F. Maugham, *Portuguese East Africa* (London, 1906) and *Zambézia* (London, 1910). The latter work was dedicated to Dom Manuel II, King of Portugal 'in profound admiration of those portions of the splendid dependency of Portuguese East Africa'.

On his expedition Maugham made a special visit to the *prazo* Lugella which had been the scene of some of the complaints. Francisco Manteiro, a prominent cocoa grower of São Tomé and the most eloquent defender of the island's use of imported labour, had recently acquired a share of the *prazo*'s lease, and recruitment had been heavy. It was thought that Lugella had been chosen because of its secluded situation and difficulty of access. Maugham found the Africans there frightened and suspicious. Many had fled the country since the recruiting began. From questioning various villagers, Maugham established the familiar pattern: the word passed down for headmen to appear at a certain place with as many men as possible. The men were told they were to go to work at São Tomé, their names were put on a piece of paper, and they were asked to express their willingness to go, which they did. After many interrogations of headmen and villagers, mostly in their language, Maugham presented the evidence.

1. That at the outset of the recruitment of natives for São Tomé there can be no doubt that coercive methods of a more or less grave kind were practiced, and there is, moreover, ground for strong suspicion that the natives may at times have been brought to the coast under restraint of a more or less severe character.

In *Portuguese East Africa*, Maugham gave his views on Portuguese treatment of Africans: 'Whilst we in our colonies have educated the native, and petted him, and done everything we could think of to impair his value as a worker by endeavouring to fit him for positions for which he is not by nature intended, the Portuguese, on the other hand, throughout the centuries of their occupation of East Africa, have never viewed him in any but a proper and practical light; for them he is first and last the "mão d'obra" (labouring hand), and any proposition tending to lessen his value in the capacity would never, and will never, be entertained by them for a single moment. I have always observed, over a considerable number of years, that in whatever direction the Portuguese have achieved but qualified success, they have always known how to deal with the Negro, and want of respect on the part of the latter is scarcely ever seen. I do not mean that this respect is extorted by cruelty; I do not believe the Portuguese master is in any sense a cruel person—indeed I must confess to having seen more ill-treatment of natives among foreigners of the Moçambique province—but wherever one may come in contact with him, whether it be Moçambique in the north, the Zambesi in the center, or Beira in the south, one will never see the insolent demeanour of the black man toward the white which is such a constant and lamentable spectacle of everyday occurrence in our Colonies and Protectorates in almost all parts of Africa.'

2. That at present the recruitment of natives is not carried out in conditions which ensure to them complete freedom to engage themselves or not as they think proper, although the prazo-proprietors may profess that it is so. . . . I am convinced that they are subject to moral coercion of a kind with which the recruiter is very familiar, namely the coercion which springs from the fact that when the native is called he does not dare refuse to obey the summonses, and once in the white man's stockade his last shred of courage vanishes, and he becomes as clay in the recruiter's hands.

3. The natives I firmly believe do not always clearly understand (*a*) how long their engagement is for; (*b*) where they are going; (*c*) what arrangements will be made for their remuneration, repatriation, etc.

Down at Quelimane, Maugham collected stories of the press-gangs organized by the local police to supply the demand for workers for the islands. Workers brought down from the interior were kept in the *quintal,* or backyard, of the chief recruiter and given large quantities of cheap intoxicants. They were perfunctorily approved by the curator, who got six shillings for each contract he countersigned, and by the medical officer, who was also paid for each worker he approved.[38]

On the basis of this dispatch and a separate report made by Maugham on the *prazo* system,[39] Grey instructed Sir Arthur Hardinge to make representations. For a number of years British subjects in Moçambique, missionaries and business men, had been harassed by local officials. Recently a missionary had been killed on Lake Nyasa by a Portuguese official and a British engineer jailed in Zambézia. The labour issue was partly a blind under which the Foreign Office told Hardinge to address 'a serious warning to the Portuguese Government in regard to the position of affairs' and to urge it to change its present policies.[40]

Hardinge had two interviews with Foreign Minister Augusto de Vasconcellos in January 1912. He told him that the British Government had good expectations that the Republic would give practical example to its expressed humanitarian desires to treat the subject races fairly and that it would carry out its

[38] F.O. 367/234, Maugham to F.O., 28 Aug. 1911.
[39] F.O. 367/234, Maugham to F.O., 3 Nov. 1911.
[40] F.O. 367/289, F.O. to Hardinge, 9 Jan. 1912.

public avowals to do away with slave-trade and the illicit alcohol traffic. In the second conversation Vasconcellos commented that the Portuguese Government, in deference to British outcry about slave-grown cocoa, had stopped recruiting in Angola 'and arranged to procure the requisite labour from Moçambique, where the natives were more civilized . . . and were, moreover, accustomed, as many of them went to work in the Transvaal mines, to employment a long way from their homes'. It would be improper to forbid, on the grounds of humanity, 'their recruitment for Portuguese plantations at São Tomé, whilst allowing it in the case of the Rand mines, where statistics showed that the mortality among the native workmen was very much higher'. If Portugal were to curtail recruiting for both areas, it would give dangerous offence to the Government of South Africa, and Portugal would be accused in the British press even more vehemently of damaging British commercial interests. Vasconcellos's remarks took much of the bite out of Hardinge's reproval.[41]

Several months later the foreign minister made formal reply to the British protest. He pointed out that his government was moved by humanitarian sentiments in Africa even when they caused, as they had in the case of São Tomé, economic loss or hardship. Workers from Moçambique for the islands were freely recruited under regulations more favourable than those of the Convention of 1909. Cases of abuse were swiftly punished. As for Maugham's report, Vasconcellos said he had found sharp discrepancies between it and the consul's book on Zambézia.[42]

[41] F.O. 367/289, Hardinge to F.O., 24 Jan. 1912 and 29 Jan. 1912.

[42] He quoted from the work: 'The present generation of the remoter prazo proprietors . . . seek first of all to attract as large a native population as possible by dint of indulgent treatment. . . . Led by men of energy and men of initiative, the coast Negro has to some extent begun to realize the dignity and necessity of labour (pp. 135–6).

'The valley of the Zambesi, in so far as it comes under Portuguese influence, has entered upon a prolonged, indeed there is every reason to hope and believe a permanent, state of peace (p. 307).

'The relations subsisting between the European and the negro are, therefore, of an eminently satisfactory character: the most unmistakable proofs of this are the aptitude the latter displays in the field of labour, and his willingness to work in the service of the white (p. 309).' F.O. 367/289, Hardinge to F.O., 1 May 1912 (enclosure).

At about the same time the Foreign Office received quite a different report on Zambézia, one which recalled the attacks of the 1880's and 1890's. The writer was R. N. Lyne, an Englishman employed as director of agriculture for the province of Moçambique. Lyne's associations with Portuguese East Africa were as long and as valid as those of Maugham. He wrote his dispatch to Consul MacDonell in the conviction that if the British Government knew about the tyranny and oppression of Africans in the Quelimane district, it would not allow them to continue. His account of the *prazo* system was the familiar nineteenth-century version: half-caste commandants in charge of native populations of 20,000 to 30,000 people, armed sepoys raping and murdering at their pleasure, the unchecked misuse of native populations of 20,000 to 30,000 people, armed sepoys MacDonell, who had served twelve years earlier in Zambézia was fully convinced of Lyne's statements and had himself been witness to some of the brutalities described by Lyne, particularly the dreaded *palmatória*.[43]

Another report, this one from Dr. Leonard Bostock, British vice-consul at Porto Amélia, gave an account of life in the lands of the Niassa Company. The administration of the interior was in the hands of *chefes do concelho* or *chefes de posto*, many of whom owned plantations. At tax collection time armed soldiers were sent out in all directions to arrest every woman in sight. They were kept at the estate of the *chefe* until their husbands or fathers paid the hut tax or until their labour on the farm was no longer needed. 'They are in fact temporary slaves.' Local police terrorized the countryside. Official iniquities were not investigated; the offender was simply asked to resign. Mortality, often the result of starvation, was high among the women forced to work on Nyasa estates. It was told that at one sub-post in the interior two or three women died each day, to be thrown into the hills at evening for the wild animals to devour.[44]

[43] F.O. 367/289, Lyne to MacDonell, 22 Apr. 1912. In submitting Lyne's report on 26 Apr., MacDonell stated that he 'was not hostile to the employment of corporal punishment. . . . In fact, I am of the opinion that such punishment, officially and judiciously administered, is very necessary and essential where natives are concerned.'

[44] F.O. 367/344, Leonard Bostock to MacDonell, 6 Sept. 1913.

The First World War brought an end to these stories. England and Portugal were allies against the German forces under General von Lettow-Vorbeck. After the war the development of southern Africa made good neighbours of the British and Portuguese communities.

CHAPTER VII

Labour from Angola

IN the first years of the 1900's the humanitarian crescendo began. No matter what the details of the argumentation, the nature of the attack or the logic of the response, the issue of contract labour from Angola to the cocoa isles came down now to its moral implications. English humanitarians undertook a vehement and often irrational campaign against Portuguese 'slavery'. Portuguese planters and their adherents put up a spirited and at times equally irrational defence. In between were two governments, embarrassed, resentful of tactics on both sides of the controversy, and hoping against hope that half measures and a blind eye would make the problem vanish.

It was neither a moral gain for humanity, wrote Roger Casement, now British Consul in the Congo Independent State, nor a useful change in tribal patterns to tear from the African family a husband or father and send him a thousand miles to learn the spiritual improvements of labour. It was wrong. Human beings were disposed of for money. And 'regular, enduring, supervised work was the badge not of free men, but of bought men. . . . For every serviçal possibly improved by his exotic surroundings, he has left behind a score—nay, scores—of his fellow countrymen morally debased and injured by every phase of his departure.' Noting that in 1897, out of 1,919 labourers recruited in Angola, twenty-eight were under fourteen years of age and 1,586 (818 males and 768 females) were between fourteen and twenty-one, Casement wrote: 'To assert that boys and girls of 15, 16, and upwards can bind themselves, with full knowledge of its scope, to a contract of exile which no one denies is for life . . . and that such assent gives to their deportation the sanction of law, is only playing with words.'[1]

[1] F.O. 63/1447, Casement to F.O., 21 Jan. 1903. The letter was drafted 29 Sept.

In a dispatch written in April 1902 Casement quoted from his diary his impressions of a week's stay on an Angolan *fazenda.* No one in Angola regarded contract labourers as anything other than slaves. 'xxx has 220 *serviçaes* (not counting children) at work. All bought—price 100 milreis each, mostly women and children, many sick. Death rate per annum xxx states is about 15–20 per cent. per 220.' The workers were not paid, but given 'vales' good only at a 'wretched shell of a store with shoddy goods and rum'. Most of the workers suffered from worms. Casement witnessed the flogging of a demented old woman for having taken her clothes off. Young people were not allowed to marry as they chose, but as their masters chose. *Serviçaes* were not allowed to go beyond the limits of the plantation. 'No change of scene,' Casement wrote in his diary, 'no change of food, no change of duty, no remission of their wearisome routine save by sickness and death. What fathers and mothers are doing today the children know they, too, will be doing in the same spot, in the same way and under the same compulsion if they live to become fathers and mothers themselves.'[2]

A departmental minute on Casement's dispatch cautiously stated, 'We need not communicate with the Aborigines Protection Society.' On 11 June 1902, H. R. Fox Bourne, none of his zeal diminished by his continuing attack on the scandals in Leopold's Congo, addressed a thoughtful letter to the Foreign Office. Fox Bourne expressed his committee's distress that a

1899, but Casement rightly supposed there had not been much change in four years.

As for the guilt: 'The guilt of the Portuguese authorities lies not in active participation in wrong doing, but in an inherited apathy of indifference to the true needs of their native subjects.

'When to this slackness of custom, which is more operative than the stringency of any code, is added the fact that labour is scarce, that without labour much of the prosperity of the province would come to an end, it is not hard to see why a government, admittedly humane, and why officials, undoubtedly kindhearted, should approve a system which takes toll of human flesh just as surely, if not so extensively, as the slave trade ever did.'

[2] F.O. 63/1447, Casement to F.O., 17 Sept. 1902. Even Brock, Casement had heard, had repented of his earlier defence of the contract labour system. And not the least of the evils in the system was the aspect it presented to the free Africans of Angola. 'I am not a slave', he said, when offered work. 'Instead of solving labour problems in Angola, contract labour only creates fresh objections in native minds.'

system of slavery under the name of forced labour seemed to be increasing in Angola, in violation of Articles Six and Nine of the Berlin General Act. Citing consular reports of the 1890's, Fox Bourne built his presentation directly upon the remarks of Consuls Pickersgill, Casement, and Nightingale. He did not wish to trouble Lord Landsdowne with unofficial reports which more than corroborated official statements. The committee was aware that neither São Tomé nor Principe, nor the ports of Angola from which the labour was sent, were within the conventional Basin of the Congo, but it did have good grounds for believing that most of the contracted labour used in the islands and on coffee estates north-east of Luanda was drawn in large numbers from the Congo Basin; and it was hoped that His Majesty's Government would inquire into violations of international obligations.[3] The most the Foreign Office would do, pursuing a deliberately dilatory tactic, was to send copies of the dispatch to Casement in the Congo and to Arthur Nightingale in Angola asking for information which it already had. The Foreign Office was not convinced that the matter was a question of slavery or that it was covered by treaty obligations. Nor did the Foreign Office want to wound Portuguese susceptibilities while extended negotiations for Moçambique labour were going on.

The Anti-Slavery Society was also vigilant. After letting West Africa pass almost unnoticed through the 1890's, the Society undertook in 1900 a programme of education for its members on the labour migration to the islands. Hardly an issue of the *Reporter* appeared without extensive extracts from the English and European press or from the letters of missionaries in Central Africa, prefaced by the editor's forthright commentary ('The Administration of Portugal in her African territories has ever been known to be inefficient and corrupt. It has been said that the slave-trade is the only trade for which the Portuguese have shown a marked aptitude . . . and the traffic in labourers to the islands of São Tomé and Principe under the so-called engagé system is practically slave trading').[4] These plain words were an introduction to a cluster of quotations. A French news-

[3] F.O. 63/1447, H. R. Fox Bourne to F.O., 11 June 1902.
[4] *Reporter*, Nov.–Dec. 1900, p. 161.

paper had printed selections from a missionary's letter which had in turn quoted an alleged commercial traveller Mr. Cooper. All the country between Lewanika and the Belgian Congo was drained by slaves from Bihé.

> Mr. Cooper had met caravans with many thousands of slaves. Their route is strewn with skeletons. . . . All this is done with the protection of the Portuguese Government; the route passed by five Portuguese forts. . . . Since Livingstone's time, nothing has changed in this unhappy country [Angola]. The blood of its children continues to cry out for vengeance! Where is the remedy? In the punishment which, let us hope, will not be long in falling on these infamous Portuguese.[5]

The next issue contained a richer assortment of indictments. The current issue of the Belgian Anti-Slavery Society provided an article entitled 'The Modern Slave Trade on the West Coast of Africa' wherein an appeal was made both to the special bureau set up by the Brussels Act and to public opinion. The article spoke of conditions in the upper basin of the Kasai, between twenty and twenty-three degrees longitude and six and nine degrees latitude, where Bihé traders came with their European guns and arms to trade for slaves from the powerful chiefs. The trade was carried on to supply the Portuguese demand for workers on the islands of São Tomé and Principe, 'and the agents for the planters are to be found at all the chief ports of Angola'. It was a continually growing demand. Conditions in the islands were good, the workers were well paid and fed, 'but the faces of all these human creatures are covered with a veil of melancholy showing that they have been deprived *by force* of that which man prefers above everything else—liberty'.[6]

A letter from M. Z. Stober, a missionary in Bailundo and one of the central figures in the evolving controversy, affirmed that slavery was not yet dead. Up-country more slaves were being sold than ever before. 'The open sore of Africa is still a long way from being healed.' Another letter, of July 1900, from a

[5] *Reporter*, Nov.–Dec. 1900, p. 162. The extract is from *Le Signal*, 3 Oct. 1900.

[6] *Reporter*, Jan.–Feb. 1901, p. 17.

missionary connected with Arnot's Central African Mission gave an account of a journey from Bihé westward.

> I have never seen such slave gangs bound west as pass us day after day since crossing the Quanza, and the many dead and decomposing bodies tell their tale—knocked on the head to end their misery, or hamstrung and left. We had to turn away again and again in abhorrent disgust. The Lord of Sabaoth avenge! . . . The crack, crack of the slaveship and the dull thud of the club on their backs is still sounding in our ears, but the sights—ah, these haunt us![7]

Both Stober and C. A. Swan, the presumed author of the second letter, were to be the principal missionary sources for British investigators and officials.

The Society kept its members informed of every detail of the trade they came upon for the years 1900–3. In the midst of repetition and indignation there was the strength of substance. In 1901 the *Reporter* printed selections from various dispatches from Colonel Colin Harding, Acting Administrator in North-western Rhodesia. In his letters and his book Harding gave one of the best accounts of the function of the *Mambari* traders in Central Africa. In a letter written in 1901, Harding observed:

> During my journey from Nyakatoro to Bihé I met five Mambari caravans proceeding to Mashukulumbwe country for slaves. These caravans are usually under the charge of Mambari traders. Eight or ten enterprising Biheans (Mambari) will combine with their followers and leave Bihé under one elected head man or captain. This distinction falls as a rule on the person who has accumulated the greatest amount of goods, or who by past experience has shown himself an adept in his pernicious profession. These caravans vary in size from 50 to 100 carriers, each loaded with goods. With these they purchase a small quantity of rubber and secure numerous slaves [the trade in rubber was almost incidental to the trade in slaves].

[7] *Reporter*, Jan.–Feb. 1901, pp. 18–19. The *Quarterly* of the French Anti-Slavery Society expressed its condemnation also. 'Of all the European colonies in Africa, Angola is the most backward as regards slavery, which is practised openly and with all of its abuses.' Of the Regulation of 1899: 'To force these natives to perform work which they refuse is to come very near to legal slavery.' *Reporter*, June-July 1901, pp. 117–18.

Arriving at a suitable locality for the trade, they separate, and going in different directions, often travelling 200 or 300 miles, they collect their slaves, and finally return to some agreed spot, where, combining forces, they form a party which no one could attack with impugnity. For the greater part of the journey the slaves are kept in shackles and roped together to prevent their escape. Ill-fed, cruelly treated, these unfortunate victims succumb by the score, and the path from Mosiko to the Quanza was lined with the remains of these unfortunates in every state of decomposition, this being noticeable in the 'hunger country' between forts Mosiko and Madito. The trees and bushes lining my path were ornamented with discarded shackles and yokes, and on more than one occasion I noticed the broken skull of a decaying skeleton, mashed to end the victim's suffering.[8]

[8] *Reporter*, Aug.–Sept. 1901, pp. 155–6. Also *Reporter*, June–July 1901, pp. 117–18, for additional information on the Harding expedition. In his book *In Remotest Barotseland* (London, 1905), Harding told much the same story. Unlike the Society and other commentators on the traffic through the interior of Angola, Harding was circumspect and sometimes generous in his remarks on the Portuguese administration. 'I regret to say that, I feel sure, unknown to the Portuguese Government, a great number of very regrettable incidents have occurred which do not reflect credit on those who are responsible for the local government of these far-away places.' Harding went on to say that he personally received every kindness from Portuguese officials (p. 107).

But no one wrote with more feeling for the horrible and outrageous degradations practised by the *Mambari*. Retelling the story he heard from an American mining engineer of his journey to Nyakatoro, Harding wrote: 'The path was strewn with the bodies of victims, heaped by the roadside; men, too old to carry their burdens, sank down never to rise again. Children, too young to endure the heat of the tropical sun, are relieved of their suffering by a stroke of the slave driver's axe, their flesh left as food for hungry wolves. Such was the sad and terrible evidence of Mr. Bricker. . . . He told us that when once returning from a walk, he stumbled over a child not more than ten years old, lying a few yards from the path, in the last throes of death, brutally left by the callous master owning him. . . . Such tales could be multiplied by many of those who have witnessed the horrors of this traffic in human bodies, and are often too gruesome in detail to be dwelt upon here' (pp. 113–14).

Everywhere was evidence of the holocaust. Around the head-waters of the Luena: 'Every day I am seeing traces of the slave trade. The wayside trees are simply hung with disused shackles, some to hold one, some two, three and even six slaves; skulls and bones bleached by the sun lie where the victims fell, and gape with helpless grin on those who pass, a damning evidence of the horrible traffic' (p. 211).

Near the Portuguese fort at Motata: 'Each passing day brings repetition of these horrid wayside scenes. Today I saw the remains of five natives in every stage of decomposition. If five were visible from the footpath, I dread to think the number that must have been dragged a short distance away and

From the Congo, George Grenfell of the Baptist Missionary Society reported that African emissaries of labour agents were freely trespassing in the Congo to satisfy the growing demand. The workers were engaged from their chief for a heavy fee and marched off, never to return.[9]

Once the slave reached Benguela there was abundant information on his treatment and fate. The Anti-Slavery Society received many communications from travellers, missionaries, and commercial men, who made the journey from Benguela up the coast on ships carrying *serviçaes*. One traveller, a missionary, had spent several days in Benguela looking into the *serviçal* system while he waited for his ship. Much of the commerce of the port, he wrote, had to do with the migration system; business men spoke openly of the market in people, of how many labourers they bought and sold during the year. Throughout Angola slavery was carried on. The missionary (anonymous, like most missionary informants, because of the fear of reprisals against the missionary or his church's programme) brought to the Society the photograph of a man with an iron collar padlocked around his neck and a length of chain coiled on his head. 'As an Englishman I am sure it is high time one of the parties to the Brussels Act brought the matter to the attention of the Portuguese Government in such a way as to compel it to fulfill its contractual obligations.'[10]

there despatched. One poor fellow had not been dead long. Lying by the remains of the fire he had ignited before his death, his gaping skull resting on his fleshless hands, his spirit had passed away without pain and without struggle. No one ever recognized his life, no one mourns his death. Other remains are found; here the skull is battered in by the trader's axe and the body clearly exhibits signs of the greatest torture and pain in the throes of death. Every sick man in a slave caravan who cannot walk is despatched in this way. In doing so they minimize the percentage of sickness and stop effectually any malingering. A man who knows that being unable to walk means instant death will do his utmost to struggle on to the end, thus often preserving his poor body for a worse fate' (pp. 220–2).

[9] *Reporter*, Aug.–Sept. 1901, p. 156.

[10] *Reporter*, June–July 1902, pp. 83–85. In an interview, the Reverend M. Z. Stober told the committee that the 1902 uprising in Bailundo had come about because of the violence done by slave-traders in the area. Slaves were most cruelly treated, beaten with hippopotamus-hide whips and the *palmatória*. Convicts exiled to Angola kept much of the trade in the highlands alive; Portuguese officials were apathetic to the mistreatment of slaves. *Reporter*, Nov.–Dec. 1902, p. 153.

On 30 December 1902 the Society sent a letter to the Portuguese legation in London inquiring whether the Portuguese Anti-Slavery Society was still in existence[11] so that they might communicate to it the stories they had received of slaving in Portuguese West Africa. Late in February a response, bearing no date, was received, apparently written by Manuel Gorjão, former governor-general of Moçambique and now colonial minister. The letter referred the Society to the many provisions of Portuguese legislation, ancient and modern, for the repression of slavery and the protection of native populations, particularly the Decree of 29 January 1903. There were officers especially appointed to look after the protection of Africans. These men in company with colonial administrators had completely suppressed the wicked traffic in slaves 'which nowadays has only an existence in the imagination of certain philanthropists'. The letter went on to quote Sir Harry Johnston's kind remarks about Angola and São Tomé. The Reverend Thomas Lewis had stated in his pamphlet *The Ancient Congo Kingdom* that it was 'a blessing for the country to be in the hands of the Portuguese, whose government is the least arbitrary with the Negro and under whom in Angola they enjoy better treatment than in other colonies'.[12] The charges laid by the Society were rejected as absolutely destitute of foundation.[13]

In Angola twenty-seven colonial officials and merchants were indicted early in 1903 for slaving and mistreatment of African workers. The governor-general in Angola was making serious attempts to halt the extravagant behaviour of some of his

[11] The Portuguese Society seems to have petered out of existence. Within a few years it would be re-established—to help defend Portugal against the attacks of the English Society.

[12] The *Reporter* noted that *they* could not find the passage in Mr. Lewis's pamphlet.

[13] *Reporter*, Mar.–May 1903, pp. 60–62. At about the same time, the *Reporter* noted that William A. Cadbury of the cocoa firm had paid a visit to Lisbon where he was joined by the Reverend Stober. Cadbury, a Quaker and a member of the Anti-Slavery Society, was to become the central figure in the controversial drama of the next ten years. He had gone to Lisbon to inquire into the charges that it was slave-grown cocoa which was being processed by English manufacturers. He was reassured by men in the colonial ministry that new legislation would dispense with whatever evils there had been in the system.

officials in the interior and to curb their readiness to deal in African labour. The charges against the *chefe* of Cambambe, Captain Diogo de Souza Laboreiro, for example, were many and varied: corporal punishment meted out to two Quissama men in prison, extortion of a sum of money and thirty head of cattle from an African farmer, who had previously been held in chains; abuse of authority against one Matheus de Barrios, detained and obliged to work in chains; the sale of three *serviçaes*; corporal punishment inflicted on one or more native chiefs; slave-dealing; 'and other crimes accumulated against him'. Laboreiro was removed from his post and ordered to stand trial.[14]

But in Lisbon the colonial ministry was more concerned for the agricultural development of São Tomé, and had prepared legislation which was designed to guarantee—and to protect—workers for the islands. The Law of 29 January 1903 was the first serious legislation to take up the problem in itself, and it was prepared, according to the preamble, 'so that the São Tomé and Principe might not lack the workers necessary to maintain and develop their agriculture'. The preamble also foresaw that the obligations of humanity would be met in the new decree. Articles One and Two stated that the emigration of Africans from Angola, Guiné, the Cape Verdes, and Moçambique to the farms of São Tomé and Principe was permitted up to the number of workers sufficient to satisfy the island's labour demands. A central contract labour commission was set up in Lisbon, on which four planters from the islands had seats. The commission, through its subordinate commission in São Tomé, would control labour procedures for the islands, such as overseeing contracts and distributing the workers to the plantations. In order to discourage the zeal of those agents who in the past resorted to the slave-trade to get workers, the payments to recruiting agents were reduced. The chapter of the decree on contracts contained many new protections for the worker, but the hard core of the legislation was found in Article 31 which read, 'Contracts will be made for the maximum period of five full years' (for workers from Moçambique, Guiné, and the Cape Verdes the period was for one or two years). Article Fifty-

[14] *Boletim oficial de Angola*, 31 May 1902.

Seven genially specified that 'when the legal term of his contract has expired the worker may refuse to be repatriated if he signs a new contract'. This was the extent of any consideration for repatriation in the new law. About 40 per cent. of the worker's monthly salary, which was about nine shillings, was withheld and deposited in the *Fazenda Pública* to be used for his return passage.[15]

This was a tough law; it provided little or nothing for the workers, and it gave over the control of the recruiting apparatus to the planters. It failed to deal with the two most disturbing aspects of the problem: the getting of the workers, which encouraged a slave-trade in Angola and beyond, and the repatriation of the workers at the end of their contracts, which in effect made their servitude a life term.

Portuguese residents in Angola were infuriated by the new law—and by earlier special legislation in favour of São Tomé. They did not like to see Angolan labour shipped off to the islands, especially under conditions which gave the colony a notorious reputation. In a pamphlet *Ao paiz* ('To the Nation') ninety-one colonists protested against laws which perpetuated forced labour. If the deputies and nobles of Portugal were to see any of the thousand savage crimes committed in Angola to acquire labour, they would turn against the new law. Once again Portugal would incur just censure for allowing violent customs to continue in the back-country. The uprising in the Benguela highlands was an example of what happened when men without conscience or scruples were turned loose on the native population.[16] In spite of its apparent humanitarianism,

[15] *Diário do governo*, 31 Jan. 1903.

[16] The Bailundo war aroused indignation in many Portuguese in Africa and at home. A letter from Novo Redondo to *A época*, a Lisbon paper, explained the cause of the rising. 'With the fall in price of rubber, up went the price of the arm, the "head of tar," as they call the black—to be contracted for São Tomé.' Traders in the interior set systematically about to collect workers. One, they promoted disorder. Two, they engaged carriers and let them steal one or two bottles of rum left purposely at hand; the thief was tied up and ransomed by his family with a number of slaves. Three, the trader encouraged his *nucama*, African paramour, to make love to a villager, who was then discovered and tied up for ransom (five to ten slaves). Four, goods were sold on credit, and after six months the debtor was obliged to give one slave for each month of non-payment. Obtaining no satisfaction

the Law of 29 January 1903 would perpetuate vices. The recruiting procedure was a farce, and life on São Tomé was anything but a paradise. One valuable colony was being gutted for the transitory prosperity of another. The writers of the manifesto took pride that they had come 'to the defence of an ideal of humanity, to prove to the entire world that the Portuguese of today like those of yesterday sustain with the same ardor and faith the glorious banner of the emancipation of man'.[17]

The sentiments of Angolan Portuguese were probably as selfish as they were philanthropic—the conduct of Angolan estate owners, for example, was generally believed to be several cuts below the standards of São Tomé—but their attack on the export system was as forthright as any English criticism. The outcry in Angola was led by a Luanda weekly, properly named *A defeza de Angola*. In May 1904 the paper ran a series of articles, the first of which began by invoking the word of Governor-General Ramada Curto, who had said in his Decree of 25 September 1900, 'It is a matter of public notoriety that many irregularities and abuses have lately been practised in some districts of the interior in the engaging of *serviçaes* to be transported from this province.' To prevent the evils the governor urged that those authorities who registered the contracts should make inquiries with the greatest care. The supervision of contracts was then given to the curators in the districts and subdistricts, as provided for in the *Regulamento* of 1899,

from the administrators, most of whom were as guilty as the traders, the Africans rebelled. 'We stop here', wrote the *Epoca*. 'Let the public make its own comments, for the standards of judging civilized men cannot imagine the horror of such revelations.' *A época*, 11 Aug. 1902.

In late September a statement appeared in most Lisbon newspapers; it had been drawn up by the principal merchants of Angola, who had also sent a delegation of important men to Lisbon to talk to overseas secretaries about the calamitous state of affairs in Angola. There was a shortage of labour, as a result of epidemics and emigration. 'The present war in the south is the result of crimes and violence towards the native races who have been sent like slaves to São Tomé. The delegates have to admit with regret that all the right is on the side of those who have risen up in revolt.' As a final warning, the delegation said that if Portugal would not act, foreigners would.

The *Jornal das colónias* (Lisbon), 2 May 1903, protested against the system, arguing that Angola needed the labour more.

[17] *Ao paiz* (Luanda, 1903).

but the labour supply dwindled, and the cocoa planters convinced the metropolitan government to suspend the offending articles of the *Regulamento,* and recruiting became free again for their contracting agents. Curto's successor in late 1900, Francisco Moncada, also attempted to put the recruiting on a proper basis; for a time he had the Luanda chief of police go on board vessels carrying workers. Some Africans were put ashore when it was revealed that they were being carried off against their will. The *Defeza* finished its first article, 'The principle is self-evident that . . . what favours few at the cost of millions is undeniable evil.'[18]

The paper was convinced that the island planters were responsible for the Law of 29 January 1903. Acting Governor-General Eduardo Costa found himself in 1903 caught between carrying out the terms of the law and heeding the angry complaints of important Angolan citizens. He tried, therefore, to see to it that those provisions which demanded that the worker contract his services voluntarily be clearly observed. The *Defeza* urged him to continue this policy. 'At least let the loyal and patriotic protests be recorded by history, the protests of those who, above all, labour to place our beloved Portugal above all suspicion and accusation.'[19]

No less disposed against the labour migration was British Consul Arthur Nightingale. Nightingale had come to Luanda in 1898; although aware of irregularities in the procurement of African workers, particularly the abuse of the vagrancy clauses in labour laws, Nightingale hoped that the growth and prosperity of Angola would gradually ameliorate these conditions. But they had grown worse, and by 1902 Nightingale agreed with Angolan colonists that the labour drain would be the ruination of the colony—and he now took a firm and moral stance against the traffic. The system was 'slavery in its worst phase, and it is greatly to the discredit of other European nations to tolerate such a repugnant traffic in human beings which was supposed to have been abolished, but which still exists in Angola under the farcical title of "contracted labour" '.

[18] *A defeza de Angola,* 19 May 1904.

[19] *A defeza de Angola,* 26 May and 2 June 1904.

In recent months the business had spread to Ambriz where thirty persons had already been indicted for recruiting without a licence. Down the coast at Benguela, 'the slave-trade is almost the only business carried on'. And on the islands the planters continued to argue that the workers never wished to be sent back to their homes.[20] 'The question is,' wrote Nightingale, 'should the repugnant trade in human beings be allowed to continue? Cannot pressure be brought to bear with the Portuguese Government to insist upon its total abolition once and for all. . . . My private opinion is that the slave-trade in Angola will not be abolished until some strong influence from outside is brought to bear on the matter.'[21]

Nightingale had many informants in Angola, particularly the British community of missionaries and merchants. One English missionary told him that when coming down to the coast in 1900 he had counted in different caravans nearly a thousand slaves being driven to the coast, most of them in horribly emaciated condition.[22] John Lucas wrote from Ambriz that most of the workers shipped out to São Tomé in the past year had been local village slaves traded for cloth or powder; some were delinquents whose chiefs sold them to recruiting agents. From Humpata, W. J. Chapman reported to the superintendent of the West African Telegraph office in Luanda that Bihé was also a hotbed of slavery. Just before he left, a caravan of 300

[20] F.O. 2/640, Nightingale to F.O., 20 June 1902. In Nightingale's view the worst phase of the business had to be seen in the interior. Nightingale enclosed with his dispatch letters from E. P. Cooper, a naturalist who went to the colony in 1897 for the Natural History Department of the British Museum, and Dr. Walter Fisher, a medical missionary, both of whom told of the horrors. Cooper wrote of the caravan route:

'After leaving the Quanza I followed the caravan path leading to Lake Tanganyika and was surprised and disgusted to find the slave-trade in full swing and also that the path as far as I went was strewn with skeletons and corpses in every state of decomposition. . . .

'The road branches E of the Portuguese penal colony of Mexiço, one branch cutting north at Kasai river and then going east to the Luva, the other keeping east past Nana Kandundu and enters the Garenganze. The former after crossing the Belgian frontier passes the forts of Mexiço Matotta, and Quanza, while the latter passes in addition the forts of Caluga Cameia and Nana Kandundu. Mind, Sir, passes within a hundred yards of the Portuguese forts.'

[21] F.O. 2/640, Nightingale to F.O., 8 July 1902.

[22] F.O. 2/640, Nightingale to F.O., 12 Aug. 1902.

people arrived there, and he was told that 500 had died on the march.[23]

Almost two years later, Nightingale saw no improvement, no hope. Neither the Law of 29 January 1903 nor subsequent legislation had achieved anything. What was needed was not new laws and decrees but some way of seeing that the old laws were obeyed. And regulations had no control over the acquisition of the workers or their forced march to the coast. One of the weaknesses of the 1903 Decree was that it did not really provide for repatriation. But, Nightingale confessed, he did not really expect to see any workers repatriated. Should the planters be willing to contract for a shorter period of time (Nightingale thought it was nonsense for the planters to argue that a long apprenticeship was necessary—especially since they gave one-year and two-year contracts to Krumen or Cape Verdeans), Nightingale thought that part of the problem might be worked out and some of the migration become voluntary—although the estate owners would have to raise the wages from the very low figure of eight shillings a month to male labourers and five shillings a month to females. But these changes would not be effected so long as the powerful bloc of São Tomé men could assert their power on the Lisbon Government.[24]

[23] F.O. 2/640, Nightingale to F.O., 2 Aug. 1902. Another channel of communication was from missionaries in Angola directly to the British legation in Lisbon. F. S. Arnot, writing from Ochilonda in Bihé, said that one no longer saw Portuguese traders chaining slaves together as in the days of old. But slaves were still readily being disposed of in Bihé. Formerly most of them had been brought from beyond the Quanza; now the villagers had 'developed the unnatural practice of selling their own people. . . . This is surely a matter for the European, Power, occupying Africa to take up and to proclaim in some way laws calculated to abrogate these customs and laws that lie at the very root of the slave trade and secure for it a perpetual supply.' F.O. 63/1447, F. S. Arnot to Martin Gosselin, 7 Nov. 1904.

[24] F.O. 63/1447, Nightingale to F.O., 5 May 1904. Nevertheless, the plantations of São Tomé and Principe were always short of workers. In 1901, 4,752 *serviçaes* (2,616 men and 2,136 women) went to the islands; in 1902, 3,499 (1,976 men and 1,523 women); in 1903, 2,864 (1,862 men and 1,002 women); and in 1904, 2,967 (1,678 men and 1,289 women). There was, in addition, an undetermined number of clandestine workers shipped to the islands, although there probably were not many of these by 1900. The mortality rate was higher than official figures admitted. Principe, with its high incidence of sleeping sickness, was a pesthole. From 12 Nov. 1900 to 12 Nov. 1901 there was a mortality rate of 21 per cent. In that period, 586 workers went to Principe and 867 died there, thus diminishing the total work force from 3,607 to 3,326.

The Foreign Office was unmoved by the many reports on the Angolan slave-trade and the migration to São Tomé which it received. To most questions it turned a deaf ear or gave an evasive answer. To the ambassador in Lisbon such instructions as were issued were equivocal. The consul in Luanda was occasionally asked for additional information, although he was not to spend any funds—or any great effort—acquiring it. The greater part of the Foreign Office's attention was given to helping to secure Moçambique workers for South Africa, and an Angolan crisis might well interfere with these projects. When Acting Consul Brock suggested that he go to south-eastern Angola to investigate an arms trade which was promoting the sale of slaves in the region and, as well, to draw up a report for Minister Gosselin in Lisbon on the effects of the 1903 Decree, it was decided that he was to be told that the Foreign Office, though glad to have his report, could not supply the funds. Such an expedition ran the risk 'of irritating Portuguese susceptibilities and the danger of learning inconvenient facts which might oblige us to make representations to the Portuguese Government—which we don't want to do'. Gosselin should be told that the Foreign Office did not see sufficient reason for the journey.[25]

In the absence of pressure from Britain whatever small measures were taken by the Portuguese Overseas Ministry were taken in response to protests in Portugal and Angola and to those made by English humanitarians. Gosselin was informed by a Portuguese colonial authority that the Law of 29 January 1903 had been issued in consequence 'of observations made in England on the scandalous abuses perpetuated in Angola in order to keep up the supply of contracted labour'.[26] When William Cadbury and the Reverend Stober came to Lisbon Colonial Minister Gorjão went to great pains to reassure them that the new decree improved the lot of the *serviçaes* and that

In the year 1900, only 350 workers were reported to have died on São Tomé estates, a mortality rate of 6·67 per cent. A number of plantations failed to record the workers who died. It was variously estimated that from 50 to 60 per cent. of the *serviçaes* died before completing their five-year contract. The death rate on some estates was often three times that on other estates.

[25] F.O. 2/883, Minutes on Brock to F.O., 28 Nov. 1904.

[26] F.O. 63/1447, Gosselin to F.O., 7 Feb. 1903.

repatriation was provided for. Cadbury said that if no substantial reforms occurred, he would recommend that English cocoa makers buy their chocolate elsewhere. With Gosselin he asked whether a British consular agent could not be appointed at São Tomé, a suggestion the Foreign Office let go by, although a licence for a vice-consul on the island was available. The belief at the Foreign Office was that there was little ground for intervention since slavery was in theory abolished and the labourers were allegedly Portuguese subjects. It was hoped that Cadbury's threat of a boycott might just do the job, for the time being, and save the Foreign Office from facing the problem of trying to force Portugal to take action.[27]

But the problem of public opinion was another matter. The minutes on a subsequent dispatch from Gosselin revealed annoyance and resignation. Now that Cadbury and the Anti-Slavery Society were 'in on the thing', it was possible that the matter would be taken up by the press and Parliament and 'an attempt made to create a feeling against Portugal similar to that aroused against the Congo Free State'. Perhaps unofficial conversations with the Portuguese minister might prevent this.[28] On 24 June Landsdowne spoke to the Marques de Soveral warning him of an outbreak of British indignation.

Throughout 1904 the Foreign Office procrastinated, finding one reason or another for standing aside. A report requested of Consul Nightingale began to assume larger importance. Gosselin said he could use a full report for private talks with Gorjão, though he did not believe much would result since São Tomé and Principe were the only Portuguese colonies paying their way, which gave the cocoa planters even greater influence.[29] The Foreign Office interpreted this to mean, 'It looks very much as if we shall merely make ourselves disliked without doing any good.' The thing to do was to return to the matter later when they had a full report from Luanda.[30]

[27] F.O. 63/1447, Gosselin to F.O., 5 May 1903.
[28] F.O. 63/1447, Minutes on Gosselin to F.O., 6 May 1903.
[29] F.O. 63/1447, F.O. to Gosselin, 24 June 1903.
[30] F.O. 63/1447, F.O. memorandum to Landsdowne, 10 Oct. 1904. Three months later Gosselin, now taking his cue from London, and the Foreign Office were still fretting about offending Portuguese sensibilities. The occasion was another projected trip to the south of Angola by Mr. Brock. Gosselin wrote,

Portugal also equivocated. Caught between pride in the development of the islands and the powerful voices of the planters, on the one hand, and the resentments of Angolan colonists and a menacing outcry in England, on the other, the Government struggled to avoid a deepening crisis. Policy became a kind of tightrope walk. Custódio Borja, on leaving the governorship of Angola, said:

It has always been my endeavour to avoid abuses inconsistent with the duties of humanity as well as with the true interests of the province. Better than any words the low number of emigrants which left Angola during the current year [1904], compared with the figures of former years, with the exception of 1903, would show what I was able to achieve. I confined myself to removing abuses and enforcing observances of the law on the authorities concerned with the export of labourers. But I did not forget that the incumbent of the high office of governor general, the representative of the central government of the country, must not only be guided in his views by local interests, but must take a large view embracing the whole interests of the nation. Therefore I raised no hinderance nor placed inappropriate obstacles in the way of the export of labour, since it was never the aim of my policy to stop the natural movement [which did not exist in 1904 any more than it did in 1900 or any other year] of emigration to the Province of São Tomé and Principe.[31]

Meanwhile the Anti-Slavery Society continued its campaign. When the Reverend Stober described his visit to Lisbon 'on behalf of the natives of Angola' in the *Angola Missionary Magazine,* the *Reporter* printed a long extract telling its readers of the revulsion in Lisbon at the 'fiendish cruelty used to keep these poor human beings captive on the plantations'. Another missionary, in Angola since 1888, wrote to the Society from the interior of Benguela that the situation in his part of the world had grown worse in the last several years. Native carriers were tricked or openly sold into slavery. Slaves and rum were the articles of commerce, and it was not unknown for a villager to sell his son for a keg of rum.[32]

'An anti-slave trade agitation directed against the Portuguese authorities will be very undesirable at present.' F.O. 63/1447, F.O. memorandum to Landsdowne, 3 Jan. 1905.

[31] F.O. 63/1447, in Gosselin to F.O., 16 Jan. 1905.

[32] *Reporter,* June–July 1903, pp. 82–84.

When Charles Swan, one of the foremost missionary antagonists of conditions in Angola, came home on furlough he gave the Society more information about contract labour in Portuguese West Africa, and the *Reporter* was pleased to tell its readers that what he had to say coincided with what the journal had previously published. Although the Portuguese had been careful in recent years to use the term *serviçal* rather than *escravo*, the difference was hard to distinguish. Mr. Swan had seen hundreds of Angolans sold in the interior and had discussed the subject scores of times with both Africans and whites. In his eighteen years of service in Angola Mr. Swan had never met a man or woman who had returned from the islands. 'A trader in Bihé said that since the rebellion he had been compelled to take out contract papers for all his slaves. At the end of five years he would simply take out further papers for another term's service, as the object of the authorities was not to put an end to slavery, but simply to get the fee payable.'[33]

When the Portuguese paper *Vanguarda* published two articles on São Tomé, the *Reporter* used them fully. The first article was entitled 'Slaves' and had to do with the refusal of the captain of a Portuguese steamer to allow Luanda merchants to board his ship to talk to the *serviçaes* aboard. A syndicate of Luanda men had insisted on the laws of the country being observed and was sending a delegation to board each ship carrying labourers in order to inquire of them if they had freely contracted. Of the captain's refusal, the *Vanguarda* wrote: 'The Angolan black does not cease, under any circumstances, to be a Portuguese citizen, and as such is a free man, and has full licence to hold intercourse with whom he pleases. . . . Portugal and her colonies are part of the civilized world, and as such cannot and will not permit slavery.' The second article dealt with the case of Cape Verdeans driven by famine to contract their services on the cocoa islands. One group rebelled against the harsh treatment and the breaking of the terms of the contract and had fled to the hills. When hunger forced them back to the estates they were bound and shipped off to the interior of Angola.[34]

[33] *Reporter*, Aug.–Oct. 1903, p. 117.

[34] 'What the planters of São Tomé have in mind,' wrote *Vanguarda*, 'is to exploit the black, to get out of him the greatest amount of work, to get him

The harshness of the attacks published in Portugal was not, up to 1905, surpassed by much of anything printed in England. After 1905, however, English commentary gradually worked its way up to a hysterical pitch, and as Portugal and the Portuguese generally came under an indiscriminating humanitarian barrage, both the Portuguese Government and the one-time enemies of the São Tomé system were driven to a defensive silence or an abusive counter-attack. Even the British Government was goaded into a kind of action by the force of public opinion, which had not been so roused against Portuguese behaviour in Africa since the days of Livingstone or the year of the Anglo-Portuguese Treaty. The peak of the authentic outcry was probably reached in 1909, but for another five years after that the flames of indignation flared high.[35]

The one man responsible for precipitating an unpleasant problem into an international controversy was Henry W. Nevinson, a name still regarded with special loathing by Portuguese colonialists. Nevinson, in 1905 one of the most famous journalists of his day—having reported the Greco-Turkish and the South African wars for the *Daily Chronicle*—had been asked by *Harper's* to undertake an adventurous journey for them for 1,000 pounds. The journalist hit upon the slave-trade. After talking to Fox Bourne and Travers Buxton (Secretary of the Anti-Slavery Society), who told him of 'dim rumours they had heard concerning a terrible form of slavery' carried on in

into the country for very little. . . . The planter sees only the man-machine in him, accustomed as he is to dispose of the black Angolan unconditionally. . . . For him the black is not to be regarded as a human being. They are not even allowed the rights of paid labourers. The black, because he is a black, has to be the eternal beast of burden, subject to all kinds of ill-treatment and insults, and to this the native of Cape Verde will never subject himself. From this inhumanity and this barbarism arise the conflicts between the planters and the contracted workers . . . in which the weaker and more righteous are always the sufferers. . . . They are deprived of their inviolable right as free men. . . .

'Here our readers have an episode from the history of shame in our Portuguese colonies, consented to and authorized by the Government, but reproved and stigmatized by all Portuguese, who will not see their country and liberty thus outraged.' *Reporter*, Nov.–Dec. 1903, pp. 137–9.

[35] At this point the controversy becomes exceedingly complicated, and for the remainder of the chapter I shall give only a selective progression of events. The full story of the final phase of the Anglo-Portuguese controversy I will develop in another volume.

Portuguese West Africa,[36] Nevinson decided to go to the islands and Angola. 'Dim rumours' was hardly the term to define what Fox Bourne and Buxton knew about the *serviçaes* scandal, but from the beginning Nevinson appropriated the issue and behaved in what was often an arrogant and guileful way, insisting always on his share of the credit, and more, for whatever success the English campaign enjoyed. On his return to England in June 1905 Nevinson was disappointed, he later confessed, by the indifference to what he had to say.

I had imagined that the British detestation of slavery would be aroused; that our Government would make representations to Portugal on the subject; that our Quaker cocoa firms would at once boycott the raw material derived from such an abominable source; and that there would be a great stir among honourable and influential newspapers. Nothing of the kind happened. A few of my personal friends gave up cocoa; Fox Bourne . . . believed my report and did his utmost to make it known; Roger Casement . . . confirmed my report in every particular from his own personal knowledge of Angola, but he was not then able to make his confirmation public; the Anti-Slavery Society, so immensely helpful afterwards, was slow in taking the question up [this statement is the result of either Nevinson's ignorance or his vanity]; the Congo Reform Association, represented by E. D. Morel, afterwards to be so true a friend, seemed to fear that Angola might divert attention from the Congo.[37]

Whatever the extent of Nevinson's egocentricity or his questionable conduct in the years following, his account of the traffic in contract labour from Angola to São Tomé was from the moment of its publication a classic of its kind. It was personal, it was wrathful, it was right, and it did the job. Nevinson had a sharp eye and a sharper tongue, but he also had something more important—a sense of dramatic proportion.[38] 'The New Slave-Trade' appeared in *Harper's Magazine* in

[36] Henry W. Nevinson, *Fire of Life* (6th ed.; London, 1935), p. 157. This autobiography is a condensation of *Changes and Chances* (1923), *More Changes, More Chances* (1925), and *Last Changes and Last Chances* (1938). The middle volume has a fuller account.

[37] Ibid., pp. 176–7.

[38] And Nevinson could write well, an art most English humanitarians had lost by the early twentieth century.

monthly instalments from August 1905 to February 1906. In 1906 the articles were published as a book with the title *A Modern Slavery*. The narrative was the story of Nevinson's visit to the island of São Tomé, his trip from Benguela up to the Katanga frontier and back, and of his journey up the coast in a steamer carrying *serviçaes*. It was an intimate, dramatic, and harrowing record.

None of the things Nevinson had to say was really new; it was just that H. W. Nevinson was saying them. Nevinson was as sceptical of man's conduct as he was indignant over his misconduct. For his first article he wrote:

> What is the real relation of the white races to the black races? That is the ultimate problem of Africa. We need not think it has been settled by a country's noble enthusiasm about the Rights of Man and Equality in the sight of God. Outside a very small and diminishing circle in England and America, phrases of that kind have lost their influence, and for the men who control the destinies of Africa they have no meaning whatsoever. Neither have they any meaning for the native. He knows perfectly well that the white people do not believe them.[39]

In Angola, Nevinson relied on consular and missionary assistance. He recognized that there was a strong feeling in Angola against the São Tomé traffic; he cited *A defeza de Angola* and acknowledged the good intent of Portuguese colonial legislation. But at that point his charity ended. After visiting a plantation 200 miles in from Luanda, Nevinson wrote, as Casement had written earlier: ' "No change, no pause, no hope." That is the sum of plantation life. So the man or woman, known as a "contract labourer", toils till gradually or suddenly death comes, and the poor worn-out body is put to rot. Out in the forest you come upon a little heap of red earth under which it lies. On top of the heap is set the conical basket of woven grasses which

[39] H. W. Nevinson, 'The New Slave-Trade', *Harper's*, Aug. 1905, p. 348. And on page 350: 'We still think of "black people" in lumps and blocks. We do not realize that each African has a personality as important to himself as each of us in his own eyes. . . . We talk a great deal about our sense of humour, but more than any other races we despise the Africans, who alone out of all the world possess the same power of laughter as ourselves. . . . The white races possess the Dark Continent for their own, and what they are going to do with it is now one of the greatest problems before mankind.'

was the symbol of its toil in life, and now forms its only monument.'[40] Although the fate of the contract labour slave differed but little from that of common humanity, slavery it was. The desperate need for labour in Angola had raised the price so high that swarms of children were growing up on plantations and passing into the life of *serviçaes*. Portuguese planters were no worse than other men, but the power they possessed over the bodies and souls of African workers was too great.

At Catumbela and Benguela, rich with the presence and the memories of slave gangs from the deep interior, Nevinson was reminded of Britain's historic stance against the slave-trade from those parts and her present lack of enthusiasm for doing much of anything. In Benguela he visited the office of the Central Committee of Labour and Emigration for the Islands, where Africans went in one door as slaves and out another as *serviçaes*. And then off to their death on São Tomé and Principe as surely as if they had signed their own death warrant. African women were openly bought and sold in Benguela for domestic and erotic use. A Portuguese official, in an 'outburst of philanthropic emotion', defended the way of life in Portuguese West Africa. 'The slave enjoys a comfort and well being which would have been forever beyond his reach if he had not become a slave.'[41]

In Hungry Country, the area from the Cuanzo to Moshiko, Nevinson found paths littered with shackles. He came across skeletons and constant reminders of the murder of slaves, but he found no direct signs of the tortures which were practised before 1902. Whatever improvement had come about was the result, he was convinced, of the Bailundo uprising. The details of this end of the traffic had been better told by others. On his way back to the coast, Nevinson reported examples of plantation slavery and of slave gangs. As he came down from the hills into Catumbela with its great courtyard, he heard again 'the blows of the *palmatória* and the chicotte and the cries of men and women who were being "tamed" '.[42]

[40] Ibid., Sept. 1905, pp. 544–5.

[41] Ibid., Oct. 1905, p. 674. This notion Nevinson grandly swept away. 'The only motive for slavery is money making, and the only argument in its favour is that it pays. That is the root of the matter, and as long as we stick to that we shall, at least, be saved from humbug.'

[42] Ibid., Dec. 1905, p. 122.

The last two articles dealt with the slaves at sea and the 'Islands of Doom'. Fearful of being poisoned, now that his purpose had been found out, Nevinson became increasingly vindictive and personal in what he wrote, and like Livingstone, in his embittered phase, Nevinson turned savagely on the Portuguese, all Portuguese, their government, and their policies in Africa. By the legal change in the captive's status, Portugal 'stifles the enfeebled protests of nations like the English, and by the excuse of law she smoothes her conscience and whitens over one of the blackest crimes which even Africa can show'.[43] At 'an exquisite Parisian déjeuner' on a model plantation, Nevinson met Joseph Burtt, on his way out for Cadbury's. According to Nevinson, Burtt remarked, 'The Portuguese are certainly doing a marvelous job for Angola and their slaves. Call it slavery if you like, names and systems don't matter. The sum of human happiness is being definitely increased.'[44] But for Nevinson, plantation life appeared hard and efficient. Nevinson preferred to spend the last pages writing of cruelties and 'native hunts' and of the moment of death which came to every worker.

What was to be done? Britain had closed her heart to compassion. What she said would have no effect; 'her tongue, which was the tongue of men, has become like sounding brass'. The only hope was America where a sense of freedom still seemed to linger. Let America declare against slavery and the abominable trade would collapse. It was better for the islands to return to wilderness than that a single slave should toil there. Nevinson spoke for the slaves. 'If the crying of their silence is not heard even by God, it will yet be heard in the souls of the just and compassionate.'[45]

The Foreign Office, which had been turning aside inquiries and letters of protest, was not slow to see that Nevinson's article was a serious threat to Portugal. In December 1905 the earlier articles had been shown to Soveral in London, who stated that

[43] H. W. Nevinson, 'The New Slave-Trade', *Harper's*, Jan. 1906, p. 241.

[44] Ibid., Feb. 1906, p. 328. Burtt is only identified as a guest. Later Nevinson revealed his name.

[45] Ibid., Feb. 1906, p. 337.

his government had always repudiated the charges and would probably soon ask the British Government to send a commission of inquiry to São Tomé to investigate the condition of the *serviçaes*. At this moment the Foreign Office optimistically viewed its position as one that 'had repeatedly called the attention of the Portuguese Government to these abuses, though it has not been thought politic recently to press the matter unduly'. Portugal continued to maintain that the regulations in force precluded any abuses.[46]

The smashing Liberal triumph in the election of January 1906 gave promise of change, and Fox Bourne asked Foreign Secretary Grey to receive a visit from Nevinson and him. Under the excuse that Consul Nightingale was preparing a special report which would have to be the basis of any representations, Grey turned the request over to Sir Eric Barrington and Lord Fitzmaurice, the former receiving the two philanthropists on 14 March 1906. At that interview Nevinson repeated the common charge that the acquisition of *serviçaes* was no different from the old slave-trade; 4,000 men and women were brought down and sold at Benguela each year for from sixteen to twenty dollars a head 'in the most unblushing way'. Barrington, in his memorandum after the talk, wrote: 'It is not a matter about which we have cared to press the Portuguese Government strongly. . . . I told M. de Soveral yesterday afternoon that the philanthropists were much excited and that it would be very disagreeable if public opinion were aroused by the fact that the Portuguese Government were encouraging something painfully akin to the slave trade.'[47]

Following the interview Fox Bourne sent a letter to the Foreign Office to the effect that Portugal was sanctioning slavery and breaking various laws and treaties. At the annual meeting of the Aborigines Protection Society on 21 March a resolution was passed protesting the traffic in slaves in Portuguese West Africa and asking the British Government to take action. At the annual meeting of the Anti-Slavery Society, eight days later, William Cadbury said that Nevinson's articles held the greatest interest (Nevinson had been asked to address the meeting but

[46] F.O. 367/18, F.O. Memorandum to Lord Grey, 26 Feb. 1906.
[47] F.O. 367/18, Memorandum of Sir Eric Barrington, 15 Mar. 1906.

was unable to accept) and bore out what he had been told in Lisbon last year. The reforms promised Cadbury in 1903, and which he had been waiting to see bear fruit, were now a dead letter.[48] In the middle of 1906 questions began to be asked regularly in Parliament.[49] Under these pressures, the Foreign Office sent a cable to Nightingale on 17 July 1906 asking him to send along his report as soon as possible.

On 20 August 1906 Consul Nightingale's confidential report, 'On the treatment of the "Serviçaes," or Contract Labourers, in the Portuguese Islands known as "the Province of São Tomé and Principe" ', was received in London. The report was a factual presentation of the history of the *serviçal* system, the legislation that created it,[50] the legislation that controlled it, and a statistical summary of each *roça* on São Tomé. Nightingale confessed to certain sympathies for the planters of São Tomé, who were taxed heavily by the Government, which gave them nothing in return (except laws giving them a labour supply). The workers were well treated in every respect, better treated probably than any other African worker on the coast. The two evils in the system were the manner in which the labour was acquired and the fact that no worker was ever repatriated. As for the Law of 1903 it was working about as well as could be expected. The contracts were legal enough, but the wishes of the *serviçal* were not consulted. Nor were the workers getting the minimum wage, as required by law—because, Nightingale was informed, it would make the older hands unhappy if new workers got more than they did. Nor was Nightingale aware of any payments to the repatriation fund. Nevinson's accounts of brutality and murder on the island could not be corroborated. In 1901 the value of all exports from the islands was 766,000

[48] *Reporter*, Mar.–May 1906, pp. 28–29.

[49] On 5 July Sir Gilbert Parker put down two questions, one to Grey inquiring if the Foreign Office knew about the allegations about Portuguese West Africa and what steps it was taking (the answer was that the attention of Portugal had been drawn to the complaints) and the other question to the President of the Board of Trade asking if the Board was aware that the cocoa imported into England was largely slave grown and what steps were being taken (Lloyd George's reply was, 'I do not see that any steps can be taken').

[50] Nightingale mistakenly assumed that the contract system grew out of the Decree of 29 Apr. 1875.

pounds sterling; in 1905 it had risen to 1,367,000 pounds sterling.[51]

The Foreign Office decided that the report did not provide sufficient grounds for representations, which might give rise in Portugal to unpleasant controversy and annoyance. One minute on the Nightingale report read, 'It would probably be best to do nothing in this direction until the negotiations about the *modus vivendi* [to assure the supply of workers from Moçambique to the Rand mines] are finished as representations on the subject would no doubt irritate the Portuguese.' A bowdlerized version of the report was to be sent to pacify, if that was possible, Fox Bourne. Fox Bourne thereupon interpreted the report as confirmation of everything he had been saying and once more urged the Foreign Office to remind the Portuguese Government of its treaty obligations.[52] He was now told that the Law of 1903 had greatly ameliorated the condition of the *serviçaes* and it would not be known until 1908, when the first five-year contracts were up, whether repatriation worked or not.[53]

Cadbury's came, inadvertently, to the Foreign Office's rescue. The cocoa makers in England were having their own problems. There was increasing pressure, some of it built up by Nevinson, to boycott São Tomé chocolate. In October, George Cadbury, chairman of the firm, wrote Sir Edward Grey for an interview. English cocoa makers were anxious to work together and were 'prepared to make some sacrifice in the interest of the natives'. They wanted to be certain, however, that any steps they took would be in harmony with any action premeditated by the British Government.[54] But no one in the Foreign Office was yet disposed to fret the Portuguese Government, and when George and William Cadbury met with Grey and Barrington, they were told that the Foreign Office would like very much to see the report of their special commissioner Joseph Burtt before considering properly whether to make representations to

[51] F.O. 367/18, Nightingale to F.O., 28 July 1906.

[52] F.O. 367/18, Fox Bourne to F.O., 24 Sept. 1906.

[53] Codrington was more forthright. His minute read: 'The fact of the matter is that the system is neither more nor less than slavery but that we dare not to say much as we might thus offend the Portuguese with whom we desire to stand well.'

[54] F.O. 367/18, George Cadbury to F.O., 27 Oct. 1906.

Portugal. Before that time, the Cadburys were told, it would not be desirable to make any public protest. Still hesitant about what to do, the cocoa people were pleased to accept that proposal, not knowing that they were being used to help guarantee a labour force for the South African mines.[55]

From here the matter was swept along to Parliament, a direction the Foreign Office had tried to avoid by sending part of Nightingale's dispatch to the Aborigines Protection Society. Demands were raised by members that the Nightingale report be published. (In the Portuguese Parliament voices were now also raised—against 'the manner in which the British Government chose to intervene in an administrative service', the 'defamatory campaign against the Portuguese administration in Africa', and 'the slurs on our national honour'.)[56] A month later Cadbury wrote to Grey that a cable in code from Burtt put the conditions in Portuguese West Africa as worse than those described by Nevinson. 'This from people who have no possible interest to serve but a simple statement of fact. The cocoa people would be interested in the result of any representations.'[57]

In March 1907 Cadbury sent to the Foreign Office an advance copy of Burtt's report. It did not tell of anything particularly new, but Burtt had impressed several people in the Foreign Office and they were ready to use his comments as the basis of a cautious move against Portugal. When by July questions in Parliament began to occur with some frequency and when the campaign in the street and the press began to become more vociferous, the Foreign Office and Cadbury again agreed to try to keep the matter as quiet as possible, to submit an edited

[55] F.O. 367/18, George Cadbury to F.O., 27 Oct. 1906; Grey to Cadbury, 6 Nov. 1906.

[56] F.O. 367/18, Villiers to F.O., 7 Nov. 1906. In the chamber of deputies on 6 Nov. the Portuguese prime minister tried to placate angry speakers by saying questions of native labour were international problems and by reminding the chamber of England's traditional friendship with Portugal.

A week earlier, in another debate, Deputy Paula Canella reminded his colleagues that Portugal had been the first country to grant political rights to Africans. Anyone who read the regulations controlling the labour migration from Angola and from Moçambique would see that they were precisely the same. How could it be that what was called slavery in Angola was not so called in Moçambique. He protested with great indignation against the English campaign of defamation.

[57] F.O. 367/18, Cadbury to F.O., 10 Dec. 1906.

version of the Burtt report to the Portuguese Government, and then wait to see if reforms were initiated. If nothing happened, the Burtt report would be publicly released and a general outcry would presumably ensue. Also, presumably, at that time English cocoa manufacturers would declare a boycott of island cocoa.[58]

Burtt's report, in a revised edition,[59] was sent out for translation into Portuguese, which caused further delays. The work had a quality different from that of Nevinson's book. Burtt was a Quaker and a religious man; he knew Portuguese, and, unlike Nevinson, was kindly moved towards the Portuguese. Since he went, in a sense, to the islands at the invitation of the estate owners,[60] he had every facility on São Tomé put at his disposal. Burtt left for Africa in June 1905. He spent five and a half months visiting plantations on the two islands and over four months in the interior of Angola, reaching as far as the headwaters of the Zambesi, some 800 miles from the coast. What he wrote was plainly put and for the most part based on Burtt's own experience. At the beginning he stated what was now the firm philanthropic position. 'The law is a dead letter, and the contract a farce. The native is taken from his home against his will, is forced into a contract he does not understand, and never returns to Angola. The legal formalities are but a cloak to hide slavery.'[61]

Burtt had no serious quarrel with the treatment of labour on the islands. On this point most writers were in agreement. Corporal punishment was used, but it was rare and was subject to fine. But the life of the *serviçal*, Burtt insisted, was the life

[58] F.O. 367/46, Memorandum, C. Lyell to Grey, 29 July 1907. Lyell said of Burtt's allegations, 'The system described is a far more flagrant breach of the Brussels Convention than anything we have heard of from the Congo.'

[59] The report went through three versions before one was agreed upon, one which would reveal but not offend, be specific but conceal sources (which were later given the Portuguese Government in a key accompanying the text). The report itself—in any version—is of much less value than the collection of Burtt's letters to Cadbury, which run to some 400 pages.

[60] On a visit to Lisbon in 1905 Cadbury had been urged to send out an investigator.

[61] F.O. 367/46, Joseph Burtt, 'Report on the Condition of Coloured Labour Employed in the Cocoa Plantations of São Tomé and Principe, and the Methods of Procuring it in Angola', p. 4. This report, dated Luanda, 24 Dec. 1906, is the original report.

of a slave. And the system placed unlimited power in the hands of the estate manager. Nor could one be sure that scandals ever reached responsible ears in Lisbon. The São Tomé people were powerful and influential. The trouble was that the demand for labour was almost unlimited. Hundreds of planters were demanding workers they could not get; weeds were choking out the young cocoa plants. The difference between the price of a slave at Ambrizette, for example, and on São Tomé was thirty pounds sterling (six as against thirty-six). These enormous profits drew legitimate traders and officials into the illicit trade.

In Angola Burtt found slavery still an accepted institution. There he saw slaves bought and sold and harshly beaten. His travels to the interior, not so purposefully dramatic as Nevinson's, added nothing to traditional reports. In Hungry Country Burtt and his companion Dr. Claude Horton saw shackles and skeletons. He discovered that the laws were but little observed in the deep interior of Angola. In the Kavungo region near the Congo frontier six Portuguese trading posts were established. They sent runners over into the Independent State to purchase captives from the rebel Valleni for guns and ammunition.

Burtt argued that the slave-trade was so dominant that 'clean-handed trade' could not compete with it. The system put a premium on rascality and created a community where only the rogue could flourish. 'For the permanent progress of a tropical colony, dependent on black labour, a sound and honest relationship between the black and white races is indispensable. Slavery makes such a relationship impossible.'[62] On his return to Luanda he talked to the governor-general who said he advocated repatriation and a revision of the system. But Burtt did not believe that he would be heard. 'The wonder is', he concluded, 'not that there is so much slaving in Angola, but that there is so little. So long as it is possible to get a high price for black labourers, so long will slavery exist.'[63]

Less than a year later, Consul H. G. Mackie, under instructions from the Foreign Office to make still another report on the system, wrote that the spectacle of the *serviçal* did not

[62] F.O. 367/46, Joseph Burtt, op. cit., p. 23.
[63] Ibid., p. 24.

create any disagreeable impression. But the system was slavery, if only because he found it hard to reconcile the indolent nature of the Angolan with the idea that he would bind himself to a contract of his own free will to work in a distant land. There was an urgent need for a commission to investigate. The alleged revelations of Nevinson had produced a deep impression in Portugal and Angola, to judge by newspaper comment and public attitudes. Whether for reasons of humanity or out of fear of further indictments, Mackie could not be certain, measures had been taken recently for the suppression of acts of cruelty.[64]

The Portuguese response in 1907 was cautious and critical. Ayres de Ornelas, the new colonial minister, an old-time associate of António Enes and a former Governor of Lourenço Marques province, gave an interview with the *Século* in which he tried to calm the troubled waters with oil—and a little vinegar.

I do not see any great difficulty in adjusting some of the existing problems. What I can affirm is that I do not believe there is any government which would not endeavour to supply São Tomé with the labour of which it makes such admirable use. . . . I recognize in Angola some of precisely the same difficulties that exist in São Tomé and which, in my opinion, arise principally from our not having yet effectively completed the occupation of the interior of Angola. Whatever the cause there is no reason why the procurement of labour for São Tomé should not be established on the same footing and with an analagous system as in the Rand. I say an analagous system because it is evident that a repatriation which we have enforced in a foreign colony, in our own colonies and among colonists of the same nation is not always necessary.[65]

Towards the end of 1907 the British Government, now that the supply of African labour from Moçambique was more or less assured the Rand, began to follow a somewhat firmer policy on the neo-slave-trade in Portuguese West Africa. Villiers was instructed to submit Burtt's report, to ask what Portugal's own investigations had revealed, and whether it was the Portuguese Government's intent to institute reforms without delay. The

[64] F.O. 367/46, H. G. Mackie to F.O., 18 Sept. 1907.
[65] *O século*, 3 Oct. 1907.

threat used was a growing popular agitation which would be embarrassing to both governments.[66] Villiers replied that he had been having frequent conversations with Foreign Minister José Rodrigues Monteiro and with Ornelas, and new regulations were being drawn up. The recruitment would be placed entirely and permanently under the supervision of government officials. Due provisions for repatriation would be published by the end of the year. The chief administrative officer of the colonial ministry would soon go to Benguela to get the new order started in an authoritative way.[67] William Cadbury, who saw Ornelas at about the same time, was given assurances that the causes of the complaint would be removed so that it 'would be impossible in the future for anyone to justly accuse Portugal of slavery in her colonies'.[68]

But with a change in the Government in Lisbon, responsible action began to drag. The new colonial minister, Augusto de Castilho, told Villiers new regulations were not needed; revision of the old ones would be sufficient.[69] A mission was sent out under Lieutenant-Captain Francisco Paula Cid, former Governor of Benguela and of São Tomé. Cid inspired no confidence in England, where his mission was regarded as a stalling tactic, or in Angola, where *A voz de Angola* wrote that when Cid was Governor of Benguela he had done nothing to stop the slave traffic out of the port and had probably assented in the export. Thus he was party to horrors 'which wound the pride of a cultured people and enrich half a dozen ambitious men at the expense of shaming Portugal'.[70]

Throughout 1908 the storm increased. In Lisbon, Villiers tried to disabuse Foreign Minister Wenceslau de Lima that the

[66] F.O. 367/46, F.O. to Villiers, 17 Oct. 1907.

[67] F.O. 367/49, Villiers to F.O., 18 Nov. 1907.

[68] F.O. 367/49, Villiers to F.O., 26 Nov. 1907. Of this remark, a Foreign Office minute reads, 'For anyone to believe this he must have a singularly large amount of faith.'

[69] F.O. 367/86, Villiers to F.O., 7 Mar. 1908. 'Very shifty', wrote one Foreign Office reader. 'Keep after them on this.'

[70] *A voz de Angola*, 23 Apr. 1907. A decree of 23 Apr. 1908 was a temporary resolution. It changed nothing drastically. It did create another supervisory board and stipulate that government agents be placed at ports which labourers were sent from, but this was about all the law provided.

campaign had commercial implications. He told Lima bluntly that the Portuguese Government could wait no longer. Once Mr. Morel got through with the Congo, Portugal was warned, he was pretty certain to turn his attention to Portuguese West Africa.[71] From Angola, Mackie wrote that not much could be expected from the Cid mission. Mackie rather thought that there had been enough denunciations by Europeans while the sufferers themselves remained unheard. 'Far reaching results might possibly be attained if the natives were called upon to recount the circumstances attending their recruitment.'[72] In Birmingham, Cadbury had given up on the Portuguese Government and was urging the Foreign Office to take stronger action. In Parliament the flow of questions on the São Tomé traffic and on what the British Government was doing about it increased. English journals and papers pressed for action.

At the Anti-Slavery Society there was a feeling that the Society might be engaged in its last great battle, and against a traditional foe. At the annual meeting in 1907, Mr. C. Wright Brooks had referred to Nevinson's book. What was to be done? England had no absolute right to interfere in Portuguese territory, but since Portugal desired to be on friendly terms, the British Government should 'put forth its moral influence'. As for the Society: 'We are a small company in a small room, but I am persuaded we represent a great moral movement in this country, for the anti-slavery sentiment which some years ago was so strong, powerful, and enthusiastic cannot be dead, but only needs to be reawakened.'[73] A resolution was passed that 'This meeting welcomes the efforts of the Anti-Slavery Society to arouse public opinion as to the continuance of slavery, the slave trade, and forced labour.'

A year later Nevinson addressed the annual meeting, saying pretty much what he had said in an article in the September 1907 *Fortnightly Review*. Three years had passed, Nevinson said, since he was in Central Africa 'examining the process of the slave trade as conducted under the Portuguese Government by its consent and under its regulations'. Two years had passed

[71] F.O. 367/86, Villiers to F.O., 4 July 1908.
[72] F.O. 367/86, Mackie to F.O., 6 Aug. 1908.
[73] *Reporter*, Mar.–May 1907, p. 40.

since he published his report, and one year since the publication of Burtt's report. Representations had since been made to the Portuguese Government. But they had abolished slavery thirty years ago and it still went on and was getting worse. Now that there was a Liberal government in Portugal, it was time to press for reform 'and not the time in which to exercise pity or patience.'[74]

Sir Charles Dilke, speaking at the annual meeting of the Aborigines Protection Society for 1908, saw no gain for English philanthropy in the Congo affair or the São Tomé controversy. Dilke, who was asking frequent questions in Parliament on conditions in the Portuguese colonies, felt that 'we have rather gone backwards than forwards in the last two or three years'. Although the English example had spread to the other nations of Europe, Dilke had the impression that ideas which were formerly universally accepted and often acted upon were no longer accepted as principles for action. 'We are all familiar with the case of Portugal, for example, whose conduct in some of her colonies is worse in some respects than any prevailing elsewhere.' The laxity of Britain's own colonial policies and of her public opinion was now a damaging force in the attempt to repress the more flagrant evils practised in some of the Portuguese colonies.[75]

In the last year of his life Fox Bourne carried on an eloquent correspondence with the Foreign Office, where he was held in small esteem.[76] Fox Bourne always gave a careful recital of evidence available, most of it culled from official publications. He had much greater scruples for the accuracy of what he said than the Anti-Slavery Society. Fox Bourne's constant contention was that the São Tomé traffic was a violation of treaty and international agreement, and 'nothing less than a complete abandonment of this survival of slave trading and slavery will

[74] *Reporter*, Mar.–May 1908, p. 52.

[75] *Aborigines Friend*, May 1907, pp. 24–25.

[76] A Foreign Office memorandum of 9 Nov. 1908 (F.O. 367/87): 'Mr. Fox Bourne . . . is the meanest looking little anatomy of a Uriah Heep. . . . I [Charles Clarke] advised him to go out himself to Angola like Mr. Burtt and Cadbury and investigate things for himself, but he was thrown into a fever of apprehension at the mere proposal.'

meet the requirements of the case'.[77] On the opening of a supplementary international conference in April 1908 to deal with the questions raised by the Brussels conference of 1890, Fox Bourne urged the British Government to press for remedial action, although 'the desire of some of the powers represented at the Conference is not so much to benefit in any way the natives as to obtain greater facilities for depriving them of means of offering resistance to unjustifiable attacks upon them'.[78]

Perhaps the finest letter written by the secretary of the Aborigines Protection Society was his last long declamation, a letter of 4 November 1908 to Grey. Fox Bourne posed two questions which he thought should be answered by those who appealed to the British public and to the British Government for effective protest against the slave-trade in Angola: what grounds are there for asserting that the evil exists and 'what warrant is there for supposing it is the duty, or even within the competence of the British Government, to interfere in the matter'. To the first question there was the over-powering evidence of Nevinson, Burtt, and others. Then Fox Bourne gave his views on various treaties which could be invoked by the Foreign Office and the various pieces of Portuguese legislation which were being violated. He concluded:

The time has, surely, arrived for Great Britain to insist upon the fulfilment of bargains which have been made with wearisome repetition during the past hundred years. . . . This should be a purely philanthropic enterprise and one that need not incur any risk of bloodshed or international complication. . . . If actual force of any sort had to be resorted to in this humane business, it would only be in legitimate performance of the nearest approach to international police work that civilization has yet arrived at. . . . The stoppage of the traffic on the costly and capacious steamers openly laden with slaves . . . would be a far easier and more speedily accomplished task than has been the stoppage of the traffic in the native dhows that formerly were clandestinely laden . . . on the East African coast. . . . Nothing but advantage can ensue if Portugal is at once clearly made aware that it will no longer be at liberty to break faith with the civilised world . . . and that Great Britain,

[77] Fox Bourne to Foreign Office, 19 Feb. 1908. In *Aborigines Friend*, Apr. 1908, pp. 129–32.

[78] *Aborigines Friend*, May 1908, p. 147.

at any rate, does not intend to be trifled with any longer and is ready to effectively claim as an indisputable right the equitable treatment of African natives which it has hitherto been content to ask for as a favour.[79]

Louder voices were being raised, in no small part the result of Nevinson's agitation, for the cocoa firms of Cadbury, Fry, and Rowntree to boycott São Tomé cocoa. In September 1907 the African trade section of the Liverpool Chamber of Commerce asked the firms to cease purchasing it. By the time William Cadbury had explained to the Chamber his firm's efforts—which led to a second, and milder, resolution on 21 October 1907—the original proposal had achieved much attention. Cadbury and Burtt went to Lisbon in December 1907 to talk to government officials and a group of plantation owners. In September 1908 Cadbury and Burtt set off for West Africa to see what had been accomplished by way of reforms. The *Evening Standard* took advantage of the occasion to publish a sharp rebuke (on 26 September 1908) accusing Cadbury's of buying slave-grown cocoa in full knowledge of conditions in Portuguese West Africa. The article made what amounted to personal charges against the integrity of Cadbury's. On William Cadbury's return the *Standard* would be sued for libel by Cadbury's and found guilty.

The *Standard* article also set off a *furor* in the Portuguese press. 'This campaign of defamation reappears periodically when the arguments addressed by the Portuguese Government and the planters to prove the inanity, bad faith, and want of foundation of these accusations are forgotten.' Let some of the 40,000 workers going to the Transvaal be diverted to São Tomé to shut up the slanderers. Cadbury was assumed to have gone off to get final facts on the beauties and benefits of the islands

[79] Fox Bourne to Foreign Office, 4 Nov. 1908. In *Aborigines Friend*, Nov. 1908, pp. 210–23. Walter Langley's reply was that the British Government was awaiting, one, the success of its efforts to get Portugal to stimulate emigration from Moçambique to the islands and, two, the report of Captain Paula Cid.

Fox Bourne, the outspoken radical, died in early Feb. 1909. Shortly thereafter the Aborigines Protective Society merged with the Anti-Slavery Society.

in order to put an end to the campaign against Portugal.[80] The *Século* complained that the chocolate manufacturers were indefatigable in their efforts to discredit. 'The best thing to do is to send a commission to the Rand . . . in order to examine the manner in which the Moçambique natives are recruited, the manner of their life, the way they are fed and treated in the mines.'[81] The *Diário de notícias* dismissed Cadbury as a troublemaker and gave its approval to the 'very correct' position of the British Government on the matter.[82]

On 4 December 1908 a public meeting of protest was held in Caxton Hall under the chairmanship of St. Loe Strachey, editor of the *Spectator*, who was now vociferously caught up in the controversy. A letter to *The Times* of 21 November 1908 called the public's attention to the meeting. The letter (whose last sentence read, 'One of our country's noblest achievements has been the abolition of human slavery, and we invite the attendance of all who view with horror the continuance of a system under which men, women, and children are bought and sold for labour.') was signed by Fox Bourne, Travers Buxton, John Galsworthy, Anthony Hope Hopkins, J. Ramsay MacDonald, Gilbert Murray, Nevinson, C. P. Scott, and H. G. Wells. The meeting was a popular and rhetorical success.

More practical success, perhaps, was achieved by a delegation of Strachey, R. C. Lehman, M.P., Reverend Robert Horton, and Nevinson to talk with Grey on 10 December. Grey asked the delegation pointedly what concrete complaint could be laid before the Portuguese which would have any effect. He got no very satisfactory answer to his question. Grey asked if they thought it a good idea for the British Government to request of the Portuguese Government facilities to permit the British consul in Luanda to satisfy himself that the labour recruitment was bona fide and voluntary. The delegation accepted the proposal as the best that could be done for the time being. If this failed, the Portuguese Government would be threatened with the publication of a Blue Book on the subject. Grey, impatient with both humanitarians and the Portuguese, was taking the lead

[80] *Jornal do comércio*, 29 Sept. 1908. The article is a remarkable piece of self-deception.

[81] *O século*, 1 Oct. 1908.

[82] *Diário de notícias*, 7 Oct. 1908.

in the Foreign Office. His minute on the memorandum of the meeting clearly expressed his exasperation with Portugal's dilatory tactics.[83]

Earlier in the year the Foreign Office had received a desolate report from Consul Mackie. Mackie's first sources for his report were missionaries in Bihé, but fearing reprisals against them he had given up the tactic, and most of the report was based on direct observation. 'The system under which labour is recruited in my district is closely akin to slavery.' In Caconda villages were systematically raided by labour recruiting parties. The captives were forced into labour gangs and sent down to the coast where they were contracted and distributed. No attempt was made up-country to distinguish between slave and *serviçal.* Englishmen working in the Benguela Railway construction and on mineral concessions attested that they had bought children and turned them over to missionaries. Children born to *serviçaes* passed into the same condition as their parents. Good treatment of slaves inland was the exception rather than the rule, and brutality and cruelty were evident everywhere. Officials of the Government had behaved treacherously towards the Africans, and certain areas of the country were empty of inhabitants, who had fled the depredations of Portuguese officials and soldiers. Mackie personally saw slave-gangs chained together.[84]

The year 1909 was the turning-point in the controversy—if it could be truly said that there was a turning-point. In the continuing history of labour problems and policies in Portuguese Africa, one year was pretty much the same as another, and 1909 was probably not too much different from 1869 or 1889, but the modest achievements of 1909—the result of private and public English action—did set the year modestly apart from the dismal succession of years before.

On the second day of 1909 Villiers spoke to the new President of the Portuguese Council Artur Alberto de Campos Henriques, telling him that the only serious difference between Portugal and England was the matter of labour recruitment. At his weekly meeting with Foreign Minister Wenceslau de Lima,

[83] F.O. 367/87, Memorandum of 11 Dec. 1908.
[84] F.O. 367/87, Mackie to F.O., 15 Mar. 1908.

Villiers was told that English humanitarian campaigns had accomplished nothing. Villiers replied that they had got Leopold out of the Congo and that Lima 'would make a mistake if he underrated the strength of feeling in England. The interest taken had aroused not merely an agitation among a group of philanthropists but a public movement that could not be disregarded.'[85] Villiers said that the gravamen of the charge was that the workers were signed to a contract they did not understand and that the way to refute the charge was to permit His Majesty's consul to satisfy himself that the workers went voluntarily.

Delay followed delay. Francisco Paula Cid had returned but was taking months to prepare his report for the Government. Lima reassured Villiers of Portugal's good intent and absolute determination to suppress all offences associated with the system, to which the English ambassador replied that his government did not doubt Portugal's good intentions, but at this point it would like also to see good works.[86] In April, Paula Cid's report was submitted, recommending sweeping changes. The districts open to recruitment should be limited; recruiting agents should be specially appointed and made responsible to the colonial government; repatriation should be obligatory.[87]

In the meantime Cadbury had returned from Angola and had recommended to the participating group of cocoa manufacturers (the English firms plus the German firm of Stollwerck) that they boycott São Tomé cocoa. Since 1906 the English firms had held off a boycott partly in response to Grey's suggestion that greater pressure could be brought on the Portuguese Government if there were the implied threat of a boycott present. Now, on 17 March 1909, a statement was given to the press.

> Mr. Cadbury has found that no adequate steps have yet been taken to remedy the evils proved to exist. . . .

[85] F.O. 367/140, Villiers to F.O., 2 Jan. 1909.
[86] F.O. 367/140, Villiers to F.O., 23 Mar. 1909.
[87] F.O. 367/140, Villiers to F.O., 7 Apr. 1909.
The Foreign Office expressed gratification at these profound charges, which would be excellent if carried out. Grey noted that he would be happier if the contracting of workers were an open ceremony instead of just something recorded on paper. Villiers was to keep pressing on this point.

His report has been carefully considered by the three firms. . . . these firms have come to the conclusion that the time has now arrived when they must mark, by definite action, their disappointment at the failure of the Portuguese Government to fulfill the pledges of reform, on the strength of which they agreed for a time to continue commercial relations with the islands.

They have therefore decided not to make any further purchases of the cocoa produced in the islands of São Tomé and Principe.[88]

Although the manufacturers held out the promise of again buying island cocoa when conditions had improved, they never again did purchase it.

The Decree of 29 July 1909 by Colonial Minister Manuel da Terra Vianna suspended recruitment in Angola for a period of three months, during which the only workers who could be contracted were those on the coast or on their way to the coast. In November the suspension was extended until February 1910 when new regulations were to go into effect.

The new regulations were contained in the Decree of 17 July 1909. They did not differ very substantially from the Law of 1903, and, again, it is difficult to understand why the Foreign Office found them generally acceptable, since the new law did not provide for mandatory repatriation and did not provide for public contracting, as Grey had insisted, but only public *recontracting* on the islands—where the British Government had no consular representative. It is true that recruiting agencies were brought under closer control and that only certain districts of Angola, where there was a semblance of real Portuguese authority, were open to recruiting. But the contracting arrangements were still flexible (Article Sixty: 'All contracts for labourers must be drawn up in the presence of the curators or their delegates, where such exist, and in their absence before the person exercising administrative functions, and no contract shall be valid unless it fulfills the conditions prescribed by these regulations'). The contract period was reduced to three years, and once more elaborate precautions were laid down to protect the health and income of the workers and to ensure his satisfactory transportation to the islands. Wages and rations were

[88] Quoted in Ilolo Williams, *The Firm of Cadbury* (London, 1931), p. 202.

fixed at decent levels and doctors' services specified. But, on the other hand, Article 112 stated that 'Natives of Africa who under Article 256 of the penal code have been condemned as vagrants may be compelled to contract for agricultural work on São Tomé and Principe under these regulations.' So long as Portuguese African labour laws contained such items as the notorious vagrancy clause, under which abuse had proliferated abuse, not much that was different could be expected in any new legislation. But the Decree of 17 July 1909 did re-establish one tradition: the creation of new Portuguese colonial legislation in response to English criticism.

In Portugal the reaction of the press to the noise in England temporarily subsided. Portuguese journals had never doubted that what was said was true; they had been forced into a defensive posture by the recurring and sometimes insulting violence of English complaints. When a group of Moçambique workers rebelled on São Tomé at the deception of a labour agent, who had told them in East Africa they were contracted for one year on the islands that they were there for three years, the *Século* noted with approval the Government's brisk orders to repatriate the workers and suspend the agent.[89] The incident also aroused protests in newspapers in Angola, Moçambique, and even São Tomé. The same paper published several illustrations from missionary C. A. Swan's *The Slavery of Today*, admitting that there was some truth in Swan's allegations. To check these crimes the guilty must be punished and the new reforms implemented.[90] In Angola, *A voz de Angola* kept up its campaign against any migration of labour to São Tomé. The paper had no faith in the new regulations.

> In this fearful decree there is not a single article, not a single word, which provides for the safeguard of the interests and liberty of the orphans....

[89] *O século*, 9 Aug. 1909.
A economista (15 Aug. 1909) wrote: 'In São Tomé the black colonists are beginning to understand that they have rights and to remember that they ought to have them respected.' The article was extremely critical of the island planters.

[90] *O século*, 10 Dec. 1909. A favourite procedure for most Lisbon papers remained the drawing of comparisons between the idyllic life of workers on the islands and the harsh existence Rand miners had to put up with.

There are no children, no parents . . . no social or human rights, there is nothing; what exists is an animal belonging to the master, under the control of the master—and as this animal becomes absolutely necessary, it is, materially speaking, treated as well as can be, so that it does not fail to give the largest amount of production and reproduction.

Conscience, free-will, dignity, social rights, these are all prerogatives of *people*, but not of native *serviçaes*.[91]

The humanitarian campaign in England paused in 1909 to take stock. New laws had appeared, a repatriation procedure was underway, a cocoa boycott had been called, and Burtt had been sent off to America by the Anti-Slavery Society to try to persuade manufacturers there to join the boycott. The Foreign Office, reluctantly perhaps, had been goaded into some sort of belated action. One of the most significant moments of the year was the publication in *The Times* (22 June 1909) of a letter signed by nineteen British, American, Swiss, and Canadian missionaries in Angola, openly and forcefully condemning slavery in the province and the farcical contracting of workers for São Tomé, none of whom, to the knowledge of the missionaries, had ever returned. Twelve of the missionaries had been in Angola for ten years or more and seven of them for nineteen years or more. For the foreign Protestant missionaries in Angola, subject as they were to official reprisals and unofficial harassments, the letter was nothing less than a statement of conscience. All in all, the assorted company of liberals and humanitarians could look *back* in 1909 with some satisfaction at their efforts during the past half decade.

Two more important reports were added to the growing literature on Portuguese West African slavery. There were Swan's very long report on his recent journey to Angola, which was submitted to the Foreign Office,[92] and shortly thereafter became the substance of a book, *The Slavery of Today*, and William Cadbury's account of his journey, *Labour in Portuguese West Africa*. Swan's narrative was a variation on a familiar theme, basically a collection of homely vignettes from his own experience or from that of African villagers and missionaries.

[91] *A voz de Angola*, 4 July 1909.

[92] F.O. 367/141, Swan to F.O., 2 June 1909.

Much of what he said had been told before (there is almost always an embarrassing duplication of incident in the literature of atrocity); some of the material gave a new, often pathetically righteous dimension to the story of Angolan slavery.

> The same Mr. —— . . . told me that a native, who had been working for him for some time, came to him one day and said his brother had been sold to Snr. ——; inquiries were made, and it was found he had been sold by his *own father* for a keg of rum! This dreadful 'fire water' had dragged the natives down nearly as low as the whites, but the whites find degraded natives play into their hands much better than others! This is the real reason why the Portuguese pleaded that the sale of alcohol to the natives might not be forbidden. . . .[93]

The crux of the matter, according to Swan, was that the officials on the coast did not do their duty honestly. If they insisted that every *serviçal* had a proper contract and had signed for his services knowingly, the nefarious traffic would die a natural death and slavery in the interior would wither away.[94]

Cadbury's volume was a sort of handbook to the contract labour system. It was a straightforward and informative presentation of the islands' cocoa industry, the life of the *serviçaes*, Cadbury's trip to the interior of Angola, his interviews with officials, and the history of his seven-year association with the problem. The work contained a battery of appendixes. It was the most meticulously proper and restrained statement to be written by an English philanthropist during the whole controversy. And it was a book which won Cadbury few friends in either England or Portugal.[95]

In 1905, 4,264 Angolans were landed on the islands; in 1906, 2,721; in 1907, 3,452; in 1908, 4,951; and in 1909, about 4,000.[96]

[93] C. A. Swan, *The Slavery of Today* (London, 1909), p. 124.
Swan told of the torture of a female slave by an 'educated mulatto trader'. She was stripped and exposed 'in a most shameful manner to the bystanders, then a stick was actually thrust up into her inside till the blood flowed profusely! . . . Surely if the men of Britain do not arise, and say this kind of thing must be stopped, the women will!' (p. 128).

[94] Ibid., p. 198.

[95] William A. Cadbury, *Labour in Portuguese West Africa* (London, 1909). A second edition, with an added chapter, appeared in 1910.

[96] These figures are approximate. There is considerable variation between official figures, depending on when they were collected and who did the col-

Angola remained the greatest source of supply. In 1907 over a hundred workers were recruited in the Cape Verdes, Cabinda, and Portuguese Guinea, and in 1908, 539 labourers from Moçambique arrived on the islands, signed for periods of from one to three years. The following year almost 2,000 workers came from Moçambique.

More important than the statistics of *serviçaes* going to São Tomé and Principe, however, was the figure for 1908 of twenty-nine workers who were repatriated to Angola.[97] After fifty-five years (1853 to 1908), a contracted worker had come back from the isles of death. In 1903, 2,864 Angolans had been taken to the islands. After five years 793 were entitled to repatriation[98] —the rest presumably having died—and twenty-nine accepted. In 1909 the number of workers repatriated fell off somewhat. Only nine chose to return to Angola (2,967 had been recruited in 1904).[99] But for the next year the figure would rise to 388 and would increase thereafter. A modest victory had been won. The islands had begun to give up their captives.

In December 1909 Lieutenant-Colonel José Augusto Alves Roçadas, hero of campaigns in the south of Angola, took office in Luanda as governor-general of the province. In his inaugural speech, the governor pledged himself to bring about reforms in the labour system 'in accordance with the dictates of humanity'.[100]

lecting. For the years 1906–9 the figures are estimates based on passenger lists, which are not always complete.

[97] Figures from F.O. 367/186, Mackie to F.O., 30 Nov. 1909, enclosures 1 and 2. Mackie got his statistics from various official publications.

In the dispatch of 30 Nov. Mackie made the classic consular comment. The new regulations left nothing to be desired [the Foreign Office had asked for his opinion], but the way laws had been disregarded in the past did not encourage him to believe they would be any better heeded now.

[98] F.O. 367/87, Villiers to F.O., 9 Nov. 1908. Villiers got his information confidentially from the minister of foreign affairs.

[99] Mackie in his dispatch of 21 Sept. 1909 (F.O. 367/141) gave the figure of seventy-eight for the first seven months of the year.

[100] F.O. 367/186, Mackie to F.O., 24 Dec. 1909.

CHAPTER VIII

The Ending

ALTHOUGH on 27 January 1910 Governor-General Roçadas issued a decree stating that recruiting in Angola of workers for the cocoa islands would commence on 1 February, there was to be no recruiting in Angola for the next three years. The humanitarians could claim a victory. The Foreign Office had made a discreet contribution. The Portuguese Government had fulfilled a clear moral obligation. For a while the angry planters had to be satisfied with a growing but inadequate number of workers from Moçambique and the Cape Verde islands. And when the recruiting of workers began again in Angola, it was under conditions which were generally admitted to be satisfactory, if not always meticulously correct. Figures for the period 1910 to 1915 are:

RECRUITED

From	*1910*	*1911*	*1912*	*1913*	*1914*	*1915*
Angola	..	..	..	1,008	1,580	4,874
Moçambique	2,444	2,840	3,473	5,384	7,893	8,375
Cape Verdes	44	270	258	148	44	966

REPATRIATED

To	*1910*	*1911*	*1912*	*1913*	*1914*	*1915*
Angola	4	385	1,550	2,071	4,198	2,876
Moçambique	272	613	834	1,310	1,562	2,141
Cape Verdes	268	88	86	182	162	960

In the same six years more than 10,000 Angolan workers re-engaged their services for a varying number of years.

A modest victory had been won. The way of life in Angola and São Tomé was not significantly altered and what seemed to be an essential attitude in the Portuguese colonies towards the use of African labour had not been seriously changed, but the system of capture, sale, and permanent captivity of workers under farcically legal terms *had* been altered and it would never be quite the same again. Subsequent labour scandals in Angola and the questionable *shibalo* system under which plantations in Moçambique were worked for the next fifty years revealed that the tradition was very much alive, but the last tentacle of the export slave-trade, now 400 years old, had been at last lopped away.

The English humanitarians could not—or would not—believe that something of real importance had been accomplished. Their protest had often been immoderate and at times irresponsible, but it could usually be justified by the enormity of the outrages they were attacking. Now their protest frequently seemed vengeful and obstinate, out of proportion, perhaps, to what could practically be accomplished. Their motives became mixed and uncertain. Not always finding a serious quarrel with the Portuguese Government, whose good intent they were bound to acknowledge, they sought a quarrel with the Foreign Office, whose efforts on behalf of the *serviçaes* were now more constant than they had been for the whole previous decade. The controversy became a kind of shouting match. The men who took over the humanitarian lead, St. Loe Strachey, editor of the *Spectator*, and the Reverend John Harris, by 1912 organizing secretary and the real power at the Anti-Slavery Society, were men of furious and flexible integrity. Both gave a sort of noisy direction to the campaign in favour of the Angolan *serviçal*; although it was not a campaign empty of achievement, it was not one that brought any particular credit to those caught up in it.

The pattern remained the same, but the issue had become more widely publicized. In Parliament questions rained down. The daily mail brought queries and remonstrances to the Foreign Office from a variety of worried groups and individuals, from churches and religious societies, and from commercial houses. They had all come lately to learn of the state of affairs in Angola and São Tomé as they had been five and ten years earlier. Meetings of protest were regularly held and resolutions passed to be sent to the Foreign Office. It was as much in its own defence as it was to goad Portugal that the Foreign Office was driven to publishing a series of White Books in 1912, 1913, 1914, 1915, and 1917.

Sir Edward Grey received a large deputation from the Anti-Slavery Society on 1 July 1910. Among the delegation were Nevinson, Lord Mayo, George Cadbury, Joseph Rowntree, John Holt, Mr. and Mrs. John Harris, and six Members of Parliament. Nevinson said that it was useless to trust the new regulations. Lord Mayo remarked that every traveller to West Africa knew of Portuguese cruelties. St. Loe Strachey said the number of slaves going to the islands increased every year. Sir Albert Spicer, speaking for the London Chamber of Commerce, said that 'they did not want trade that was the result of cruel and unnatural conditions'. Canon H. S. Holland read a letter written to him by the Archbishop of Canterbury. 'I rejoice to hear that you are taking up this terrible matter of the San Thomé cocoa plantations. If the allegations made are substantial, and I have seen no real refutation of them, it seems to be the clear duty of those who have at heart the well-being of the less civilized races of the world, to sound a vigorous protest and to invoke every aid that can be enlisted for bringing such dark deeds to an end.'

Grey said it had been his task since taking office to gather the facts of the system, particularly the evil of the recruiting on the mainland, and to bring them to the notice of the Portuguese Government. He did not want to derogate the sovereign rights of Portugal or to hurt their political susceptibilities. He was convinced that once they were fully aware of what went on they would take stringent action. Now recruitment had been suspended and new regulations drawn up. He was not aware that there was any need to criticize them yet. To criticize the administration of laws in foreign territories was a delicate matter. He trusted that past evils would be eliminated and that the Portuguese Government would realize that it was in the best interests of both countries to avail themselves of the helpful interest of all those who were concerned with the problem.[1]

[1] *The Times*, 2 July 1910.

The *Diário do noticias* (4 July 1910) applauded the interview. In a long article, the *Diário* gave high praise to Grey and moderate praise to the good

The militant English humanitarians were no longer content to wait. On the occasion of the formation of the Portuguese Republic in October 1910 Strachey gave the new government a sharp warning. The British Government should not recognize the new régime until certain pledges were made. Slavery, slave-raiding, and slave-trading must cease in the Portuguese African territories. If the Portuguese Government did not put its house in order soon it would run the risk of having heavy pressure put on it by countries other than Britain. 'The fierce slave trading that has been going on in Angola is disturbing the minds of the natives throughout West Africa not only in our possessions, but also in those of Germany, France, and, still more, of Belgium.'[2]

Meanwhile the Foreign Office was receiving vaguely encouraging reports from its new consul in Luanda, Frank Drummond-Hay. There was no migration from Angola, and conditions on São Tomé were still very good. Repatriation was a great problem, and Drummond-Hay questioned whether it was to the worker's advantage to be shipped back to Angola.[3] In a private letter, Drummond-Hay wrote:

> My candid opinion is that the Angolan *serviçal* is in Paradise at São Tomé in comparison to his native home, where he would be caught and sold again by his own people if he came back, and repatriation would certainly do away with his freedom. He is far better off where he is. He is rather a lazy devil and always looks for a change to something else and does not like regular work which is so good for him, and that is why he says I want to return to Angola but cannot say which part of Angola as he does not know.[4]

In November the Anti-Slavery Society sent a small delegation, including Burtt, Nevinson, and Harris, to Lisbon to prevail on the new government to speed reforms. On the very day

intent of the philanthropists. In conclusion the paper assumed that the affair had now come to an honourable end and there was no longer any reason for the British boycott of island cocoa to go on.

[2] The *Spectator*, 15 Oct. 1910, pp. 588–9. In the same issue a letter from John Harris, citing Colin Harding's account of events in 1902, also warned the Portuguese Government to change its ways.

[3] F.O. 367/187, Frank Drummond-Hay to F.O., 20 Oct. 1910.

[4] F.O. 367/187, Drummond-Hay to Tilley, 21 Oct. 1910.

of their arrival (14 November 1910) the formation (or re-formation) of the Anti-Slavery Society of Portugal was, fortuitously, announced. The minister for foreign affairs, Bernardino Machado, welcomed the delegates and praised them at great length for their dedication to the cause of humanity. He stressed the traditional ties of friendship between the two countries. 'Let the Anti-Slavery Society continue its propaganda on behalf of the African races in general and let the delegates repeat their visits with the certainty that the opinion which prevails abroad will penetrate the public mind in Portugal.' Let the Society discuss with the Portuguese Anti-Slavery Society such matters as were proper to both countries. The ultimate solutions to these problems, however, must rest with the governments.[5]

The new governor-general of Angola, Manuel Maria Coelho, spoke more directly of his government's plans in Angola. His first step would be to suppress recruiting agents and to turn the job over to responsible government officials who would receive no pay for their services beyond their salary. Emigration would be entirely voluntary. For a while repatriation would be compulsory. These would be the first acts of his administration. 'We must show that Portugal cannot continue to be accused of slavery by the civilized world. The only practical way to obtain this result is the compulsory repatriation system.'[6]

The issue now came down to repatriation—and the problems it presented. Through 1910 and 1911 the Foreign Office constantly pressed the Portuguese Government for action. The difficulties of repatriation were many, more than enough to thwart

[5] F.O. 367/187, Villiers to F.O., 22 Nov. 1910, enclosure. See also *O século*, 19 Nov. 1910.

[6] Interview with *A economista*, 6 Nov. 1910. Governor Leotte do Rego of São Tomé took an idealistic view of the problems. 'Everything depends not on complicated and confused regulations, made generally under the influence of momentary impressions, and not in harmony with the real interests of the colony, but on the good faith, the sincerity, and the honourableness of all those who have to do with the matter, agriculturists as well as the authorities of the colony and of those places where recruiting operations occur. The question . . . might be solved and without further embarrassment as long as we always proceed with loyalty and in the spirit of patriotic sacrifice, never losing sight of the fact that above all we have to live up to our good traditions of a civilised and humanitarian nation. . . .' *Boletim oficial de São Tomé*, 17 June 1911.

the efforts of an inadequate, though well-intentioned colonial staff. The managers of estates effectively discouraged many of their workers from returning to Angola. Large numbers of workers had spent the greater part of their lives in island slavery and had no genuine desire to return to a land they but dimly remembered. The original wrong which was done them now made voluntary slaves of them. And there was the problem of what to do with the workers brought back to Angola. Through 1911 and 1912 both British and Portuguese reports told of the obstacles and frustrations faced by workers and officials.

Drummond-Hay wrote in May 1911 that he had been informed by Vice-Consul Lionel Fussell at Lobito that repatriated *serviçaes* hung about the local stores spending what they had on drink. Then they drifted around to the compounds. Some sought to be recontracted for work on the islands. Fussell surmised that 'they had become too civilized to desire to return to the crude mode of living in which they were brought up'. The same situation was said to apply at Novo Redondo. Repatriated workers were given the choice of staying on the coast or proceeding inland to their own country. Most of them stayed on the coast where there was no place for them. The governor-general spoke of establishing settlements in fertile areas for the repatriates.[7] Three months later Acting Consul Robert Smallbones reported that the latest load of *serviçaes* to arrive had created a disturbance and most of them were clamouring to be sent back. Smallbones believed that unless the repatriation were carried out in good faith it would be a failure.[8]

On this point he was in agreement with the ubiquitous Luanda *Reforma*. The first groups of workers sent back, the paper claimed, contained people born on the islands. They were sent with no money and no knowledge of their destinations.[9]

[7] F.O. 367/234, Drummond-Hay to F.O., 15 May 1911.

[8] F.O. 367/234, Robert Smallbones to F.O., 25 Aug. 1911.

[9] In a Lisbon paper, Hermano Neves wrote an article, 'A Pavement of Good Intentions in São Tomé. Repatriation, its Farce and its Tragedy.' He argued that repatriation was inhuman. Landed in Benguela, without friends, money, or employment, the *serviçaes* were dying on all sides, fifty allegedly being found dead on Benguela pavements at one time. The Government should have taken time and set up an agricultural colony before allowing repatriation to proceed. *A capital*, 8 June 1912.

Some of them, after twenty years on the islands, arrived in ruined health. They had to live on the charity of people in Angola.

The unscrupulous and almost criminal manner in which people from São Tomé have been sent to this province cannot continue ... It is not just that those who have enriched themselves at the cost of the hands of Angola should send those hands back to the mother colony when they have become useless . . . It is probable that this form of repatriation is a stratagem which will, on account of the protests that will be raised against it in the province, enable the planters to argue that repatriation is unproductive of any good results, and that the truth is, as they have said all along, that the people who have once gone to those islands never want to leave them again.[10]

The *Reforma* was essentially right. During the first years of repatriation, for one reason or another—some of them devious—workers were given but a fraction of their withheld wages. The old and the sick, some of whom had spent virtually a lifetime on São Tomé, were dumped in Angola. It was believed that the planters got rid of a number of workers recruited before 1903 in order to avoid paying repatriation wages. The issue of the repatriation fund, which had been mishandled and loosely supervised, caused English humanitarians great distress and was one of the major targets of their latter-day offensive.

In a remarkable report Drummond-Hay told of the *serviçaes* repatriated during the second half of 1911. The simple facts spoke for the whole drama of São Tomé:

Seventy-nine went to Benguela. The ages of fifty-seven of these are given ranging from 27–54 years. In nineteen cases it is not stated how long they stayed on the islands, four spent nine years there, fifteen ten years, thirty-four from ten to twenty years, and three twenty-five years. Their destination was in no case known. . . . Twenty-two received no bonus. . . . Six brought children with them.

Twenty-nine went to Loanda. The ages of twenty-seven of these are given: they range from 24–72 years. In two cases it is not known how long they stayed on the islands, twenty-one stayed there from ten to twenty years, one twelve years, two fifteen years, and three thirty-four years. They are all reported as returning to their native

[10] *A reforma*, 19 Aug. 1911.

place. This may, however, be only a phrase. . . . None of them received a bonus.

Seventy-one went to Novo Redondo. Their ages were unknown in eighteen cases, the ages of the other fifty-three ranged from 27–72. In fifteen cases the length of their stay on the island is not given. Five spent from ten to twenty years there, the rest in an average spent over twenty-six years there. Their destination was unknown and they received no bonus.

I . . . beg to draw attention to the fact that 122 *serviçaes* out of the total of 179 received no bonus [withheld pay]. This seems impolitic and unjust and cannot further the ends of repatriation.[11]

Gradually the difficulties were overcome. By 1913 the complaints were diminishing. Workers were now returning with their withheld wages and they had not been on the island so long or enslaved in such remote areas that they did not know their homelands. The slaves brought down from the highlands of Angola and beyond the Angolan frontiers in the late nineteenth and early twentieth centuries had died or chosen to remain on the estates, and now it was the return of Angolans to Angola. By 1915 the circle of migration and repatriation was about as honest and efficient as it would ever be.

But that happy state would not be reached without difficulties. The British Government had assumed that the Republican Government would issue far-reaching legislation to reform the migration system. The Law of 13 May 1911, however, was merely a modification of the *Regulamento* of 1899 and reaffirmed, in Article 1, that 'every native of a Portuguese colony is under the moral and legal obligation to procure for himself and acquire by work the necessary means of subsistence. . . . He has full liberty to choose for himself the way in which he wishes to fulfill the obligation, but if he does not fulfill it in any way the public authorities may force him to do so.' The Foreign Office decided it was 'a decree for the enforcement of labour. . . . The whole principle of forced labour when applied by Portuguese officials is devious in character. . . . The contract labour is thoroughly bad in terms enacted.' Although contracts for the islands were cut to two-year terms, there was still no

[11] F.O. 367/285, Drummond-Hay to F.O., 18 Mar. 1912.

provision for compulsory repatriation.[12] The Foreign Office felt that once again it had been had, and disappointment over the new law was one of the main factors leading to the publication of the White Book of 1912.

Another reason was the harassment from humanitarians. John Harris had gone to the islands (for two days), Angola, and the Congo in 1911 and 1912. He now spoke and wrote with added authority, and for the next three years it was his voice which rose stridently above almost all others. Sent out by the Anti-Slavery Society, which he dominated on his return, Harris took charge of the campaign. In articles and letters to the *Manchester Guardian*, the *Contemporary Review*, and the *Spectator*, Harris told the same story that had been told so many times before. In a book *Portuguese Slavery, Britain's Dilemma* (London, 1913), Harris gave a selective account of Portuguese conduct. His dismissal or disregard of Portuguese efforts since 1910 to improve the system was typical of Harris's kind of blind humanitarianism. The attack made by Harris was that not all of the workers had been repatriated, that the repatriation fund had been misused, that conditions on the islands were not as good as they were reported to be. On the basis of these allegations, reinforced by familiar horror stories from the past, Harris kept the fires of indignation stoked. He used the same perverted technique in his voluminous correspondence to the Foreign Office. When the first White Book came out Harris (and Buxton) wrote Grey claiming a verdict in favour of the Society's actions, saying that slavery was still slavery, and that Britain should withdraw from her alliance with Portugal if things didn't improve (just what things, Harris did not specify). Foreign Office commentary was that Harris was not 'over-nice' in his use of 'facts' to support his theories. He should also be rebuked for quoting from the White Book out of context.[13]

After a meeting with several men in the Foreign Office, Harris wrote them that St. Loe Strachey and he still agreed that

> . . . we should push our policy vigorously throughout the country, not only because we believe it is an expedient policy, but because

[12] F.O. 367/234, Drummond-Hay to F.O., 24 Nov. 1911. Minutes on decree are enclosed.

[13] F.O. 367/286, Buxton and Harris to F.O., 8 Nov. 1912.

we believe it is absolutely sound. I feel very strongly that either we should maintain our present attitude or give it up altogether, because the moment we admit the Portuguese system is that of ordinary contract labour, with abuses, then my committee would, in my opinion, be compelled to drop the question and concentrate its attention on our own system of contract labour. I do not hesitate to say that once you have got the 'labourer' on the mainland plantations, or on the cocoa farms of the islands, he is, in the main, treated in a more kindly manner than the majority of the coolies under our own system; but there is a vital difference between the methods by which the labourers have been obtained.[14]

In his threat to expose labour conditions in British Africa, Harris was renewing a charge which the Society had made from time to time over the decade: that working conditions and the treatment of workers in the South African mines were bad, Portuguese defenders of their own contract labour system had been saying since the 1890's that African workers in Moçambique and the cocoa isles were better off than African workers in the mines, where treatment was harsh and often brutal. They cited extensive mortality figures to prove their point. Portuguese and humanitarian accusations found support in occasional articles in South African newspapers or in the reports of government committees.

Usually on the basis of what Harris was writing, the *Spectator* kept insisting that England should break the Anglo-Portuguese alliance guaranteeing Portugal's colonial rule. Strachey was convinced that slavery was still the absolute reality in Portuguese West Africa.[15] The White Paper seemed to justify its position. Since a repatriation programme was 'not really repatriation at all . . . substantially slaving goes on as before'. Quotations from the White Book were misused, taken out of time and out of context. A great deal was said in the *Spectator* about sleeping sickness on Principe but nothing about the three-year ban on recruitment in Angola—the humanitarian's unique triumph—and nothing about the fact that labourers for the islands were now coming principally from Moçambique,

[14] F.O. 367/286, Harris to F.O., 24 Oct. 1912.

[15] The *Spectator*, 23 Mar. 1912, p. 465. The journal entrusted the moving of this proposal to the Liberal party and to the public action taken by the Anti-Slavery Society, which was made up mostly of Liberals.

as humanitarians had urged for years, recruited in about the same way as the Witwatersrand Native Labour Association recruited for the mines. When the second White Book was published in 1913, the *Spectator* saw the Foreign Office 'hard at work explaining away the forty thousand slaves who work in the cocoa plantations of San Thomé and Principe [trying to prove] that slavery ceases to be slavery if it is carried on under a respectable *alias*—as, for example, contract labour. . . . They are trying to bury the body of Slavery in a very shallow grave and with an altogether insufficient quantity of earth.'[16]

In one of its moderate moments the *Spectator* published a three-instalment essay by Lord Cromer in 'Portuguese Slavery'. It was a serious and understanding article. Cromer had been involved in the controversy for a number of years; he knew its history and he knew the problems. He attempted to put the issue into a moral and historical perspective. He admitted that the excesses of the past had diminished and that the Portuguese Government was recently endeavouring finally to suppress the trade in slaves. But the repressive nature of life on São Tomé where 700 workers, according to Consul Smallbones, were forced against their will to recontract their services on one estate in 1912, created a régime of forcible engagement which was, even by Sir Edward Grey's definition, slavery. He recommended that the planters of São Tomé be encouraged to substitute a system of free labour, which was already succeeding with workers from the Cape Verdes and Moçambique.[17]

During a full debate in the House of Lords on 23 July 1913 and at a public meeting, under the auspices of the Anti-Slavery Society at the Westminster Palace Hotel a year earlier, the Foreign Office and Portugal were equal recipients of sustained criticism.[18] The speakers at both occasions quoted liberally from Livingstone and Harris, since there was not a great deal of current fact for the humanitarians to use. The Archbishop of Canterbury could say that the White Books left him with an uncomfortable feeling, but the White Books revealed only that

[16] The *Spectator*, 17 Aug. 1912, p. 225.

[17] The *Spectator*, 8 Mar. 1913, pp. 389–90.

[18] The *Spectator*, 16 Aug. 1913, pp. 235–7, 23 Aug. 1913, pp. 268–70, and 30 Aug. 1913, pp. 304–5.

there were still abuses in Angola, vestiges of the slave-trade, and in São Tomé, the forcible retention of workers, which two governments were making honest efforts to eliminate. Not since the 1850's had such a concerted effort of persuasion by the British Government and direct action by the Portuguese Government been taken.[19]

At Luanda, and at Benguela and São Tomé, where there were now British vice-consuls, the work of investigation and report was the primary task of consular representatives. In a 26-September-1913 dispatch, Smallbones reported that the work of repatriation was still not as successful as it should be, and he had reached the conclusion that repatriation should now be made absolutely compulsory. The number of those who had chosen to remain was very small and he had been driven to this recommendation after witnessing for more than a year the tactics used by the planters to keep their workers and after seeing the pressures they could apply to a weak-willed *curador* in São Tomé to bend him to their will.[20] From Lisbon, Lancelot Carnegie wrote the Foreign Office that in his discussions with Prime Minister Afonso Costa he had stressed the repatriation issue. Costa admitted the difficulties, said he was negotiating for more ships to carry the workers, and was trying to avoid the consequences of the workers being dumped on the mainland. His government was doing everything it could to implement an entirely new system of labour in the African colonies (in which endeavour it would fail, as had every government before it).[21] Consul Hall Hall admitted that there were elements of truth in the Society's pamphlet, *Slavery in West Africa* (by

[19] For a report of the meeting, see *The African World*, 19 June 1912, p. 464.

[20] F.O. 367/336, Smallbones to H. Hall Hall, 26 Sept. 1913. Earlier in the year Smallbones had reported that 'repatriation is being carried out loyally and in the right spirit', although their original contracts were a sham and their recruitment a farce. 'What is going on now is the emancipation of an unfree people. . . . Steady slow liberation appears particularly necessary both for the industry . . . and for the "*serviçaes*." In my humble opinion, universal compulsory repatriation of all "*serviçaes*" coming from Angola would be impolitic. Nor am I prepared to advocate the compulsory repatriation of those who have finished their contracts, as long as repatriation is carried out as at present.' F.O. 367/355, Smallbones to F.O., 29 Apr. 1913.

What changed Smallbones's mind was a closer visit to the islands and talks with managers of estates and people in the curator's office.

[21] F.O. 367/357, Lancelot Carnegie to F.O., 15 Nov. 1913.

John Harris in 1913), but that for many accusations proof and facts were wanting. Hall agreed that so long as large numbers of workers remained on the island, slavery could be said to exist there. But he was confident that most of the workers now going to the islands went of their own free will. Nor could he agree that Portuguese laws were never kept. Nor was it true that workers were still not receiving their withheld pay. But he did agree with the Society that repatriation should be made compulsory. Slavery was a traditional way of life in Angola ('the natives are naturally prone to be slaves, just as . . . the Portuguese have proved themselves naturally prone to be owners of slaves'), and for their protection, repatriation should be insisted upon.[22]

In almost all of the discussions the Portuguese Government was courteous and correct towards the British Government and made only remotely critical remarks about what seemed to almost all of Portugal an unjust humanitarian campaign. José de Almada, First Secretary to the Colonial Office in Lisbon, wrote a number of letters to the *Spectator* and *The Times*, citing statistics and legislation, trying to correct the impression which had been created by John Harris. The reaction in the Portuguese press and in public opinion was more bitter and vehement. But one of the most biting replies in the long and unpleasant campaign belonged to the old soldier and colonial servant, Alfredo Augusto Freire de Andrade. In an open letter to William Cadbury, prompted by a misguided article on forced labour written by Cadbury and E. D. Morel for the *Nineteenth Century Review* (October 1912) Colonel Freire de Andrade spoke out his country's sense of injustice. Departing from the generally accepted colonial idea 'that the native never willingly works', Freire de Andrade argued that Portuguese native labour laws corresponded in their demands and in their punishments with those of other colonial powers. It was

[22] F.O. 367/337, Hall Hall to F.O., 25 Nov. 1913.
In June 1913, Hall Hall, after talking with a Boer hunter and a German fertilizer salesman, both of whom travelled widely in Angola, said he was informed that 'the day of slavery' is ended. Strong action by Governor-General Norton de Mattos had put a brusque end to domestic slavery in Angola wherever Portuguese authority extended. F.O. 367/355, Hall Hall to F.O., 21 June 1913.

necessary for the civilization of Africa that the native peoples be obliged to work. He agreed that contract labour, in the eyes of some, might not differ greatly from slavery, but if this were so then Portugal stood guilty with other colonizing nations in Africa and Asia. But the assertion that slaving in Angola existed as it did in the fifteenth century was maliciously false. Point by point he hammered at Cadbury's alleged inaccuracies and misrepresentations. He used the White Books with the same skill as Harris and the *Spectator*, but to demonstrate the reverse, that Portugal's policies were sound and right. He made the usual comparison with the Rand mines' labour recruitment. Then, going to the nub of the philanthropic complaint, he wrote:

Now that repatriation has begun there would seem to be no further ground for growling. But . . . you seem to insist on the Government's freeing the boys who are legally engaged and are not and never have been slaves, and, further, that they shall be transported to Angola and established in places previously arranged for. For you this simple course is sufficient. It comes to this: to please you the Government should ruin the colony of São Tomé by taking from it 30,000 natives who are performing useful and light work, who are well fed and well looked after, and paid in Angola. . . . Natives left to themselves never willingly do any work, and as the Government would have none to give them at Angola, and would therefore refuse to feed them, no doubt you would accuse it of ruling them under a system of wholesale starvation. Should the Government give them any labour, you would naturally not fail to accuse it of practising slavery. Is this what you are aiming at? . . .

The unfair way in which you allude to the White Book is obvious, keeping back anything favourable to us and then leading up to conclusions which are conducive to your case. . . . The results of our efforts, as set forth in the White Book, are vitriolic to you. . . . You say that the recruiting begun in November at Angola is 'apparently' being made under the old system, although you know what is going on in São Thomé, and that such a statement is utterly at variance with the truth.

And here I will stop as I am sick of the whole matter.

Against such bad faith, prejudice, and sheer pig-headedness argument is perfectly useless. You have made great wealth by means of the cocoa bean, worked by the poor natives of São Thomé and natives in other parts of the wide world, and you exploit them and the Europeans who are helping in the amassing of your fortune. You have, therefore, ample means at your disposal—money, publicity, and . . . everything that money can buy—and you are using these means to slander our administration. I, on the contrary, have nothing of the kind, having all my life worked for my country, and her good name, and this is not a sure means of accumulating riches.

Perhaps in what I have said I have spoken plainer than civility requires. . . . It is irritating to me to see that the efforts we are making with sincerity and good will to better the condition of things are persistently ignored or falsely represented and treated with contempt.[23]

By the middle of 1913 the controversy was shifting on to foolish and fragile grounds. The Anti-Slavery Society, at last convinced that a process of repatriation, albeit a slow one, was underway and that recruitment in Angola was being conducted more or less satisfactorily, began to inquire into labour conditions in Angola itself, into the régime of forced labour and domestic slavery. The Society began to push the Foreign Office to appoint Sir Roger Casement as a special commissioner to investigate conditions. The Foreign Office, realizing that whatever abuses Casement might come upon would bear the stamp of his reputation, turned aside the proposal and told the Society it would ask Consul Smallbones to make a full report. In August 1913 Lord Cromer proposed to the Foreign Office that it act as intermediary in the dispute between the Society and the Portuguese Government. Although no one took Cromer's suggestion very seriously, Sir Eyre Crow wrote in a memorandum: 'The root of the existing distrust is their belief, for which there is a real foundation, that the anti-slavery agitation is intimately connected with a movement favouring the transfer of their African colonies to Germany. For this belief the *Spectator* has been mainly responsible. . . .'[24]

[23] Freire de Andrade to Cadbury, 30 Dec. 1912. Extract in F.O. 367/334, Sir A. Hardinge to F.O., 30 Jan. 1913. The letter was printed in the *Revista colonial* (Dec. 1912). Cadbury's article was not consistent with his usual attitude of objective questioning. He, too, seems to have been caught up in the heat of the campaign.

[24] F.O. 367/336, Memorandum of 30 (?) Aug. 1913. It is difficult to know the extent of German participation in these late years of the quarrel. A number of humanitarians were of a 'pro-German' sentiment.

But by the outbreak of the war in 1914 the heat was dying out of even these peripheral discussions. The White Books for 1914 and 1915 had largely to do with such semi-technical matters as sleeping sickness in Principe, difficulties of repatriation from certain estates, and statistics of recruitment, repatriation, and payment. In September 1914, Vice-Consul Lewis Bernays reported from São Tomé that 'conditions have wonderfully improved in the last few years, and I think we are slowly approaching a time when the liberty of the *serviçal* will be almost beyond question'.[25] In 1916 Hall Hall sent a full, and in a sense final, report to his government. The situation was not perfect. Many workers were still on the islands who should have been repatriated, but it was now obvious they remained there from choice or because they had no place to go where they could be taken care of. The death rate for the islands was high, running about 5 per cent. a year. On the other hand, the 'methods now adopted for obtaining labourers are quite satisfactory'. Deferred pay was being paid in full. Many workers were choosing to return to the islands, and Hall Hall was convinced that almost every worker who did go there was generally aware of what the contract stipulated and where he was going. 'I have the honour', the consul wrote, 'to state that in my humble opinion, the present conditions under which native labour is engaged for and employed in those islands are such as to justify the purchase of cocoa from San Thomé and Principe by Messrs. Cadbury and other British firms.'[26] A year later Joseph Burtt wrote that 'a great human drama has been acted and it has ended happily'.[27]

In 1915 the *Reporter* had printed a selection of letters, some of them solicited, from missionaries in Angola, on the current state of affairs in the colony. The commentary was not altogether cheerful, but it stood in dramatic contrast to the letters missionaries had been writing to the Society over the last fifteen years. From Kavungo, near the Rhodesia and Congo frontier:

[25] Lewis Bernays to Hall Hall, 14 Jan. 1914, in *Africa No. 1* (1915). Cd. 7960 (London, 1915), pp. 18–19.

[26] Hall Hall to F.O., 30 Oct. 1916 in *Africa No. 1* (1917), Cd. 8479 (London, 1917), pp. 66–68.

[27] Quoted in E. D. Morel, *The Black Man's Burden* (New York, 1920), pp. 156–7.

'I do not know of a single case of white men dealing in or possessing slaves at the present day. I can also add my testimony to the untiring efforts of the present official at Kavungo of putting down any suggestion of slavery and his desire to stamp it out once and for all. . . . One is thankful to be able to say that the dark days of slavery seem to be over in this part.' From Nana Kandundo, a missionary who had given valuable assistance to the Society in its campaign, wrote: 'I know that the Portuguese authorities are actively engaged in stamping out the slave trade. . . . Many slaves kept either by Europeans or by fellow Africans . . . have received letters of freedom from the Portuguese captain. . . . The captain also seeks to check the cruelty with which his soldiers not infrequently treat the natives. . . .' From Bihé another missionary reported that in the past eighteen months he had not heard of a single slave bought or sold by Portuguese traders. 'My conviction is that Government officials have sought to put a stop to slave traffic.' An American missionary from Bailundo: 'Much has been done. Looking back ten years one can see a decided improvement. The Government and the better class of public opinion is opposed to it [slavery], and, given a fair chance and proper encouragement, will in time, correct the evil.' From Chisamba: 'The Government desires to do well by the natives and to abolish slavery. . . .'[28]

After World War I the Society and the *Spectator* returned to the fray from time to time. The Society continued to press the Foreign Office for a strict accounting of the *serviçal* traffic to the islands. The Foreign Office tactic was to ignore these dispatches whenever possible. A memorial to the Foreign Office was circulated among delegates at the League of Nations. Cadbury, Nevinson, and Burtt made occasional comments deploring reported new acts of discrimination against the *serviçal* and the alleged high death-rate. The attacks did not have the bite of a decade earlier, and the Foreign Office felt justified in not reappointing a consul to São Tomé in 1920. The Portuguese

[28] *Reporter*, Apr. 1915, pp. 14–18. Two missionaries in Bihé dissented from the prevailing view. Slavery did still exist, mostly Africans dealing in Africans; the authorities were cognizant of what was going on and often connived in the business. The *Reporter* did not give the names of the correspondents.

Government remained sensitive to the issue, and in 1921 forbade recontracting on the islands. It appeared that conditions were about as good as they would ever be, given the traditional Portuguese attitude in Africa towards native labour.

Reliable statistics for the period 1916–20 are:

RECRUITED

		From Angola	From Moçambique	From Cape Verdes
1916	To São Tomé	3,573	5,439	86
	To Principe	660	..	677
1917	To São Tomé	1,918	3,499	47
	To Principe	465	148	279
1918	To São Tomé	937	570	4
	To Principe	779	192	140
1919	To São Tomé	5,399	68	68
	To Principe	985	18	190
1920	To São Tomé	3,220	447	198
	To Principe (6 mos.)	185	9	121

REPATRIATED

		To Angola	To Moçambique	To Cape Verdes
1916	From São Tomé	2,949	2,433	44
	From Principe	186	14	802
1917	From São Tomé	2,553	420	30
	From Principe	118	12	305
1918	From São Tomé	1,484	1,404	15
	From Principe	82	2	472
1919	From São Tomé	1,333	1,248	71
	From Principe	420	63	468
1920	From São Tomé	1,826	1,044	39
	From Principe (6 mos.)	136	1	115

RECONTRACTED

		From Angola	From Moçambique	From Cape Verdes
1916	On São Tomé	1,775	1,661	4
	On Principe	22	7	186
1917	On São Tomé	2,706	6,065	19
	On Principe	112	29	324
1918	On São Tomé	1,566	6,970	25
	On Principe	142	60	596
1919	On São Tomé	3,550	7,451	23
	On Principe	133	62	534
1920	On São Tomé	1,050	3,021	14
	On Principe (6 mos.)	51	61	209

The mortality rate from 1915 through 1919 was 5·35 per cent. on São Tomé and 3·95 per cent. on Principe. From 1908 to 1920, 34,281 workers had been repatriated from São Tomé and 7,376 from Principe. In 1920 there were about 39,000 workers in São Tomé and over 4,000 in Principe.[29]

Throughout the 1920's a diminishing group of humanitarians made desultory protest against forced labour in Angola and the traffic to São Tomé. As the big Portuguese West Africa colony slid into bankruptcy and the concerns of Lisbon for the African population dwindled, a number of familiar abuses crept back into labour relationship between Portuguese and African. The famous *Report on Employment of Native Labour in Portuguese West Africa* (New York, 1925) by the American sociologist Edward A. Ross brought back a host of memories from earlier in the century. Ross visited in Angola in 1924, and his series of laconic case histories of the plight of workers and villages in the Angolan highlands were part of a familiar pattern of accounts from that colony. The report was circulated at Geneva and was given a rebuttal by the Portuguese Government.

From then on, the subject of slavery and contract labour in the Portuguese African colonies trailed into oblivion, although conditions in the 1930's and 1940's were scant improval over those in 1925. Not until the late 1950's would the issue flare into controversy again, this time to occupy the attention of the world.

[29] Statistics from *Native Labour in West Africa* (Lisbon, 1921). This is a pamphlet put out by the Sociedade de Emigração para São Tomé e Principe in answer to the memorial circulated at Geneva by the Anti-Slavery Society.

Note on Sources

MUCH of the material for this work was drawn from the Foreign Office records and correspondence in the Public Records Office, notably some 800 volumes in the Slave Trade Series F.O. 84 and the various consular series for Africa and Portugal, F.O. 2, F.O. 63, and F.O. 367. These dispatches from Angola, Moçambique, Zanzibar, Nyasa, South Africa, and occasional files from Madagascar and Comoro as well as the correspondence between London and Lisbon are extremely valuable for any study of Portuguese Africa. Parliamentary debates on the misuse of labour in the Portuguese African territories were another source.

For the humanitarian protest I have used principally the Anti-Slavery Society's *Reporter* and the *Aborigines Friend*, published by the Aborigines Protection Society. Various missionary publications and correspondence have been helpful, although I have seldom made direct use of this material. The periodicals which I consulted for the entire period were *The Times*, the *Spectator*, and the *Fortnightly Review*, while for particular periods I used other English periodical sources as cited in the notes.

My most important Portuguese material has been the official Portuguese government gazette, the *Diário do governo* and the official gazettes (*Boletim oficial*) for the colonies of Angola and Moçambique for the years 1850–1915. Whenever possible I have consulted various Portuguese and colonial newspapers and journals.

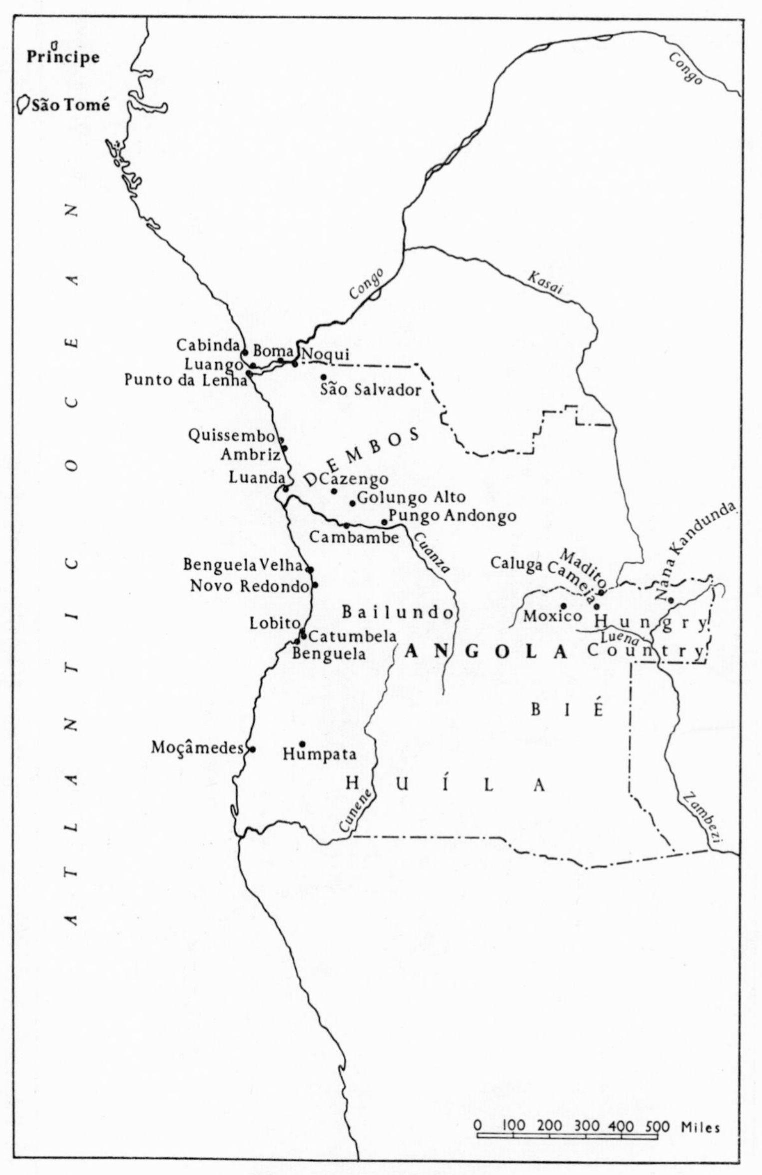

Map 1. Angola, 1860–1910.

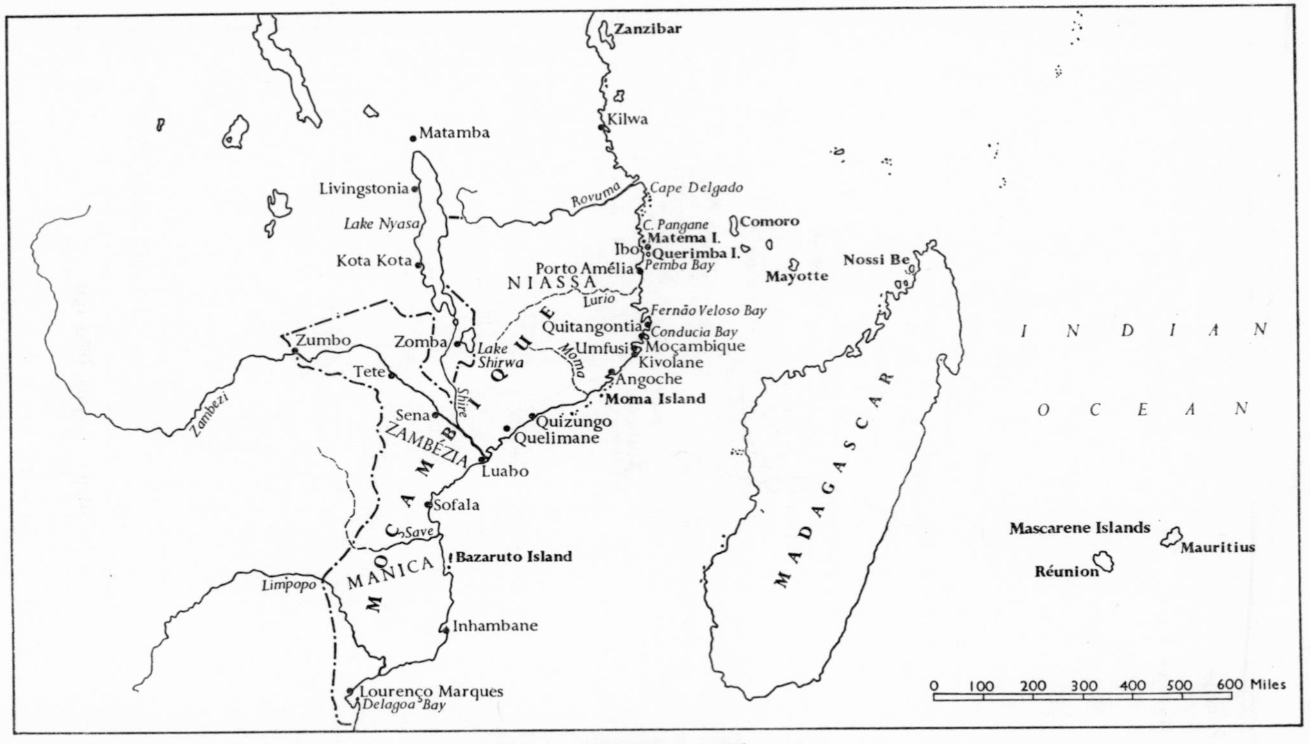

Map 2. Moçambique, 1860–1910.

Index

INDEX

INDEX

PRINTED IN GREAT BRITAIN
AT THE UNIVERSITY PRESS, OXFORD
BY VIVIAN RIDLER
PRINTER TO THE UNIVERSITY